More Praise for *Spanish Recognitions*

"Piercing historical insight . . . it hardly matters where you go . . . Settle is terrific company." —Paul Mansfield, *Daily Telegraph*

"Ms. Settle travels to Spain and the reader is the beneficiary of her insightful peregrination. She strikes out on her own, weaving masterfully the contours of Spain's people, history, and mountainous landscape into an entertaining, personal narrative."
—Gary Shapiro, *New York Sun*

"A lively tour . . . it diligently uncovers the past's legacy the way a traveler does . . . with the feeling that each discovery has been made for the first time." —John Freeman, *Newsday*

"A dramatic, intelligent, curious, and empathetic writer . . . [her wanderings] are recalled with delicious, plainspoken eloquence."
—*Booklist*

"More than a travel narrative, this book uses historical vignettes coupled with personal observations to show us the heart of the country."
—*Library Journal*

"A graceful memoir of solo travel in post-Franco Spain, bookending the author's equally graceful *Turkish Reflections* (1991). . . . Travel-writing in the tradition of Jan Morris and Paul Theroux, recounting sojourns that are never entirely comfortable, never really dangerous, but full of surprises and pleasures." —*Kirkus Reviews*

"Settle, an 'eighty-two-year-old grownup,' delights in discovery, is curious about the old, possessing an intellectual-quest spirit and ageless wisdom. Clearly in love with the 'people so beautiful,' 'the scene so handsome,' Settle invites readers to follow in her footsteps and see out of her eyes." —*Publishers Weekly*

"Illuminating anecdotes. . . . Richly illustrated with both historical and present-day images. . . . Settle has a gift for crafting mellifluous prose." —Chris Springer, *International Travel News*

SPANISH
RECOGNITIONS

SPANISH RECOGNITIONS

The Roads to the Present

MARY LEE SETTLE

W. W. NORTON & COMPANY

New York • London

Copyright © 2004 by Mary Lee Settle

All rights reserved
Printed in the United States of America
First published as a Norton paperback 2005

"Love Letters in the Sand," words by Nick Kenny and Charles Kenny,
music by J. Fred Coots. Copyright © 1931 by Bourne Co. and
Toy Town Tunes. Copyright renewed. All Rights Reserved.
International Copyright Secured.

For information about permission to reproduce selections from this
book, write to Permissions, W. W. Norton & Company, Inc.,
500 Fifth Avenue, New York, NY 10110

Manufacturing by the Maple-Vail Book Manufacturing Group
Book design by Charlotte Staub
Cartography by Adrian Kitzinger
Production manager: Amanda Morrison

Library of Congress Cataloging-in-Publication Data

Settle, Mary Lee.
    Spanish recognitions : the roads to the present / Mary Lee Settle.—
1st ed.
        p. cm.
    ISBN 0-393-02027-4 (hardcover)
    1. Spain—Description and travel. 2. Settle, Mary Lee—Travel—
Spain. I. Title.
    DP43.2 .S48 2004
946—dc22   2003022814

ISBN 0-393-32717-5 pbk.

W. W. Norton & Company, Inc.
500 Fifth Avenue, New York, N.Y. 10110
www.wwnorton.com

W. W. Norton & Company Ltd.
Castle House, 75/76 Wells Street, London W1T 3QT

1 2 3 4 5 6 7 8 9 0

CONTENTS

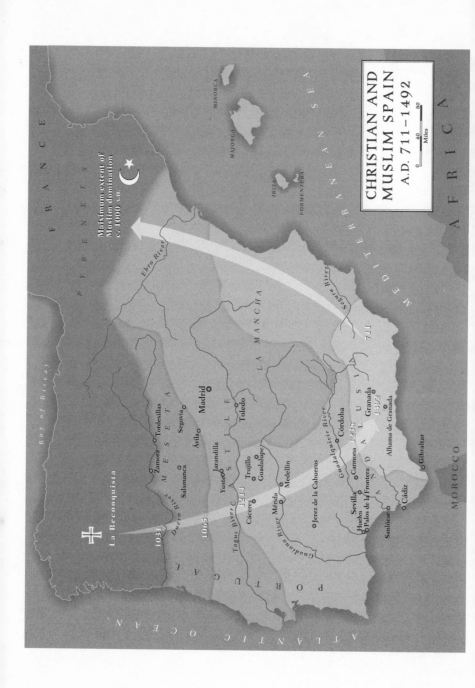

CHRISTIAN AND
MUSLIM SPAIN
A.D. 711–1492

0 40 80
Miles

SPANISH
RECOGNITIONS

A TRAVELER BETWEEN

 To be alone by choice is one of the great luxuries of the world. I went to Spain alone. I wanted to discover it, not have it pointed out to me by friends, guidebooks, experts, or that most powerful of modern Big Brothers, controlled tourism.

I knew just enough Spanish to eat, ask directions, and find the bathroom. But I did, or thought I did, know more of Spain's history. After all, I had written about Ferdinand and Isabel in the fifteenth century; I had traveled the main battle lines of the Spanish civil war. How wrong I was. What I did not know was more important than any of this—its land, its mountains, its rivers, and how they had formed its people and its past.

I stumbled onto Spain as surely as Columbus had stumbled on America while looking for someplace else. I had to shed what I had learned, a Spain from books, from visits as a tourist, from other people's eyes and my own study, what I thought I knew, my someplace else. I hoped not to impose all that. With half my country beyond the Mississippi, and the whole peninsula of Florida named in Spanish, I am ashamed of my ignorance and acceptance of that form of censorship, the official history of our past.

There is a wonderful Scottish word for what I hoped to do. Snerge. To snerge around, stick your nose in, as curious as a cat and as quiet. I wanted to earn again the child's eye of discovery.

I had found out that it had to be unplanned, as it had been for me in Turkey when I landed there by accident and stayed out of affection. I found that with little plans and a hanging-out peace of mind, I could come upon Spain instead of grabbing at it, as I had found Turkey, and out of it would come this book, I hoped, as a twin to *Turkish Reflections*.

They have so much in common, two countries rising like the horns of a bull at either end of the North African and Middle Eastern Fertile Crescent. They have the most profoundly effective of ancient and modern borders, the borders of religion. Both have been Christian and Muslim; Turkey replaced orthodox Christianity with Islam; Spain replaced Islam with militant Christianity. They both began as warrior nations. They both have residues of their opposites. The Arabic language creeps into a Turkish sentence, place names in Spain are often Arabic, place names in Turkey reflect the country's ancient Christianity.

So I packed my profound ignorance of Spain's physical geography, two guidebooks, a Michelin road atlas, a Spanish-English dictionary that seems to have been designed for businessmen and people on the make. What is your name? Would you like to dance? *¿Dónde están los servicios?*

I took books: *Don Quixote*, of course. whatever I could find of Federico García Lorca, Spain's greatest modern poet, with side-by-side Spanish and English so that I could learn the Spanish words and rhythms. The poems of St. John of the Cross and St. Teresa's dear autobiography went with me, and an old topographical map.

It was as natural for me to take the map as for city people to leave such a thing behind. Spain is the second most mountainous country in Europe, and those kilometers take longer if you are driving up hill and down dale. I am from the mountains. Part of my family have been engineers for nine generations, from the late seventeenth century, when they were surveyors who went, as Jefferson's father went, into the Alleghenies to find a high, wild, lonely country too full of trees, bears, panthers, naked warriors, and tangled impassable rhododendron. I cannot remember ever getting into the back seat of my father's Buick without checking to see where the brass plumb bob was so I wouldn't sit on its sharp end.

I also took a plastic plate, knife, fork, and spoon so I could eat in whatever room I landed in, a sixty-watt bulb to read by—which turned out not to fit the lamps, so I had to learn enough Spanish to buy another—a point-and-shoot camera, and a few hangers to put my wash and wear and wear and wear stuff on in hotel bathrooms, since with an international lack of trust, most hangers in hotels are hooked to permanent rails so you can't hang them over the bathtub or take them away.

I needed the dinnerware because the Spanish have dinner very late and they have it with partners, or in family groups. It was never lonely in my room, or in my mile after mile of walking, but it was lonely the few times I tried to eat in a restaurant alone at night. By the way, the first thing I noticed that had changed since Franco's time was that when I went to Spain in 1970, and had to dine alone, an American flag was set on the table to show I was not a whore.

Oh, and so I don't forget, I took neverending curiosity, without which we might as well stay at home and grumble.

Spain is a new country, the youngest in Europe. The new women there are so completely emancipated that they move through their jobs, through the streets, through higher education, and through acceptance as if they had inherited it. Maybe they have, from their grandmothers, who manned the barricades in the Spanish civil war. Or maybe it is what is left of the pride of the *hidalgo*, the best of it, without the prejudice and the scorn that defaced it. They seem to have been able to skip shrillness. They are polite, dignified, and I never in the time I was there saw any young woman, whether she was the cleaner of a room in a hotel or a bank teller or a shop assistant, who did not seem to be poised, neat, attractive. There are so many beautiful young men and women. The flags and the barricades are remembered, but the manners are not forgotten.

We go to Europe as visitors, thinking we are going among strangers and finding that they are our kin. We see the "historic sights." We are led with care by the modern industry of tourism and we come home remembering in our mind's eye these planned sights as we keep postcards, or photographs. I do this, too, for erudition can never replace wonder. I take tour buses, and stand in awe where awe has been so earned, by the past kept so alive, by the ancient hospitality so present, by the manners of the most elegant people in Europe.

But sometimes it is meet, as in the Prayer Book, to go beyond and see around, and ask why. The obvious, the everyday, the peripheries of a glance would have been so easy to miss unless I walked, strolled, sat around, used the guidebook and the experts but didn't let them use me. I went there hoping to be neither tourist nor expert, but a traveler between them, as Ibn Battuta had been in the fourteenth century, Washington Irving, Kinglake, the gloomy

Richard Ford in the nineteenth, and D. H. Lawrence in the twentieth.

What I remember most vividly was the unexpected—a young motorcycle cop in Castile who spoke English and was so polite and led me out of town at about seventy miles an hour through heavy traffic. How did he know about my Indy 500 secret soul? Or I see and hear yet the happy small boy on a corner blowing an ancient ceramic whistle that sounds like a canary, and is shaped like a tiny pitcher. Behind him rises the great façade of Our Lady of Guadalupe, where Columbus brought the first two Indians to be baptized. The small black Byzantine statue of the Virgin, probably seventh century, is said to have been found in the thirteenth century. Her worship was taken to the new world by the *conquistadores*.

If I wanted to understand this new country in this new millennium, I could not ignore the Spanish civil war, which began in 1936, and really ended only with the death of Franco, Spain's dictator for thirty-five years. Spain has, in this century, gone through one of the most catastrophic civil wars in her history. It was the watershed that has formed modern Spain.

Like so many of my own generation who were beginning to pay attention to what went on beyond their own streets, I fell in love with the Spain of that war. It used my innocence and tested it. And it has been ever since the first passion that calls me back to Spain.

In the summer of 1936 I was seventeen. I followed, day by day, the explosion of Spain's cities, the pictures in *Life* magazine, the beginnings of a new language of familiar places it would take fifty years for me to see, Belchite, Valencia, Barcelona, Madrid, and, the most immortal of all, Guernica. I remember them as battlegrounds in the only country in the

Europe of the thirties whose democratically elected government stood up to the attempted takeover by the fascists led
by the Spanish Army. The first Spanish I learned was the cry
from the Republican barricades defending Madrid: ¡No
pasarán!—They shall not pass.

It was heady, it was brave in a worldwide depression when
we longed for courage and had not found it, not in Germany,
not in Italy, not in the country after country that were falling
into the trap of Hitler's terrible promises, not in what we saw
as the timidity of the democracies, including our own. Spain
gave us hope, even as our own country was finding diplo-
matic ways to stay neutral and let a democratic government
fall to the influence of the Soviet Union, the only country to
send official help. Now we can judge securely by the facts of
the wild decisions, on the left and the right, the takeover by
Germany for war exercises, the backing of Italy for Franco's
side, and the threats to withdraw support that the Soviet
Union used to strengthen the communist minority in Spain.

That was then and this is now, and we know too much
about the Spanish war, but then, it was simple, a black-and-
white war, a right side and a wrong side. Thousands of volunteers went to Spain to help the republic, many of them
American. Of course, at seventeen, I wanted to go. We all
wanted to go, and so many of us did. If we were naïve, thank
God for naïveté; maybe it breaks the barriers of cynicism.

So I expected to see the old wounds, the old fears, and
instead I found the elegant, dignified children of new Spain.
I walked in strange cities among strangers, until they
became, not known but recognized, not understood but
accepted, as dreams are accepted. When strangers become
familiar you are at home anywhere.

So I drove where the road led me, with only enough planning to get to a chosen city or village by evening. I was seeking more than looking and I didn't even want to define what I was seeking for fear of losing surprise.

I wandered through medieval kingdoms, ancient tribal divisions of prehistoric Spain, through the seven hundred years of the *Reconquista*, north to south, river to river. Four of Spain's five main rivers flow west into the Atlantic—the Duero, the Guadiana, the Tagus, the Guadalquivir. Only the Ebro flows east-southeast taking the falling water from the Pyrenees into the Mediterranean. It was as if the people looked to the Atlantic eons before there was a Columbus.

But most of all, I think, there were three cities where I had longed for years to go, not to see the places necessarily, but as we go to Monticello or to Mount Vernon, or wander across the battlefields of our civil war. We long to go to where there have been people who formed our lives, a sense of touching them by being there. Is it so strange to want to walk where they have walked, or be where they have been? It is one of the basic reasons for travel.

The first was the city of Avila, where St. Teresa was born and grew up. She is that practical, down-to-earth, tough saint who had the guts to slap the papal nuncio. Then I went to see where the queen of Castile, called Juana la Loca, had been locked up for over forty years as a political prisoner, and so I went to Tordesillas. I wanted to follow the routes of St. John of the Cross and Lorca, whose paths had crossed in Granada, centuries apart in life but contemporary in spirit.

Lorca had been the first to guide me to a longing for Spain. I read and began to grow close to his words in the first year of the Spanish civil war, my freshman year in college. I knew nothing about him, his life or his death. I had found a play that gave me hope that there was a man with passion and love enough to face his world, not as he hoped it to be but as it was, and his world was Andalucia, in southern Spain.

Then, for years, I had the recording of Germaine Montero reciting Lorca's ode to a friend, a bullfighter who had been killed in the ring, and I can still hear her voice with that profound echo throughout the poem, *a las cinco de la tarde*, the grief, the bitterness in that repeated line, the official time of day when the bullfights begin. There were the poems of love and of joy for his country, his cities, without pretense and without bombast, his *Gypsy Ballads—Sevilla, Granada.*

So along with Miguel de Cervantes, whose saintly mad comic Spanish Hamlet is the ever contemporary guide to Spain for all of us, I had Lorca to tell me what I might look for. His essay about the *duende* would lead me to what I had not known, for we have no word for it. I was to find it was the essence of Spain.

What is it, that moment, that quality which, when heard or seen or read or remembered, makes your hackles rise? It is the essence of true pitch; it can be found in a note of music, like the augmented seventh chords in the last act of *Don Giovanni*, a drive in golf, a knife-clean dive, a performance that catches fire, a perfect marriage of passion, precision, and chance.

It cannot be planned or summoned. It is there, or not there. How I began to find it is the path of this book.

MADRID

 When I landed at the international airport, I could have been anywhere. After the rudeness and the rush, and a certainty that I would never be understood, I escaped to Madrid. I stayed for the first time in the old city, where the Moors had built an *alcázar,* a fortress against the Christians in the north, sometime in the eighth century, and turned a tiny village that had been there since Paleolithic times into what would become, in the sixteenth century, the capital of Spain.

Madrileños still consider the area around what was the *alcázar* and has grown through the centuries into a gargantuan palace as Madrid's true center. All buses, gossip, stories seem to start at the old *Puerta del Sol,* which had been the entry into the medieval town. I walked out of a small hotel into a strange country and a strange cityscape, and did what I have always done on my first day in a new old place. I forgot the guidebook, strolled, got lost, turned the wrong corners, and began a voyage of discovery that would take me over so much of Spain.

I wanted to bide my time, and be surprised, and to have

those glimpses of familiarity in cities, that depth of memory where directions are inherent, the weather taken for granted, where holes in corners are as well known as the lines in your hands, and you seem to pass places you have lived, been happy, been sad.

My wandering began where the narrow, intimate streets had been carved by animals and people walking through eons of time. As I stared at the tall seventeenth-century houses along paved lanes, my feet found a shape I could not see. It was the inevitable hill, the center of all old Spanish cities, hidden by paving, concrete, brick, stone, over the city that had grown slowly until Philip II, he of the Invincible Armada, chose it as the first permanent capital of Spain.

I heard ancient church bells, and the swish of wheels and the rush of traffic. Overhead the signs were advertisements for a new "Euro" city, and below them, paying no attention, some old ladies sat on benches in front of a small café, and I was caught in their laughter as I passed. Had some of these women donned the coveralls of the *guerrilleros*, taken their rifles and ridden buses to the university front in the Spanish civil war? Their grand- and great-grandchildren, thousands of young people, erect and beautifully dressed, gestured at cell phones or gathered in fast-talking groups that made it clear to me I would never learn Spanish. It is the fastest language I have ever heard. I could not think, much less speak, in that avalanche of talk, never too loud, always somehow urgent.

People sat in groups, or comfortable and alone, at tables under umbrellas in the sunlit cafés, reading papers, resting, simply watching. They were the *madrileños*, some of whose DNA was buried eons deep beneath the streets, to whom the

Hapsburg monarchs who first made Madrid the capital of Spain were new people.

The street still seemed uncrowded, the movement graceful, people physically aware of each other, which to me was startling after the rush and blindness of crowds in our own American cities. Children ran across my path while their parents sat and gossiped. I remember the smell of wine, and the *tapas*, the appetizers that are so often the delicious substitutes for dinner as the Spanish go from café to café in the *paseo*, that evening stroll and gossip, as traditional and formal as evensong, which can go on as late as midnight.

For the first of so many times I was aware of there being no family or group where the children were not as at home in the wide sidewalks and walking streets as the grownups. In Spain no one is left out when it is time for the morning walk or the *paseo*, as if they all were in large shared living rooms.

I had been in Madrid once before, but that time, I was looking for what I already knew to be there—the Prado, the university on the western fringes of the modern city. This time I longed to stumble on what I did not know, to be surprised, to see the city itself and what it might be hiding.

So I followed along the roads of Madrid, layer by layer, century by century, as well as I could, and it was all there, all I had hoped for. Of course I went again to the Prado, but this time to visit Goya, not to take in, grab, rush, see it all— just to be there. The late eighteenth- and early-nineteenth-century city belongs to Goya. He made it his by seeing into its essence, and by painting its life and its deaths, its people, its picnics, its *fiestas*, changes, fears, and even its miracles.

Francisco de Goya y Lucientes, the rough peasant from Aragon, arrived in Madrid in 1780 with the dung of the village still on his boots and made a time immortal. He is, for me, the greatest guide to Madrid, who in his time wandered as I was wandering, and taught me to see as he had seen, with clarity and passion.

He became the court painter, and the courage with which he painted those almost brutal portraits of the family of the reigning king, Charles IV, is, to me, astonishing. He worked then, during what is remembered as the Enlightenment, led by one of Goya's patrons and friends. That civilized man, humanist and minister of the Enlightenment, Jovellanos, sat for Goya, so quiet, so contemplative, so sad.

I had thought, and even read in guidebooks, that the Prado had once been a palace, but it hadn't. What it had been had to do with kings and their tempers and the times, and the awesome power of despotism. When there is an enlightened despotism, as there was for such a short but memorable time in eighteenth-century Spain, the despotism has often wiped out the enlightenment.

The heir to the easygoing, feckless Charles IV was his pompous son, Ferdinand VII, whose portrait by Goya, with its royal robes, shows the petulant face of a spoiled child. No king was ever more loathed by the Spanish. During his reign intellectuals, artists, liberals, the icons of the Enlightment, fled the country for their lives. Goya was one of the many who escaped his rule by leaving. He died in exile in France. Unamuno left in the 1920s, and Ortega y Gasset during the civil war. Manuel de Falla, and Spain's finest painter, Picasso, died abroad. But they carried Spain with them as surely as their own skin.

The Prado had been a half-finished building that was to be a museum of natural history, left over from the Enlightenment when Ferdinand ascended to the throne. The only act he seems to have carried out that was not appalling was to have it finished in 1819. That is the irony, for the Prado is the exiled Goya's monument, as in so many ways Madrid is his city.

To walk from the *Puerta del Sol* along the wide boulevards past the huge neoclassic buildings, the triumphal arches, under the shadows of the old trees that seem to line every street, is to walk through centuries of change back into eighteenth-century Madrid. I was guided there and introduced to Jovellanos by reading Carlos Fuentes. His book *The Buried Mirror* told me more of Madrid and the way it had been than any other contemporary writer, maybe because we both recognize Spain as a mirror of the deep past of our own new world.

The wide boulevards, the parks, the classic buildings of the eighteenth-century Enlightenment are those of Jovellanos's time and influence. But some say that Goya's dreamer at the table in the "black" prints with the awful birds of nightmare around his head is Jovellanos, too. For when enlightenment goes out, the inevitable darkness of brute stupidity comes as it did at the end of his career. He was its victim, one of the stoic, grace-saving Spaniards of which Seneca was one, and Cervantes, St. Teresa, St. Ignatius Loyola, Unamuno, Ortega y Gasset, Federico García Lorca. They have appeared from time to time, it seems, when needed, as living sparks of truth in what has seemed too often in the past a smoldering fire of reaction. Some of them managed to live through hard times. For others, the decision to stay cost them their lives. They have, over and over again, saved the communal sanity of this wild, incisively elegant country.

Bismarck said, "Of all the nations I admire the Spanish the most. How energetic these people must be! Their governments have attempted without exception to destroy their nation but have never succeeded."

In historic time the hilltop settlement that was the old Madrid had grown from a primitive redoubt of piled stones to a fortress—Celtic, Iberian, Roman. Those ancient stones were incorporated into the ever-changing frontier post between the Christian Visigoths and the Moors. When the Christians captured the little hill town after several centuries of war, they made the Moorish *alcázar* into a Christian palace, which has grown into one of the largest in Europe. It looks north.

North, to the Romans and then the Moors, was enemy territory. North meant the wild Lusitani, then the Vandals, Visigoths, Christians, names to strike terror before, by some metamorphosis of time and the censorship of legend, Christian and Visigoth melded together, and the once feared and hated Gothic became an ideal of aristocratic chivalry.

In 711 A.D. the Berbers from North Africa were hired as mercenaries to come to what is now Spain, then a Visigothic kingdom in what had once been Rome's most valued colony. In the series of raids and murders that decided kingship among the Visigoths, Rodrigo, the king's brother, had invited them. Roderigo won the throne, and the mercenaries stayed, finding better pasture than they had left in North Africa. Since they had brought no women with them, they married the women they found there, and another element of the marvelous heritage of the Spaniards was added. Roman Christians and what was left of the Visigoths fled to the wild Astorian mountains into the far north. The Moorish invasion and the Christian *Reconquista* dominate seven hundred years of Spanish history. They lasted from the eighth century to 1492. I would travel in their wake.

When Philip II chose Madrid, then a small town, as his capital, it is said that he chose it, unseen, from a map, because it was at the center of Spain. Around it was an empty tableland that had often been a battleground. Madrid sat isolated in the center of a web of new roads reaching out across the empty country to the distant cities of his kingdom. The king who ruled over more territory than any Spanish king before or after him sat like a spider in his retreat of a palace monastery.

The greatest "portrait" of Philip II is a building that lies in a valley north of Madrid. It is the monument Philip built to himself, the carapace of the king below the heights of the Guadarrama mountains. The Escorial is the coldest imperial building I have ever been in. It is magnificent. It contains thousands of works of art in galleries so lofty that a slight mist seems to cling to the carved ceilings. I suspect it has always been as cold, dead, and impressive as it is today. It houses more than seven thousand relics of saints, including heads, limbs, and entire bodies. Thousands of masses were sung in its chapel. A perpetual drift of liturgical chanting echoed for centuries through the huge palace monastery, museum, royal cemetery.

As I wandered through it, I came at last to Philip's own quarters, a small, simple room with a desk, a *prie-dieu*, and a narrow cot. Somehow the private man seen there in what he had chosen for his lair seemed pathetic, touching.

So by European standards, Madrid is a young capital. The ground where I wandered through crowds of people still has its individual cast, its city-statehood ignoring its national status. The people who seem to have been there forever, the same and not the same, have grown warier perhaps, and more sophisticated. Their civic pride exists below the changes in building, in space, in growth, even in politics. They are first *madrileños*, then Spaniards.

All this in one walk through the city? No. A gradual recognition, a growing familiarity and surprise. I had not expected the sense of intimacy I found in the grand capital of Spain, the home of the Prado, the grandiose boulevards, the great parks, the tour buses, the Madrid of the tourists.

Goya's paintings in the Prado came alive again for me. It had been in the *Campo del Moro* below the palace hilltop that the terrible execution of the *guerrilleros* of Madrid by the soldiers of Napoleon took place. It is made into an immortal damnation of war in Goya's *Second of May*. Those who are waiting for death in that painting fought with whatever weapons they could find. It was the uprising from the depths of the earth of Spain against the invasions of Napoleon, the beginning of Spanish resistance that fomented the Peninsula War. Like Picasso's *Guernica* in the modern civil war, Goya's paintings, along with his etchings *The Horrors of War*, are terrifying icons that plead for a peace that has over and over been snatched away.

I decided not to take one of the many tour buses parked and waiting in the *Puerta del Sol*. But where I dodged buses, crowds, newspaper stands, cafés, car after car, was where Goya's *Attack on the Mamelukes by the Madrileños* had happened the day before the executions of the second of May.

Around me strolled the population of today, young and attractive, a genetic elegance that Spaniards, from hints of their prehistoric art, have had forever, heads up, pace calm, presence sure. Here and there I passed people so beautiful I turned my head away to keep from staring.

Spain is old, but the Spanish are young, one of the youngest populations in Europe. I had a sudden thought that everyone who could must have mourned the death of Franco in 1975 by getting pregnant in the first few years after the end of his dictatorship.

In the spring of 1936, after a hard-fought election, a republic had been elected for the second time in Spain. There had been an earlier attempt at democracy in 1931, but it was soon put down by a dictatorship. When it failed, a new election was called in 1936; a new republic was won by the democratic forces in a rare combination of left-wing parties called the Popular Front. Only a few weeks passed before the reactive forces under Franco rose in revolt against the elected government. This time it did not succeed until a three-year civil war had been fought.

By the early fall of 1936, the university west of the city was the scene of fierce resistance by the people of Madrid and the volunteers from other countries who flocked to Spain to defend the republic. Many of them were liberals who defended the republic because it was the elected government. Many were members of the radical wings of the Popular Front, made up of trade unionists, Communists, Syndicalist Anarchists, Trotskyiites, and every left-wing group in between.

Every political philosophy in Europe in the mid-thirties tried to steal the Spanish civil war and make it their own. On the right, the army, the Falangists, the royalists, and, alas, the princes of the Spanish church were aided by the well-armed Nazis sent by Hitler, and the Fascists sent by Mussolini. But it began and it remained a Spanish war between authority and the consensus of the elected republic that had been brewing for centuries.

I drove through the rebuilt university, and on a corner along the way I glimpsed the Florida Hotel, a little place where Hemingway and so many others had stayed to tell the world what was happening in Spain. There was no Goya or Picasso to paint it and immortalize it forever, but there was and is memory, and pride, and still a motto, *¡No pasarán!*, which the *madrileños* will never forget.

The fighting went on from academic building to building, then floor to floor, but Madrid stood firm. Armed men and women went out to the university on buses by day to fight and came home at night the same way. *¡No pasarán!* The Communist woman known as *la Pasionaria* used the phrase in the fiery speech in Madrid. It became a worldwide motto for the resistance to Franco. Madrid was not conquered until the Republic lost the war three years later.

One day I sat, as I did so often, in the *Plaza Mayor,* that beautiful and terrible space. It is surrounded by sixteenth- and seventeenth-century façades with balconies, which once were hired out for whatever spectacle was offered in the space below. The statue of Philip III in the center of the plaza looked arrogant, his shadow shortened by the noon sun. A bird sat on his head.

Once the *autos de fe,* the "acts of faith," which were the trials where the Spanish Inquisition condemned converted Jews, Protestants, and Spanish heretics, had been held there. It was in this space that high galleries for judges and spectators were built. Those deemed guilty were paraded by to entertain the court and the *madrileños.* Thousands of what were now termed Old Christians watched as *converso* after *converso,* the name for the Jews who had been forcibly converted, with heretic after heretic, *alumbrados,* who believed in silent prayer, and Protestants of many sects were marched into the plaza dressed in the ignominious yellow penitential garment, the *sambenito,* and the tall yellow miter, for public trial, as the crowd threw stones and garbage at them. Even the bodies of the dead, some of whom were declared heretical if they had been buried according to Jewish rites, were exhumed and carried in the procession, with the yellow miters on their skulls, and the yellow of the *sambenito* on their skeletons or putrid flesh.

It was at an *auto de fe* in the *Plaza Mayor* that the feeble-minded last Hapsburg, Charles II, celebrated his wedding and was allowed, as a great honor, to light the fire to burn the convicted Jews and heretics. They were burned outside the city walls after the procession, since so many people whose palaces were gathered around the *Plaza Mayor* in the small streets to be near the palace, like chicks around a great hen, had complained of the smell. It was in the *Plaza Mayor* that a bullfight in the painting by Goya had been held.

I lounged in the sun at a table in an outdoor café. The plaza was silent and nearly empty except for a few shoppers, the inevitable strollers, some people who had stopped where artists had set up their easels across the great space in the shade. I finished reading the Paris *Herald Tribune*. I flipped through a guidebook with some disdain. I knew so much, after all.

The name Goya stopped me. Something of Goya I had never heard of. The mention of an obscure hermitage by the river that had been decorated by him; out of the way, the obscurity that draws me. On my map I found my way and walked first to the parapet beside the eighteenth-century monster of a royal palace. The green ceiling of the thick woods of the *Campo del Moro* far below me hid the path to the river.

I looked beyond it, beyond the great *mesa,* north to the mountains where there is almost always snow. I had expected to see the river away in the distance. There was only the great modern city.

I walked downhill as water flows; it is a good way to find one's city in Spain, river and hill, the two ancient marks. I wandered within the woods. In one of the many sieges of the old town centuries before it became Philip II's sixteenth-century capital, there had been the bright Moorish banners. Philip had had the trees planted to provide a private hunting ground. Beside it was the old road uphill that switched back and forth as old paths have always done to ease the uphill climb. It had not changed shape but it had become a highway with fast-moving traffic. The sleek, small, feisty automobiles that the Spanish drive so well had long since replaced the carts of vegetables and fruit that had once labored up the hill to the city market.

So I dodged cars in some vague hope of getting to the river. The riverbank was gone. It, too, was a highway. The only concession to what had once been the country were the fine trees. Where there had been meadows and orchards, where a chapel had stood, where on San Antonio's day there were swings and rides and picnics by the water, there was, as in all modern cities, the international stateless flow of traffic at evening.

But there was still the old name, San Antonio de la Florida. It was where once the seamstresses of Madrid had come in their best embroidered shawls on San Antonio's feast day to throw thirteen pins into the holy water font. When they thrust their hands in the water, the number of pins that stuck to their palms would tell them the number of suitors they would have in the next year. There had been beggars and procuresses, thieves and dandies, boys and girls and music and dancing.

Then the riverside became fashionable. The old chapel was pulled down to make way for rich estates. The Duchess of Alba built a fine mansion and entertained there. She is supposed to have been Goya's mistress. She had been the model for his twin paintings *The Naked Maja* and *The Clothed Maja*. Queen Maria, whose portrait in the Prado by Goya, the court painter, depicts a bad-tempered witch, decided that she, too, wanted to be out of the vast palace on the hill. She moved down to the riverbank and built a fine house. In 1799 she ordered a small royal chapel built for her family and hired Goya to decorate it. He was fifty-three years old and the most famous artist in Spain.

There it was in the evening light, a small neoclassic chapel. Beside it a replica stood, twin simple neoclassic hermitages. The parish church had been cloned from Goya's hermitage when someone who loved art and had the ear of the court saw that smoke from the votive candles was harming the murals covering the cupola and the arches of the original chapel.

At the door of the second chapel a bride and groom were poised to enter the church, she in a grand white wedding gown and an heirloom veil, he in black tie. Elegant guests waited to follow them, the women's clothes and jewels an astonishment of riches and fashion, the scene so handsome it could have been the eighteenth century haunting the evening.

The twin churches, the clarity of the air by the river, even with the traffic, made a pool of quiet in the midst of the impatient city. A little sign pointed the way into the *Museo de Goya*, a dedication to the most truthful, courageous painter Spain has honored. To paint or to write without the obscuring gloss of fear or favor is the stuff of genius. Goya, the rough peasant, the darling of the court, had it. At a time in the late eighteenth and early nineteenth century, when the Inquisition was still in force, when the French Revolution had produced a trembling reaction in courts all over Europe, Goya recorded what he saw.

I looked up at the cupola with its skylight, like the sun. He had painted a balcony rail around the base of it, as if to hold back the crowd of people who were witnessing the miracle when San Antonio, to try to prove that his own father was not a murderer, raised a man from the dead to bear witness. The crowd seemed to have come from some space of the city beyond the church to cluster around the balcony rail, high above me.

There they are at their moment of miracle. Some watch. Some marvel. Some crane their necks to see what the others are watching. Some pray. Most are indifferent. A boy has lost a shoe. An old man, San Antonio's father, looks whipped by sorrow and fear. The dead man, exhausted and pale from his grave, is held up by his arms at his moment of speaking to clear San Antonio's father's name. He is about to name the killer. From the midst of the crowd the killer runs away into that sky space from which they have all gathered.

San Antonio is the kind of poor young priest Goya saw every day in the streets of Madrid. He stands a little above the crowd, on a rock. There is a simple halo, as if the sun had rested around his head for that moment.

All around the balcony are the people from Goya's Madrid, those who had met for so long in the place between the river and the church before it had been swept away by fashion. Three girls gossip; only one of them seems entranced by the moment. A beggar, or a thief, scans the crowd. A woman has thrown a shawl over the balcony rail, and sits behind it, staring at a young man who raises his arms in ecstasy. Or waves to a friend. Or simply stretches his arms because he is alive.

An old, veiled woman, a procuress, looks straight down at me, and all of us who, for nearly two hundred years, have looked up at the crowd who line the balcony rail. Perhaps she is watching Goya's patroness, the well-known ugly adulteress, Maria Louisa, the queen of Spain. The old procuress is the only one who looks down, connecting the painted crowd that lines the cupola with those who watch from below.

Behind a young man and his sweetheart, he turning, astonished at the miracle, a little afraid, she oblivious of all but him, there is a man with his back turned, his clothes seventeenth century, red and yellow, colors of the Inquisition, which was still a force to be feared when Goya painted the chapel. The cupola is haunted by Goya's choices.

Below the crowd, in the arches, the life-sized angels have wings, but what imperious bird wings! They also have the faces of people Goya might have met at court, or in the theater, or on the streets of Madrid. There was much criticism of this at the time. They were said to be too beautiful, and, frankly, too familiar, to be angels. One, the most ethereal, looks disturbingly like the Duchess of Alba. They are portraits. It is said that all of the crowd are portraits, some found in the streets, some in the court, some close friends of Goya.

I sensed a new thing, familiar in stills from modern movies. Goya has painted a moment in time. Some of the faces are brushed with the speed of their movement. Some are faded in the distance. Some are caught when movement has obscured them. Goya has done this, captured a glimpse in passing, as if we, too, are passersby in a Madrid street, ignoring the miracle.

As I recall that place I am there again, and will be. It is a pause in time, and it is so astonishing that it is almost unbelievable in memory. But perhaps the most essential way for me to know I had seen great art was when I left it, and walked out into the street, where, for a moment, I could see with the eyes of the painter. I left that small, deceptive place expecting to see miracles, and expecting them to be ignored by most of the people who passed me in the street, people who, for a little while, had Goya faces.

CASTILE

Ring roads, beltways, *periféricos* are the modern circles of Dante's Inferno. I see the cars going on forever, their drivers tailgating, cursing, speeding, spreading deadly fumes, never exiting, forever and ever deserving the hell they have made.

I loved it. I was enjoying flying along the *periférico* around Madrid in a beautiful small rental car, a *Real;* stick shift, balance and weight perfect for speeding. It lived on diesel, fifty miles to the gallon. I was getting used to keeping to the eighty-mile-an-hour flow of traffic, and beginning to slide past slower cars.

I was letting the land sweep by, with that chosen ignorance that presents a world to tourists as if there were an empty space between "historic" sights—as if blood had never been shed, or there had never been harvest, birth, death, or a patient way of traveling deep into a country. It was time to find an exit and get off.

I found one northwest toward Avila, on the north side of the mountains, navigating by the sun, and the Sierra Guadarrama, that protective wall of granite and snow that I had watched from the palace hill in Madrid. Well-kept roads went from town to town as they always have, the routes of the Lusitani, the Roman legions and the Castilian armies.

I had all day to roam. After all, I was alone, and almost asking to get lost. I was looking forward to discovery, not to being tied to that deadening word, itinerary. How can you know ahead what you are going to see, find, lose, discover, any more than who you are going to fall in love with the day after tomorrow or another time? I was content, at the right speed, in the right place at last.

How peaceful the countryside was. It seemed that on every distant mountain ridge, at the highest point of the horizon, a tiny fairytale spire rose into the endless sky. Was it bluer over Spain that day than anyplace else I had ever seen? It seemed so. The spires were to me what I had dreamed they would be from my childhood, castles in Spain.

But I was beginning to recognize the names of villages and towns from my research on the Spanish civil war. The road ran through the battlefield of Brunete, the landscape that after sixty years had become this peaceful and beautiful place. I drove slowly through towns where I passed flowering vines that tumbled over the walls, and houses that seemed to be asleep, and where one of the most terrible battles of the twentieth-century civil war had been fought.

From Las Rosas, north of the Madrid front, through the Escorial in the northwest, and south to the road from Madrid to the west, was the village of Brunete, which had given this confused and deadly battle its name, the Battle of Brunete. It had spread over an area larger than Rhode Island.

Brunete engulfed the Escorial, which was turned into a hospital by the Republican army. In this bloody landscape, under the brutal sun of July 1937, thousands of men on both sides had been killed. The Republican armies had been thrown up against crack Spanish Nationalist troops from Africa, and strafed from the air by the dreaded Messerschmitts and Henckels of Hitler's Condor Legion. Nazi Germany was using the Spanish war as a training ground. That would be evident in the world war that started three years later.

The Republican troops were sitting ducks in this deceptive landscape. Now I was seeing why. I was passing the *arroyos* and the low foothills of the Guadarrama mountains. On a landscape that was flat on the military maps, these were the traps.

Two brigades of American volunteers fought there with the International Brigade of men and women who were soldiers, nurses, and drove ambulances. They came from all over Europe and America to help protect the newly elected republic. Nine hundred young Americans had formed two brigades, the Lincoln Brigade and the Washington Brigade.

Six hundred of them were killed at Brunete, many of them still in their American clothes and their city shoes. The survivors formed the famous Lincoln Brigade out of what was left. As the Lincoln Brigade they were to fight through much of the rest of the war, their ranks swelling as more and more volunteers arrived. After World War II, the survivors were hounded from job to job, lumped together as "premature anti-fascists" by a reactive American government, along with most of the people who had volunteered for any of the allied forces in the two years before the United States entered World War II in 1941.

These were things I did not want to remember. I had been one of them. I had volunteered for the Women's Auxiliary Air Force before America entered the war.

I drove, slower and slower, caught by my own knowledge of a time and a landscape that had been so terrible, for we who have been to war, no matter where we were, have crossed a line into a memory that is more than a memory; it is a reliving, and will be there as long as we live. My hands were shaking on the wheel, and I had to stop beside a country road that seemed to go no place in that vast space. How many of my countrymen must have sat beside those roads, exhausted by heat, fear, and thirst? I remembered the story of an American volunteer who had stumbled, half drunk with fatigue, into the Escorial. He wandered through the great rooms, where hundreds of beds had been set up for the wounded, but he could find no place to lie down. Finally he made his way up some stairs and into a small, bare room where there was a single cotlike bed. He fell on it and went into what he called a sleep of the dead. His dirty shoes stuck out over the end of Philip II's bed.

That is the kind of memory we have; a small space and a few minutes, not an overall intelligent mental map where the results are known, the causes listed, there are vectors and sectors, and a totally false bloodless understanding.

I had started out that sunny morning for Avila, to a saint and a walled city, and the controlled, cleaned-up past of one of the countrywide Spanish *paradores*. The ruins of old monasteries, castles, and fortresses have been made into a series of the most comfortable and beautiful places to stay in Spain. I longed to get back to that innocent morning, but it had disappeared.

Somehow, in that crisscross of roads that must have confused those new civilian soldiers, who did not know the land and did not speak the language, I had gotten lost as well. I found my way to a first-class road, and joined traffic north to go where the long line of cars were going, anyplace away from what I had remembered.

Through the tunnel that has replaced what once was *El Alto de los Leones,* the naturally fortified mountain pass south to Madrid, and Andalucia, I came to a new country, and the oldest and once the wildest part of Christian Spain. Every day's travel would bring the hard knowledge that Spain, the most mountainous country in Europe after Switzerland, is formed as a state by its physical land. Its rivers have divided it into valley after valley, with its towns and villages castellated by the mountains that separate them. Once they were isolated; they still retain their independence and their pride. The few *mesas,* and the great *meseta,* are almost the only tablelands.

After the open fields, the low hills, and the *arroyos* south of the mountains, the road curved and plunged around sharp curves and steep rocky outcrops, sometimes through cuts in raw rock. It was unexpected, this rough landscape. Those fairytale spires I had seen in the distance on the crests of the sharp granite mountains, the "castles in Spain," were the ruins of watchtowers and brutal heavy fortresses in what had been a no-man's-land between the Gothic Christians and the Moors for so many centuries.

I had entered the kingdom of Old Castile, the font of the ever-present, ever-haunting past of Spain. William Faulkner once said, "The past is not dead. It isn't even past." Perhaps there is no place in Europe where it is truer than in Castile, where the past seems more alive than the present. In order to understand that the land I passed was something besides the blank space that kept apart two "lovely old" cities, museums that seemed to be kept alive for tourists, I had so much to learn about where I was.

For more than five hundred years the armies of Castile had fought across this mountainous place, and built the castles that I was seeing against the sky. They had imposed upon the petty kingdoms and the Moorish sultanates two extremes, iron religion and urban freedom. Its rulers had committed terrible acts that left scars. After so much war, the northern land was desolate, and almost uninhabited, except for soldiers posted to forts at the border, sometimes through years of peace. Villages for their wives and children grew up near the barracks as in the frontiers of the American West, forming the beginning of the great cities of Castile, the land of castles. The old Roman fortified towns, the Moorish cities were ruined and empty of people. With promises to the more intrepid settlers, made by the ruling aristocracy, the adventurers and the landless were persuaded to venture into dangerous, wild country, and from those settlers around the abandoned fortresses, new cities were born, at first rough and isolated.

Gradually, through the years, the land opened up to farmers, adventurers, those on the run from whatever trouble, poverty, or crime they were escaping in other, more civilized places. The promises that drew settlers, as in the American West, were land and freedom. As new Castilians they were invited and protected by the king, whose ambition was that the vast area of land be populated.

There were the incentives, the promised safety, all made legal by the frontier *fueros*. The word means charter, but it had among the Castilians a force beyond its meaning. The *fuero* stood for independence, for a perpetual legal right to freedom in a world that too often resorted to slavery. These royal promises are still the basis of Castilian local pride.

The great cities of Castile—Segovia, Avila, Burgos, and the

rest—started as these frontiers. The reign of Ferdinand and Isabel began at a time when these cities were becoming rich, and there was perpetual trouble between the cities and the power of the *grandes*, those descendants of the soldiers who fought the wars against the Moors and had been granted huge tracts of land, the *latifundios* that would be the pride and the scourge of Spain. With the true political genius they were to show over and over, Ferdinand and Isabel chose to protect the cities.

One of their royal tasks was to recognize that long-held passion for urban freedom. It may well have been the reason that they had no permanent court, no single capital. Their court was mobile, moving from pride to pride through a series of highly individual cities and states.

What power Castile flaunted over its poorer and less belligerent neighbors and much of the new world has long since disappeared. But there are ghosts that still affect the modern world of Spain. So much war has rolled over this part of Spain that, like the ever-surviving ants, the local people have had to build back, and build back trying to replace what they remember.

The Castilians are still quick to resent interference with the historic privileges they have earned by blood and by the danger of the very building of their cities. Spain is still wary of the easy compromises of a national state. It is one of the most potent strengths behind the movement to return ancient works of art to their *patrias chicas*, their little countries. The center of life is still local, to the political and economic annoyance of those who would rule from Madrid, and the amusement and lack of subservience of those who sit in the evening in the small-town *plazas mayores*. The most sophisticated Spaniard will speak with pride of his village, the family tap root, his *patria chica,* even if his family has left it long ago.

Castile had produced tyrants and reformers, saints and geniuses, and the most famous queen in Spanish history. She was Isabel the Catholic. There was not one city I went to that had not been touched by the decisions, the strengths, and the weaknesses of that round-faced, nervous woman, the patron housekeeper of Spain. She is so much an icon that it is not easy to find out who she was, her childhood, her training, and the learning she took for granted. And it is impossible to accept the overwhelming shadow that Castile still throws all the way to the Mediterranean without knowing the woman who, more than anyone else, helped to cast it.

She inherited the same kinds of fights, prejudices, gossip, and corruption found in most families fighting over wills, power, and money. But what did she, the person who was Isabel, think, accept as her right and duty? During her turbulent childhood, there was constant family quarreling. Family quarrels among absolute monarchs are affairs of state. Their caprices, prejudices, and early rigid training cast long shadows.

What expectations did Ferdinand and Isabel carry? They had both been made heirs, he of Aragon and she of Castile, by blood, trickery, envy, and conquest that went back to the Visigoths, who had been in Spain since the fall of the Roman Empire.

This was a woman who, in her early adolescence, tricked the king of Castile, her easy-going half-brother, Enrique IV, into naming her as his heir by promising that she would not marry Ferdinand. She was already the veteran of years of civil war over her succession. She was an active force in the faction of *grandes* who supported her claims and spread the word that her niece, Juana, Enrique's daughter, the true heir, was illegitimate.

She had two suitors, one the widowed king of Portugal. The other was the heir to the kingdom of Aragon, Ferdinand. But the king of Portugal already had an heir, so her own children would not be first in line for the combined thrones of Castile and Portugal. So she ignored her promise to her half-brother, and secretly negotiated to marry Ferdinand. There was one problem. They were cousins, and the church did not allow a marriage of close kin under the canon laws of consanguinity. Ferdinand and their supporters faked the permission of the pope.

They were both broke. They borrowed the money to marry in the city of Valladolid. She was eighteen years old. Ferdinand, at seventeen, had already led an army by the time he was thirteen. They had known each other for four days.

Their marriage is seen historically as the first step in the modern union of kingdoms that was becoming Spain. But that is the trouble with history. The people who set it down know what happened. History looks backward. What the new young monarchs thought they were doing at the time may have been another matter.

Isabel had grown up under the influence of a militant Catholic church, and the myths of the great crusade of the *Reconquista*. It had already for four centuries been the powerful force that kept the kingdom at war, pushing ever south, recalling what had become the legend of a great Gothic kingdom that was being revived. Like many political legends, it was not true.

What she and Ferdinand accepted as their first duty was to continue the crusade to revive the Visigothic kingdom as they had been taught it had existed when the *Reconquista* began in the tenth century, with a series of border raids carried out by what the Moorish rulers thought were mountain savages.

When the Moors arrived in 711, the Visigoths were swept north, over the mountains, beyond the Guadalquivir River, then the Guadiana River, then the Tagus, then the Duero. They were left only the small territory of Astoria. Here they stayed for three hundred years. Finally, they combined with the local Astorians, Roman Catholic Christians, Celts, and Basques into a Catholic country that was to move south for the seven hundred or more years of the Christian *Reconquista* of Spain. Finally, by the time of the death of Isabel, the Visigothic heirs had captured the water, pasture, and loot of the whole of Spain.

The prejudices and the weaknesses that the Visigoths had brought so long ago to Spain were, alas, still alive, and revered. One was a tragic and ominous concept that had once been tribal and was later to become the land of *limpieza de sangre,* the Visigothic belief in purity of blood, Gothic blood. They scorned intermarriage with the natives. They were loudly and dangerously anti-Semitic. Anti-Semitism became lethal in fifteenth- and sixteenth-century Spain. The dreadful laws of *limpieza de sangre* were turned against the Jews, who had been an important and integral part of what held the kingdoms together for centuries.

The effect of the Visigoths on the Spanish past has almost entirely died out of Spanish memory, but it has been a hidden force into the twentieth century. It created fierce prejudice, violence, and the most arrogant class consciousness in Europe, mostly with the official seal of the monarchy, and the backing of the church.

Only one year before Isabel's birth, the leading royal historian of Castile, Diego de Valera, had written to the heir to the Castilian throne, "You shall have rulership over all Spain, and you shall reform the imperial throne of the noble race of the Goths, from whence you come."

That was the heritage Isabel and Ferdinand took pride in, along with most of the Spanish ruling class.

The reality of their barbaric Visigothic ancestors was to grow into an ideal of the Gothic that was to remain popular reading until the nineteenth century and Sir Walter Scott. (He, by the way, was accused by Mark Twain of starting the American Civil War.)

In the sixteenth century Gothic romances had been the childhood reading of St. Ignatius Loyola, the creator of the Jesuits, the Society of Jesus, and of St. Teresa, the patron saint of Spain. The popular passion for Gothic legend, Gothic ideals, and Gothic romances was given loony immortality by the genius of Cervantes.

Even official art was affected: Jesus' hair and beard grew blonder and blonder. His eyes turned blue. He became more a saintly Christian martyr than a wandering Jewish rabbi whose words changed the world. His mother, Mary, became the ideal of Gothic girlhood, her face pale, her hair blond, her robes the blue of chastity, her age fourteen or so. The underbelly of such an ideal was uncivil; contempt for the "other," whoever the other might be—the Jew, the intellectual, the dark-haired Mediterraneans who had been in the southern mountains and the beautiful *vegas,* those green Spanish valleys, along the clear waters, since before the Phoenicians, the Romans, or the Moors.

But also by the fifteenth century the concept had become lightly comic. Pedigrees were for sale, Gothic ancestry was a matter of pride ("I am Goth from father to son, all the way back," one *hidalgo* said on his deathbed). The privileges were taken for granted by those who had them and sought by those who did not. And not all the privileges of *limpieza de sangre* were those of social and family pride. They were the legal preconditions to holding civil office, to entrance into the universities, and to entering some of the monasteries and the higher echelons of holy offices.

Corruption and mountains, ideals of some long-lost knight-hood, and Christian martyrdom were the wellsprings of Castilian power and legend, all in the narrow valleys and the sharp mountains of this rough land I drove through on the way to someplace other than I had planned on that first Saturday morning in September, on my first day out of Madrid.

I dawdled behind and in front of a line of strangers along a road in Old Castile. We followed each other with that infinite impatience we harbor in crowds that mean no harm. At last I saw a sign. We were not trundling along to Avila, but to Segovia. I didn't care.

We moved toward the steep hill that juts out over the Castilian plain on a high promontory that looked in the distance like a cliff. That sharp cut has for so many centuries made a perfect castle sight to look for enemies, north and south. Segovia is a truly permanent border city between the conservative north, Old Castile, and Spain south and east of Madrid.

The massive Roman aqueduct for which the area is famous was etched so high against the hard blue of the sky that I had to lean down in some danger of being rammed by the car behind me and crashing into the car before me so I could look up to the second stone tier, more than a hundred and fifty feet above me. The late morning sun etched the arches of stone with shadows in niches that once had held votive statues. The smaller stone arches that carried the vast heavy riverbed were so far away they seemed frail. They held up a narrow river that had been forced to flow along a streambed carved in grooved stone. The aqueduct had to be as high as the hill of Segovia, for the city depended on the downflow of water, inch after inch, for miles from its source, using gravity to keep it moving. It was still being used until a few years ago to provide water for Segovia as it had done since it was a Roman city in the first century A.D.

I drove in my turn past the arches that held up the aqueduct. Large squares of stone held carved names. I wondered how old they could be. I wanted to stop but was trapped by traffic. The line crept uphill toward the *plaza mayor*. We drove through streets the width of twelfth century travel by foot, horse, or mule. Our cars nearly touched the sidewalks on both sides; sometimes, we brushed against window boxes full of flowers.

Like everybody else, I was looking for a place to park. I found it downhill near Segovia's *alcázar,* one of those fortresses first built by the Moors on Roman bases, then by the Castilians on Moorish ruins, a truly fairytale castle with the valley far below that I had driven through disappearing beyond the horizon.

It was Saturday, the day that Spanish families from Madrid go to the country. A surprising number of young men and women were sitting under the trees and around the low stone walls as if Segovia were a park. There were few foreign tourists. You could tell them, us, me, by cameras.

For the first time I went into a market. For the first time I bought bread and cheese and figs and a small bottle of wine—in Spanish, of a kind. I joined the picnickers on a stone bench below the city wall. And after lunch and the sun

I drowsed in the grounds of the castle with hundreds of other visitors, my back against an old, gnarled tree, and had my first *siesta,* that wonderful, civilized, Mediterranean afternoon when everybody goes home and the shops close, and the city sleeps, tourists or not, to open again at five o'clock.

On that first day I had already found a civil war, escaped into the wrong city, learned *siesta,* the Spanish for figs and red wine, and above all, strolling. The Spanish are the most accomplished strollers in Europe, and they are elegant about it. They don't stand in the middle of the street and make you go by in the gutter, as in some countries. They are infinitely polite. But they do stroll, and in that beautiful city in the late afternoon I strolled, too.

Along the old street leading up the steep hill from the castle, I was awed by medieval houses that the people of Segovia have taken for granted for over seven hundred years. I stopped and looked for the first time at the still-defiant, unchanged pride of Castile—a carved coat of arms, a street, a church tower, a statue of someone honored in a plaza with no explanation to tell us, the strangers, who it might be. The Spaniards welcome us and let us look, too, but they often do not explain. I went later to several cities where there were no tourist brochures in English or, as far as I could see, any other language but Spanish. What has survived is still for them, their own.

The oldest buildings in the city are like Gothic outcrops of granite that seem to grow from the hill rock. By the fifteenth century Segovia was rich. It was because of the sheep, and the methods of grazing. The constant movement of livestock, the grazing and water rights so fiercely protected, the branding, the yearly sales, the contempt for fences made any attempts by free peasants to farm almost impossible. A year's food could be eaten away in a night by passing herds. The people began gradually to move into the cities, and survived by learning trades.

The raising and shearing of sheep, the spinning of yarn, the carding of wool, everything to do with woolen cloth, was the leading industry of Castile, and it brought more riches than even the glittering gold from the new world. Segovia, like Avila, Medina del Campo, and Burgos, became a city of leather workers, weavers, spinners. A new urban force was gaining power, that of the industrial merchants, and craftsmen and women, the weavers, the carders, the spinners, whose skill was becoming famous all over Europe.

While I was looking at the cliff-high ancient city walls that were built so long ago to contain and protect Segovia and its people, I stumbled on another of those wars in Castile that seemed never to have ended. I saw a hint of it first in a street, and then in a plaza with an unknown man on a plinth. The street was the *Calle de Bravo.* It is the memorial to Juan Bravo, whose statue stands in the plaza. His house is still pointed out. He was not a peasant, a shepherd, or a weaver, but a king's representative, a *regidor,* one of the proudest of royal appointments.

In every town I was to see later in that endless political chess board, battleground, and frontier, the cities in the *meseta* of Castile, there was either a *calle des comuneros* or a street named for one of the leaders. Unlike any fighting that had gone before, it was a civil war between autocracy and the voices of an army of urban citizens that reached across class, generation, and economics. It was the first civil war in Europe that can be called modern.

There had been so much civil strife, family against family, brother against brother, peasant revolts, wars of succession.

This war had begun in Segovia, and it was new, but was it more even than that? It began as an uprising of the leading Castilian cities against a foreign king. It was a tax revolt. But more than a hundred years before the English civil war, it would grow into the first uprising in Europe to demand elected instead of appointed representatives and regular meetings in the *Cortes,* the Spanish Congress, which up to then had met only when the king required it, and that was usually to raise money.

In 1520, a civilian militia was formed out of the need for liberty against a tyranny that was draining the country into hunger and the loss of the hard-earned *fueros.*

Nothing could have been less welcome to me than to think of civil war after the morning spent crossing the battlefield of Brunete. But in Spain history intrudes everywhere. It is not something apart; it is in the stones, the towers, the narrow streets.

In the late afternoon, I toiled with the crowd up the steep hill street toward the *plaza mayor.* In Segovia it is the main gathering place to look at the cathedral, which overwhelms the plaza. The evening was lovely, and the slanted sunlight glistened on the delightful pinnacles of the Lady. The huge gold wedding cake filled the sky in front of us, a Flemish delight. It is the famous cathedral built after the revolt of the *comuneros,* a monument to the first Hapsburg king. It is so large, so bright that at first you do not notice its neighbors. But it has taken from 1525 until now to look at home in this ancient city of Romanesque and Visigothic granite buildings.

Long before I knew what I was seeing I stopped and stared at the huge pavement of stones, where the first blood was shed in the war of the *comuneros.* On May 30, 1520, a gentleman rode into Segovia, maybe up the same steep hill I had climbed. He came from his estate on his mule, in his scarlet cloak and scarlet doublet with his gilded sword and dagger. He had been warned not to go into the town, where the mob had already killed two of the king's catchpoles, the tax gatherers. He had scorned the warnings.

After all, he was Rodrigo de Tordesillas, an appointed delegate to the *Cortes,* a *hidalgo,* a member of the minor nobility. Like the rest of the gentry and the grandees, he paid no taxes. It is no wonder that the goal of a successful businessman would be to reach *hidalgo* status by whatever means he could. The peasants and wool workers bore the full burden of taxes, sales tax, head tax, any tax the government could think up when they needed money.

The *hidalgo* in the red cloak had just returned from the king's business, the meeting of the *Cortes.* They had just raised the taxes of the working artisans and the poor by nearly 50 percent. He, after that persuasion known as *douceur,* had helped to swing the votes to satisfy the king's demand for money. *Douceur,* the greasing of the palm, the polite gift of money, was not thought of as bribery. It was simply a tip, a privilege of office. Everybody understood that. What had he to fear from the rabble of Segovia, most of whom worked in the wool trade that had made Segovia one of Castile's richest medieval cities?

He tethered his she-mule and entered St. Michael's Church to report to the city fathers. The mob followed him into the sacred building. They dragged him out of it, toward the gibbet where the two catchpoles lynched the day before still hung upside down. He was already nearly dead from beating as he was half-carried across the *plaza mayor,* his scarlet cloak dragging in the dust and animal waste of the market.

When had the seeds of that inevitable revolt been planted? Had it had been as far back as the birth of the Castilian cities? Had it been planted by Ferdinand and Isabel, whose legend, still held to so grimly in Spain, is that they were the king and queen of a golden age? There was, for a while, a golden age, but it was Columbus's discovery, by accident, of the new world that made them so powerful. Up to that time they had stripped the public as clean as they could to pay for the incessant war against the last kingdoms of the Moors. Isabel had sworn a sacred oath to rid the country of infidels. It was a time when she, as a fundamental Catholic, would never have questioned her duty.

In 1516, their grandson, the eldest son of their daughter Juana who had married the Duke of Burgundy, inherited the throne of Aragon on Ferdinand's death. Ferdinand had been chosen to act as regent for his mother, Juana, queen of Castile. After a royal fight in which the grandson's faction overwhelmed Ferdinand's faction, Charles was named regent of Castile instead. He was "His Sacred, Caesarean, Catholic, Royal Majesty, [now self-styled] king of Castile and León, Duke of Burgundy from his father, King of Aragon, Count of Barcelona," and soon to be emperor-elect of the Holy Roman Empire after Maximilian.

He had never been in Spain. He spoke no Spanish. He was a gangling, awkward, unattractive boy of eighteen, jerked by the puppet masters who had raised him in the court of Flanders. The only image of him I know is a small poly-chrome statue in the chapel at Granada, showing the huge jutting chin that would be known as the Hapsburg chin. That small portrait is, like many of the contemporary polychrome portraits, one of the fine works in that essentially Spanish medium. As soon as his body would obey, he grew a beard, which he wore until his death.

He came to Spain for the first time in his life, not to rule but to exploit, as he was told. After all, it had only been fifteen years since the death of Isabel, and two years since the death of Ferdinand, and they had left incredible pickings for a new regime. The new world promised riches; the wool trade of Castile promised even more. His claim to the throne was considered fraudulent since his mother was still alive. His advisors were bumblers. The election of this stupid boy as the Emperor Charles the Fifth of the Holy Roman Empire was mostly paid for by Segovia and the other cities of Castile.

Whatever Charles's advisors could do wrong, they did. The looting was public. Two of his entourage were each allowed to take three hundred horses and eighty pack mules loaded with fine clothes, jewelry, furniture, silver, and gold bullion from the new world to Flanders. Charles went back to what had been his home all of his life, leaving Flemish courtiers and clergy to govern his new realms of Castile and Aragon.

The populace watched the gleaning of their country for two years, and then, when the new king returned, demanding the 50 percent raising of taxes to fight in middle Europe and buy the title of Holy Roman Emperor, the cities of Castile finally revolted. That was the beginning of the revolt of the *comuneros*.

The mob murder of the man in the scarlet cloak was only the start of the two-year civil war whose memory is still guarded all over Castile by street name, by statue, by long-remembered pride. After the war, the *grandes*—who had stayed aloof from the quarrel between the cities, which they despised, and the court, where they sulked at having lost their old control when Ferdinand and Isabel sided with the cities—realized they had to make a choice. They sent their mercenary troops to bolster up the royal armies. It was the final stand of the *comuneros*.

Charles brought with him promises for a new era in Spain, to repair the devastations of war, and five thousand of his best Flemish guards. It was the beginning of the years of Flemish influence, some of which can be seen in the Prado, with its fine collection of sixteenth-century Flemish art.

It was then that Charles built the cathedral that is the pride of Segovia. But if the cathedral was in its time a modern imposition on an already ancient town, even more so is the castle that grew out of the Moorish *alcázar*, another out-of-place and out-of-time delight. It is a pure nineteenth-century fantasy of what maybe a medieval castle ought to look like, reconstructed when the palace barracks was set afire by army cadets who wanted to go to barracks in Madrid. It will forever now be known as the one castle in Spain that Walt Disney decided was perfect; it was copied at Disneyland, the same pinnacles, the same towers, the same illusions.

AVILA

 I expected the "city of saints and stones," but I did not know about the roses, and the farce, and how brutal the walls were. I came there in the evening from Segovia, less than an hour away to the east. The light at the end of a day made the fortress city in the distance look like a flat wall of gray stone against the sky, without density or weight. As I drove nearer the heavy architecture, the towers stood out above the hill ahead of me, and the walled city seemed as terrible as it must have been when it was built as a military refuge.

This is the only city in Castile with its medieval walls intact. All of the Castilian cities must have looked like it in the eleventh century, when they were fortified against their neighbors, and when the constant danger of raids was modified only by the weather or the time of year—safer at harvest, safer in winter. There were seasons in bloodshed.

Avila is now a modern city, but I forgot that when I drove to its walled center. The road began to climb toward the *parador*, one of those government hotels housed in historic buildings that are the pride of Spain, and should be. This one, built against the inner side of the city wall, promised a sixteenth-century palace—a palace to stay in while I followed the footsteps of a saint and mystic who lived in poverty and prayer.

As I drove under a heavy arch between two sky-high towers, I could almost feel some phantom iron gate crash shut behind me. If there are ghosts in Avila, they are heard—the clang of iron, the forges, the ironclad wheels of wagons that trundled over the cobblestones, the shouted orders, the pounding feet, the knife-bright clash of swords, and the lances held shoulder high by knights on their galloping horses, coming to the shock. The incessant tolling of bells, for the hour, for the dead, for warning and for prayer, had long been silenced, but not the faint echo from a church far away in the valley. I was afraid.

A wedding reception was being held at the *parador* when I arrived, the second one I had seen, a tradition of five o'clock marriages in Spain. It makes sense—the *siesta* over, the *paseo* just beginning. The bride in white with her long train, the groom in black tie, were going up the wide steps into the *parador*, followed by a close-packed crowd of guests as I went by. I had trudged so far in Segovia, and driven so far through what seemed, on looking back, to be centuries, that I felt tired and sweaty and wanted to dump luggage and crash, have a drink, have dinner, face Spain again in the morning.

I was trying to maneuver the car from a narrow cobbled medieval street into a medieval gate where a medieval building housed the *parador* garage when I ran into a dog's tail of Gothic incivility. It was the only time in Spain I encountered rudeness. Three of the wedding guests had to stop walking for a minute while I maneuvered the car. One of them strode up to the car and commanded me to move out of the way, taking up more time than if he had let me go on turning. He was elegantly dressed, as correct as if he were in uniform, all aristocrat, all good tailor, very tall, thin, and arrogant as hell. The word arrogant is said to have come from the manners of Aragon.

I simply turned the key and stopped the car until he finished waving a rolled umbrella, blathering in a Spanish so fast I could not understand a word. He strode back to the other wedding guests and I moved the car. I see him now, a prisoner of that outmoded view of himself, his clothes rich, his manners somehow threadbare. I was beginning to be personally offended by Avila, and sorry that I had come, but I had come as a pilgrim to a saint, and I knew I was going to stay.

So I parked the car, took my bags and laptop into a lovely ecclesiastical entry, struggled, overloaded and grubby, to the reception counter, snaking through a genteel riot of wedding guests. When I had found my room I could still hear them, so I decided to go out into the city for a while; the loud buzz of the wedding reception was engulfing the first-floor rooms.

I stepped out onto the cobbled street into an ancient fortress, rejecting and cold, made of granite by giant children with all their innocence and their brutality. Eighty-eight towers, in a vast rectangular wall with only nine gates like the one I had passed through. The towers nearly seventy feet high, the two hundred turrets on the high walls between them, all seem still ready for the archers; and always, for me, that ghostly sound and the smell of sweat, fodder, and horse manure—the cavalry of knights, playing and practicing at war, a long-gone, bloody children's game.

There were expensive modern shops within the walls, along cobbled streets that were still filled with people for the *paseo.* Soon the tension, the sense of capture, began to fade, and I remembered why I was there and why I would stay and search until I found a saint among the stones. The twilight was beginning to fade.

Later, and in other cities, I would join the *paseo* with a sense of belonging and being welcomed, and if I did not go to stroll among the strollers, I was conscious of missing some appointment I had not made. It would become, to me, the best time in a Spanish city, friendly. Not relaxed; never that.

That first evening I was utterly alone under the wall's dark shadows. To tell the truth, I hated and feared Avila at the beginning, among strangers. The architecture was, to me, a powerful stone rejection. Then I came to a huge arch where a gate had been, and I walked through it into a more casual, easy atmosphere. That gate would become, for me, the whole time I was in Avila, an escape route. It is the *Puerto de San Vicente,* which leads out toward the Church of St. Vincent beyond the northeastern corner of the old city. I would start from there, over and over until it became familiar. Later I realized that it was, too, for St. Teresa.

Just outside of the walled city is a long spacious plaza, with a Romanesque church at the end. The streetlights were beginning to shine in the deep twilight. It was the ancient *mercado grande,* where people go at evening, and the shops are attractive. It has been there since the eleventh century, the market space, the place for riots, fairs, fights, and *autos de fe* beyond the walls.

It was turning dark in Avila; the streetlights were too low to light the looming dark towers. I made myself walk slowly back toward the *parador,* hoping and praying I would not take a wrong turning. Finally I was there. I went into the bar for a drink. There were the bride and groom, she still in her white wedding gown with her satin train huddled in her lap, having a drink with the last of the guests.

I took my drink out into the garden, back into a softer darkness, scented with flowers. Then I saw, in the faint light of half-hidden torches, an ecstasy of roses in the *parador* garden. The roses were old, taller than my head, espaliered against the inner side of the city's wall, their branches leaning into the evening. There were places to sit, stone benches that may have been there forever or put in yesterday. It didn't matter. I was already beginning to accept living in one of the oldest and the most complete medieval barracks left in Europe.

The next morning it was time to do what tourists do, find the shape of where I was by walking. I walked along the outer side of the great wall, and there were roses everywhere, softening with their color and their scent the gray stone harshness of Avila. Shops were cut into the wall itself. The trail of roses led along the wide, well-kept lawn between the wall and the road.

I passed the apse of the cathedral, thrust out into the road, a rounded projection almost in the center of the eastern wall. It was built there as part of the defenses of the city. No place in the city reflects the past of Avila more than this building. It was the first Gothic cathedral built in Castile. Its dour simplicity astonished me, after the gold Flemish Lady of Segovia.

It was in that cavernous space bound by gray stone that one the most ridiculous farces ever in Spain was solemnly planned, part of that much fought-over inheritance to the throne of Enrique IV, which was to end with the accession of Isabel as queen of Castile. If ever a city needed a farce it was Avila.

The nobles were ranging around Castile, choosing their own heirs to the throne and generally overstepping their privileges. Those who were to meet in Avila had chosen Isabel. After all, everybody knew her; they had seen her grow up. She had been brought up and educated by the nuns in the Convento de Santa Ana, below the fortified hill, a pleasant walk in the country beyond the walls.

A meeting was called in Avila, and *grandes* and churchmen assembled in the cathedral from as far away as Toledo. They decided to depose Enrique IV for what they saw as his sins against his sovereignty. So they had a large platform built in the *mercado grande* to mount a fake trial. The people of Avila crowded the plaza as if for a royal spectacle, a fair, a celebration. The Spanish have ever loved an excuse for a *fiesta*.

A stuffed dummy representing Enrique was placed in a regal chair. There were speeches, accusing the king of four sins. First, he had offended royal dignity, and at this point the archbishop of Toledo lifted the crown from the dummy's head. Then the Count of Plasencia accused the dummy of bad administration of justice, and removed the sword from his side and held it high. The Count of Benavente took away his scepter and accused the dummy of bad government. Finally Diego López de Zúñiga made a "harsh and brutal" speech, and knocked the dummy of Isabel's half-brother out of the royal chair.

I was beginning to see a Castile that is so concentrated on the memory of Ferdinand and Isabel and their family that they seem still to own it—family farms, family quarrels, family births and deaths, disastrous family wills. Isabel tried and almost succeeded in running Spain from the grave. I could not escape her legend, her molding of a state. All through the reign of Ferdinand and Isabel, the two had treated Avila as a home. When they had to face their worst personal tragedy they came back once again to the place where Isabel had been a child and brought the body of their son and heir, Prince Juan. He lies in the Royal Convent of St. Thomas, in the chapel palace they built for him.

It overlooks the Adaja River, southwest of the walled city, an outgrowth of stark Gothic known in Spain as Isabelline. All the new riches of the Indies were spread around the simple figures of poor and sacred saints. It is lavish rather than baroque; it has no wit; it is splattered everywhere with gold and more gold. If the Escorial is a portrait of Philip II, this sad place, part monastery, part palace, is that of Isabel. I see a sad, hard-working woman who wanted to put everything in order, religion, children, investments, and Spain, before she went to bed. It was Juan's death that led finally to the disastrous ascension of Juana as queen of Castile.

That had been Isabel's worst nightmare; she saw in her daughter's recalcitrance her own mother's madness, which had darkened her childhood. So she tried, as she did everything else she touched, to control it by putting a codicil in her will to keep Juana from having the power to rule Spain; it was a decision that was to haunt Spain, a long shadow, that, on the surface, was a triumph of planning and for a while resulted in the greatest empire the world had ever seen. It was a danger she could not see. She had tried, though, and what she did cast a defining shadow over her daughter's life and the life of the state for four hundred years.

In 1521, the city fathers would gather again in Avila's cathedral, at the invitation of the dean, who was a member of the *comuneros*. The cities sent delegates to Avila for a meeting to define their terms for peace with Isabel's grandson, the young Charles I. It was in this chapel, now part of the cathedral museum, with its flags and its knights, and its darkness, that the voices of the common weavers, carders, and industrial peasants were first heard in debate in Spain.

This room was where they first demanded that the *Cortes* meet at regular, announced times and, even more frightening for the urban *hidalgos,* a popular vote for its members instead of a favored appointment, which often had been inherited, father to son. It was not what many of the city fathers who had joined the *comuneros* desired at all—they had only wanted to get rid of the foreigners who had come with royal power to leach the country of its wealth.

Charles blamed the Jews for the revolt, which probably had the effect of inflaming the already rampant prejudices of the city fathers. There were many Jewish families in Avila; some had been converted for several generations and had married into "old" Christian families.

One child of this mixed blood was doña Teresa Sanchez de Cepeda y Ahumada. She was six years old when the *comuneros* meeting was held, old enough to be aware of it and more certain to be aware of the legal action that her father was taking. Her father and uncles were in court presenting very expensive papers to prove their *limpieza de sangre,* pure Castilian Christian blood "all the way back," with branches connected, however tenuously, to every leading family; as the dying *hidalgo* said, " pure Goth all the way back."

It is no surprise that a family would do all that power and money could to protect their own, even though the protection was fairly useless among a cynical population. It was no different in Avila. The little girl who was to be St. Teresa lived in a highly dangerous atmosphere. Her own *converso* grandfather had been humiliated in an *auto de fe* procession

in Toledo, forced to wear the shameful *sambenito*, the penitential garment that was hung later in his local Christian
church to shame the family forever. He had been accused of
being a lapsed Jew. He had moved his family to Avila, in
those days far enough away from Toledo so that there was at
least hope that the shame would not follow them, but Avila
had the prejudices, the envies, and the ears of a small city.

As I went about the streets, exploring and finding what I
had not come to see, St. Teresa and Isabel became more intertwined. They shared the same streets, the same churches,
even the same convent where Isabel lived all through her
childhood, and St. Teresa took her vows as a nun. She was to
live in the Convento de Santa Ana for more than twenty years.
Family tombs were of the blood of both of them, the city their
homes in their most vulnerable years. The nunnery is still
there, where Isabel was sent away from her mad mother, and
Teresa lived with more than a hundred nuns in a convent that
was in her time more like a genteel boarding school.

Isabel's worst effect on the life of St. Teresa was obvious. It
had been her own fanatic Catholicism that had made her
known throughout Europe as Isabel the Catholic, fed the
flames of old Visigothic prejudice, and strengthened the
Spanish Inquisition. She had two fanatic Catholics to influence her, Torquemada and Cisneros, Cardinal Jiménez, who,
except for his religious puritanism, was one of the most enlightened men in power in the country. They decided to cleanse
Spain of religious dissidence, and on the way make more
money for the once empty royal coffers. The so-called New
Christians were easy prey. At first, there were gross, brutal confiscations and executions, tortures to extract confessions from
frightened people. It became quickly an international scandal,
the beginning of Spain's bloody reputation in Europe.

A *converso* could be arrested for the most innocent of old Jewish habits—washing on Friday, putting clean linen on the beds one day instead of another, changing into clean clothes for Saturday. Treatment of *conversos* was not only fanatical, brutal, and merciless but thorough. There were mass confiscations of their property, some of which went to the crown, the rest to the Inquisition for "expenses." Many of the fine sixteenth-century buildings so admired today were built with this money.

The whispers in her lifetime throw a bright light on the sheer courage of an embattled half-Jewish woman who became, along with another Jew, St. James, the brother of Jesus, the patron saint of Spain.

At the southeastern corner of the walls is the *Puerta del Alcázar,* the huge gate that opens into the *Plaza de Marcado.* Beyond it, her hands clasped, I found Avila's St. Teresa. It shows her as she might have looked had she been a dream, a vision, a beautiful lady, ideally calm, not grief stricken but sad. The statue is lovely. I am still furious.

This is the woman who said, "God deliver me from silly devotions and sour-faced saints," and who loved Seville because "there is no suggestion of that nonsense about my supposed sanctity."

Is this the woman who slapped the papal nuncio, told the king of Spain to shut up, had an argument from time to time with God himself? What she looked like is known from a contemporary portrait and many contemporary descriptions. In the only portrait of her that was made from life she was fifty-two years old, deep in the work she chose, or that she believed chose her. Her face is slightly plump, her eyebrows strong and black. This is a portrait of a brave, slightly ironic, intelligent woman who looks tired, and beyond the fatuous "holiness" she despised, a woman who has shed fear. It is endearing that she complained that she looked ugly in the painting, for she had been a beautiful woman, and still had about her that small human vanity.

Surely I could find some glimpse of her in the city where she spent her life up to the age of forty-five; something besides the hard stones and the sanitary and diminished images, for most of her far-reaching decisions were made in Avila. It was here that she found her path.

When I came to the house where she was born, I found that it had been replaced years after her death by a grander one. As a baroque convent, it was far from the first broken-down little institution she founded in Avila "that would just do for a convent, though a very small one . . . equipped so we could live in it. It was very rough and ready, and no more was done to it than was necessary to make it healthy to live in. This is always the proper way of doing things."

There was little money but what she could scrounge, no houses, no furniture (which is what she called the straw mats that were the first beds put down for her nuns). She was to start seventeen Barefoot Carmelite houses, none of them with more than thirteen nuns to pray for Spain's sins during what she called "a world in flames."

The flames were of the fifteenth- and sixteenth-century wars of religion in Europe, and the Thirty Years' War in which, it is said, a third of Europe perished, as the mercenary soldiers, both Catholic and Protestant, destroyed everything in their paths. *The Miseries and Disasters of War*, the series of etchings of the atrocities in the Thirty Years' War by Callot, are superb illustrations of the conflict. They were an important influence on Goya when he drew his series *The Horrors of War*. The Catholic leader in this long series of religious wars was the Holy Roman Emperor, Charles V, who once had been that unattractive eighteen-year-old boy led by the nose by his "advisors."

As a bright, loving, vivacious, and very pretty young girl, Teresa had been put in a convent school by her father because he feared that in her zest for life, she would, frankly, get herself into trouble. She confessed in her autobiography as one of her many temptations the reading of novels, the same kind of Gothic romances on which the local priest laid blame for the "madness" of Don Quixote. Amadís the Gaul, the knightly hero of the most famous lay book in Spain, was her hero, her ideal of manhood.

Her father put her there because of gossip about her behavior, innocent but wild; if there was excess it was of a joy that never seemed to leave her. She had to be taken away when she nearly died of an illness that has never been defined, but which seems to have been a hypersensitivity that kept her in terrible pain. During her recovery she secretly began her life-long discipline of silent prayer, a way of worship much punished by the Inquisition.

Against the will of her father she ran away and took her vows as a novice in the Carmelite nunnery of Santa Ana, the same building where Isabel had been kept as a child. It was Teresa's first step toward the woman she would become, whose message would reach over Spain, the Catholic Counter-Reformation, and then beyond those confines to the world. Her message is in the books she wrote, the vast correspondence she kept up with those she loved, her holy metaphors, her ecstatic visions, her down-to-earth images, her wit.

The Carmelites in Avila where Teresa took her vows had long since dropped the early strictures of the order, which had been started outside Jerusalem over a thousand years before. For twenty years as doña Teresa de Cepeda y Ahumada she had a private apartment in Santa Ana, where she led a social life she was coming more and more to despise. She had a servant, visitors, many friends outside the confines of the nunnery; at the same time and in the privacy of her inner sanctum, she was being slowly drawn toward what would be her life work.

In the convents of sixteenth-century Spain, aristocratic and rich nuns called themselves *doña*, Lady, and were allowed a servant, good food, visitors, and carefully censored books. Convents were good places to stash the well-born illegitimate, younger daughters to save the dowry, and wives who were tired of their dreary husbands. Although the convents required a dowry, too, it tended to be less than in the marriage market.

Teresa was slowly learning to discipline her energy, her romanticism, her intelligence, and her faith in life and God, into a new channel. She had guidance from her confessor, who told her to write her first book, her autobiography. Water, its flow, its cleanliness, its refreshment, its power, was forever to be her metaphor.

She would be the most influential person ever to come from the city of Avila. In a world of total masculine authority, in the years of "a world in flames" she started the reform movement of the Carmelite order, and took it back to the vows of chastity, poverty, and obedience to God that its nuns had taken when the order was started.

She obeyed the interior visions that instructed her to do her work. She disciplined herself to keep the vigil of her prayers for years until she had been freed of fear into a clear path of service. She went into this path sick and frightened; she came out cleansed of the guilt she had been taught, the frightening place she had been born, into in an ugly world. She walked in pure joy and wit into a wide path of service. The fears that had been mountains for her diminished into nothing. And she wasn't afraid of God, the king, the papal nuncio who tried to stop her, or the devil himself. If courage to follow what she believed to be her work sustained her, humor and love blessed her, and a strength beyond the frailty of her body drove her. That was where her sainthood lay. She was far from the kind of puerile mystic, all draperies and tears, that she found some-times amusing, sometimes a nuisance. And she was the only woman ever to become a doctor of the Roman Catholic Church. Avila lives on her fame.

But Avila in the sixteenth century rioted when she opened her first reformed convent in a poor tumbledown house with four Carmelite nuns. She was reported to the Inquisition for her habits of prayer, which were seen to be dangerously like those of the *alumbrados,* whose cult of inner prayer made them heretics, and who were being jailed or burned all over Spain. In many ways they resembled the Quakers, who were persecuted in the seventeenth century in Old and New England.

Those who reported her to the Inquisition must have known that she was in great danger, not because of her beliefs but because of a father's wealth, a father's blood. To report her was very nearly an attempt to kill her.

Mystics see her in constant ascendant ecstasy when she was so embarrassed by the phenomenon that she asked her fellow nuns to sit on her and hold her down when there were strangers present at mass.

While the official church condemned, St. Teresa prayed for those who had gone so far in reform that they were all lumped together as "Lutherans" and burned when they were found out, often within the church hierarchy itself. Her reform stayed within the limits of the church, perhaps because she, as Cocteau said about genius, knew "how far to go too far."

To me she is one of the bravest women who ever lived, and a writer of pure honesty and essential truth, however obscured by the language and metaphors of her time. Often misconstrued, and misunderstood, her words shine through bad translation and that censorship known as editing or good taste, orthodoxy, and sanctity. She said herself that one of the things that made her happy when she was starting a foundation in Seville was "that there is no suggestion of that nonsense about my supposed sanctity." Barefoot Carmelites was the derogatory term for her foundation because the nuns and she herself wore the simple sandals of peasants; with a certain wit she took that name for her new foundations—the Discalced Carmelites.

Direct contact with God without going through the discipline of the church had led many a heretic to be burned at the stake. Even some of the leaders of the church who dared to touch the idea of reform and humanism fathered by Erasmus were accused of the heresy of Luther and jailed or sent to the stake.

She could not but know what she faced. But in her own eyes and in her own experience, she went, armed with the trust in God that gave her courage. Beyond the criticism of her own religious order, she traveled across Spain, not preaching, not converting, simply setting up small foundations of reformed Carmelites, who were sworn to go back to the ancient pure rites and laws followed so long ago on Mt. Carmel. She did as a woman what St. Francis of Assisi had done as a man.

When I walked along the old streets of Avila where she

had walked, I was sometimes overpoweringly conscious of her; it was impossible not to be. Her actions and the legends about her are mapped there, one church where she was christened, one where she prayed, a house she visited, a monastery where she confessed. After a time I saw her everywhere, away under the tourist signs and the little train that took tourists on what I dubbed the St. Teresa express around the walled city.

But it was outside the walls that I met her first, and even that may have been legend. The Church of San Vicente, which was begun in the eleventh century and which stands outside the *Puerta de San Vicente*, is to me the most beautiful Romanesque church I have ever seen. The south porch has life-sized figures of patriarchs, and saints, as so many other churches. But watching them as they looked down on me, I knew that a great sculptor had conceived them. He is said to have been Master Fuchel, one of the few medieval architects and artists who is known by name for works that were usually anonymous. The figures are formal, with the elongation of Byzantine bodies.

What was it that set them so beyond the usual ecclesiastical sculpture of the time? I went back whenever I passed and looked again as I would stop in the Prado in Madrid to see the Goyas, and then leave, as I did many times there, without stopping to see anything else. It is *duende* in stone, the presence like no other, no matter the formality, or the time created. It is the rare shock of recognition, the chill, as of falling in love.

The interior of the church seems intimate; its almost gold light pours down through the sky-high windows of its tower into the narrow nave to bless the people below instead of diminishing them as the Gothic vaults tend to do. Almost at once, when I went in by the porch door instead of the main Romanesque door, I came to the tomb of the three Christian children, San Lorenzo and his sisters, who had stood up to be counted as Christian in the Roman Empire, whose rulers had set out to destroy Christianity as a dangerous cult. Their poor little provincial martyrdom had taken place in the first century A.D. on the spot where the church was built.

The tomb has bas-reliefs, and little primitive marching Roman soldiers. It has something else, too, that goes beyond the usual memorials to the usual martyrs. It has an ironic magic, the horrible mundanity of people doing a job, as if the Roman soldiers who carry out the tearing apart of the children's bodies by stretching them on crosses were simply obeying orders without emotion or hatred or much interest. It made me wonder what in the modern world that we take for granted would be looked on with horror by future generations. The tomb, too, is said to have been carved by Master Fuchel, with that uncatchable spirit in his hand and eye.

The bas-reliefs of course are brutal, but incredibly strong, not with the obscenity of agonies as many of these memorials are, like are stone tabloids of their time. There is something else, a reality, beautiful, not to be forgotten. The soldiers, the children, are all playing their roles in a *duende* of sculpture, too, for the crime of defiance.

It is that word, defiance, that made me begin to recognize the essential quality of the Spanish hero. It was there in Avila, the bastion of authority in stone, with those children, and with St. Teresa. She is more akin to those children than to the St. Teresa of modern Avila.

This was the first glimpse I had, a spark, a flicker, of the essential quality that has been honored though the centuries in Spain. For me it had no name yet, but I recognized it. It was not rebellion, and it was not resistance. It was the pride and courage to defy the accepted mores, and to face tyrants without fear, whether the tyrants be kings or windmills. It is, to me, why Don Quixote is the essence of a Spanish hero. He is the tragicomedy of Spain, their Amadís, their Hamlet, their Charlie Chaplin, their clown, their sorrow.

The Church of San Vicente is where doña Teresa de Cepeda y Ahumada went to pray, in the crypt, and received the revelation that set her on her road to her life's work. I read about her lonely prayer in St. Vincent long before I ever saw Avila. I could not verify it in any guidebook or official brochure. But then, so much is left out, so much has been hidden by orthodoxy, fear, and historic good taste, that it does not surprise me.

She walked down the dark, damp stairs into the crypt, as I followed so many centuries later, into the shrine of the Holy Virgin. Had there been no votive statue of the Holy Mother, no votive candle casting shadows on the dark wall, the crypt would have been like one of the dungeons the medieval world used for prisons. It was there that she knelt and prayed for guidance, and was given the permission and the duty to do no less than to reform the Carmelite order to what it had once been. She prayed to blot out the remission of the strict rules, and the easy life of the nuns, who, while living Christian lives in the eyes of the church, were comfortable, well fed, well clothed, and, even within the nunneries of the Carmelites, had a social hierarchy that imitated the world outside the walls.

It was a scandal and a nuisance, as so many revelations are, and it put Teresa in great danger, from punishment by her own superiors and by the Inquisition. She walked, not serenely, but unstoppable, through rules, through dirt roads, winter and summer, on and on for the rest of her life, some-times staying in palaces, sometimes hovels. She was a friend of hermits, one especially—Philip II, the king of Spain, who lived piously in that one small room at the Escorial. Another, Peter of Alcantara, was so lean and holy that St. Teresa said he looked like a twig. Today, you pass foundations begun by St. Teresa in Spanish cities other than Avila. They are no longer in the simple houses where they originated. Still, they provide an interesting contrast to the fine medieval and Renaissance monasteries that have been turned into luxuri-ous *paradores*.

St. Teresa has been seen through history in many ways. To some, she is a will-o'-the-wisp that we try to catch and pin down. Bernini saw her in her most famous ecstasy, when she was pierced in her heart by an angel with a gold spear. So many see his view of her as orgastic, as they must if that is the way they see.

We see from where we stand. So I can only say who she was to me. She was, as most women writers are, myself included, Mary and Martha, too. Martha still argues with Mary day after day as we leave the last of the laundry, the dried tears of chil-dren, the demands for living "standards," the criticism of the established, usually male, literary dictators. We go to our cor-ners, our rooms, our hiding places, and do our work, often, as she did, feeling guilty, as she wrote once, because her share of the spinning had not been finished.

But I think she knew the other side, too, the relief from Mary's work that is Martha's. She must have known that escape from the concentration that leaves behind killing fatigue, the disquiet that follows the demanded quiet, and often, in her case, the physical pain. No wonder she wrote that God was in the pots and pans.

She was so wonderful a writer. She compared herself once to a small donkey, the comparison was apt for her, too many burdens, too many strings . . . a busy contemplative, an oxymoron of a woman. She had the genius to soar to her heaven and then stumble to earth and take us with her in a daily metaphor. She wrote, "Such was the vision that the Lord was pleased to send me that by comparison everything here on earth seems, as you might say, like a smudge of soot."

Her dear friend was Spain's greatest contemporary poet, St. John of the Cross, whom she teased by saying that he insisted on saving mankind even though they hadn't asked. She had the true simplicity of a poet, and if her humility was, to us, a little overdone, she was of her own time and her own language, and in her simplicity and her honesty not only one of the greatest writers of Spain but one of the greatest women writers anywhere and any time.

She wrote in the language and the images of her time, as we all do. The popular Gothic romances her father forbade gave her castles for her visions. She has more in common with those who catch the glimpses she caught and struggle to put them into words than she had with any of her sixteenth-century neighbors in Avila. Longing without a name and fulfillment glimpsed are more of her company than almost anyone she could have known in her time except St. John of the Cross.

She would have recognized Thoreau when he wrote, "It was not corn I hoed nor I who hoed corn." Marlowe's "See how Christ's blood streams in the firmament" was of her visions. Nearer our own time, the words of Yeats, "It seemed, so great my happiness, / That I was blessed and could bless," was of her experience.

She was probably the only person in Philip II's lifetime who told him to shut up. No matter that in Avila she is today a censored, polite and pious tourist attraction, with her own little railroad, so visitors will not have to walk up those hard hills and trudge down into those steep valleys as she did. To Federico García Lorca she not only had *duende,* she was *duende.*

If she sassed the king of Spain, she had no fear of a greater power that she saw as her friend. Once her mule shied and threw her as they were crossing a creek. She sat there in the water and shook her fist at the sky, and called, "No wonder you have so few friends if you treat the ones you have so badly."

She was a tough, persistent, loving woman, not abstractly, but touchingly, blessed. She was a visionary who was as down to earth as a broom; she was human, vulnerable, and stubborn. She could dance, sing, play the castanets, compare the whole of life to a night in a bad inn, and fall in love. She is said to have once taken the cape and made three passes at a fighting bull.

It took years of agonizing illness to cast out of herself fear, entangling society, shame. After the years of her self-doubt, her attempts to cleanse what the world she lived in had taught her was sin, she came out on the other side beyond fear—fear of the Inquisition, fear of the absolute monarch, fear of the church hierarchy.

This is the woman who wrote the book of her trials, her autobiography, with such humanity and simple honesty that it is the book read in Spain second only to *Don Quixote,* with whom she has much in common. Imagine a nun, forty-four years old, which was considered in her time an old lady, who stood outside the walls of Avila, took off her sandals, brushed the dust of the city from her feet, and said, "I will not take with me even the dust of Avila," and then walked out into the alien world.

TORDESILLAS

 My road to Tordesillas was fifty years long. It started for me, by accident, in the Reading Room of the British Museum. I remember the day it began, one day out of so many years that I spent there working on *The Beulah Quintet*, the smell of leather, print, ink, and winter clothes around me. The Reading Room was a huge circular space under an etched gray glass dome so far above me that it might have been a part of the lowered sky, because it was February, the gray month that in England never seems to end. All around the curved walls there were open shelves so high I had to reach for the books on the top shelf. The long desks, with their seats on both sides, fanned out from the center of the room like the spokes of a wheel.

I remember the new blue leather of the desk, where I had chosen my seat for that morning, my papers resting on it, the time of waiting crawling by. Around me a hundred people worked in a concentrated silence as if a vast chess game were being played.

I had long since learned to sit at the end by the open shelves and browse among books that went back several centuries while I waited for the research material I had ordered. When my books were delivered, I would disappear into the wilderness, the battles, the convict ships, but in the half-hour I had to wait, I could go, choosing by chance, anywhere in the world at any time.

There was a wall of large leather volumes nearest my desk. I got up to look at them. They were the printed state papers of England, going back more than five hundred years. I chose a book at random. I remember letting the book fall open; I can hear it again. It was like the old magic of dipping in the Bible to tell a fortune or receive guidance. I read the official reports of two people cast ashore by a storm in the English Channel and being sheltered for their first night in a castle in Dorset. It mentioned the fact that the woman showed great courage. The man was the Duke of Burgundy, son and heir to Maximilian, the Holy Roman Emperor. His wife was the heir to the great Isabel, queen of Castile. Later I was to finish *O Beulah Land* in a tower of what was left of the castle that had sheltered the royal couple.

I began a habit of choosing a seat near the state papers. I found that Philip, the Duke of Burgundy, had died, and randy old King Henry VII had proposed marriage to his widow, Juana, queen of Castile. The negotiations went on for some years between Henry and her father, King Ferdinand of Aragon. It seemed that Juana had little to do with the matter. Kings, queens, dukes, princes, famous battles, and Shakespeare's historic plays marched through those pages.

I tried to find something of a queen of Castile, who had disappeared so quickly out of Spanish history. She would not go away. I even wrote a play about her, but it did not exorcize her demanding ghost. At first all I could find out was her legend, presented as official history. It is a story loved by the

Spanish. There has even been a new film about it. It made Juana into a wild woman, mad for love, who ranged for years all over Spain, traveling only at night, to take her husband's body to Granada, where he had asked to be buried. She was said to have opened his casket and kissed his feet.

All that remained of her, or seemed to, were several very famous romantic portraits of the mad queen, one turning away from priests who were trying to help her, one standing in the middle of a field with the coffin beside her on a famous night when she refused to go into the planned stopping place because she found out that it was a nunnery instead of a monastery, a sad, mad queen who hated women because of her obsessive passion for a philandering husband. For centuries Spain and the world have known her as *Juana la Loca de Amor*, Juana driven mad by love.

It offended me. Why was so little known about the man and woman who inherited the throne from the great Isabel? There was something wrong, too many questions unanswered, too many people whose interests were involved. I began a year's long search. Much of what I was finding out did not fit the sorry official story.

When Isabel died and Juana inherited Castile, one of her first acts as queen was to lift the Holy Inquisition in Seville, which was so brutal that it had become a scandal in the rest of Europe. She demanded an investigation for the first time since the Inquisition had become a legal arm of the Castilian and Aragonese monarchies. This certainly did not fit the picture of a withdrawn, demented woman. For Juana and Philip to challenge the Inquisition was to call up ecclesiastical power against them.

I thought that it had to be Juana's decision, for Philip cared little for Spain except as a money source. He was a handsome, much-loved rake, said to be sweet and gentle with the ladies. Juana was the most intelligent of Ferdinand and Isabel's children.

What had influenced her decision? There were whispers of heresy. There was no way the Inquisition could take the queen of Spain to the stake for heresy. But the church did have the power to ruin her by labeling her as mad.

The second fact that did not fit the legend was the death of Philip. He had played tennis in Burgos, drunk a glass of cold water, and was dead before the week was out. He died on September 25, 1506. But the glass of cold water was unimportant compared to the fact that plague was killing people all over Castile, and especially in Burgos.

Had he caught the plague? Or was his convenient death part of his bitter fight with King Ferdinand for power? The Spanish Catholic Church, the most authoritarian in Europe, which saw itself in a centuries-long crusade against the infidel, may have wanted to rid itself of this happy-go-lucky nuisance of a man.

Isabel had quarreled with Juana when she tried to keep her from leaving Spain to join her husband on her first visit from Antwerp as heir apparent. To stand up to Isabel was a brave act. Since standing up to authority was and is one of the main attributes of a Spanish hero, that seems to be another reason why her decisions may have been cast about publicly as neurotic at best, mad at worst. After all, to have the heir apparent of the queen of Spain as a heroic anti-autocratic figure is a nuisance in a power struggle. Was that dilemma part of the choice of a legend of madness?

So Juana had been trammeled, first by her mother's iron will, which had ordered that if Juana were uninterested or unfit to rule, King Ferdinand should be appointed regent of

Castile until the majority of the eldest son of Philip and Juana was of age. Although Ferdinand and Isabel, as we know, were joint rulers of Castile and Aragon, both countries had retained their separate identity. On Isabel's death, Ferdinand had no official power in Castile.

A three-cornered fight raged around the new queen, first between Philip and Ferdinand for her loyalty, second between Ferdinand and the *grandes* of Castile, who had never liked him and who broke the will by exiling him from Castile and appointing Cardinal Cisneros as regent. Maximilian was thinking of invading Spain to claim the throne for his grandson Charles, the seven-year-old son of Juana and Philip. Juana had been a valuable property for the power seekers when she inherited the throne. As a widow she was an inconvenience.

The personal denigration of Juana was, to me, where legend and reality met and clashed. It seems to have begun five weeks after Philip's death. His body had been filled with a calcium derivative, a kind of quick lime, and enclosed in a lead coffin inside a wooden one, the traditional way to bury a plague victim. His coffin was placed in the crypt of the monastery at Miraflores, a few miles outside of Burgos. On All Souls' Day, the second of November, five weeks after his death, Juana went to the monastery to do what Spaniards have done for centuries on the Day of the Dead, open the casket and say a prayer.

When the coffin was opened, the calcium had already almost obliterated Philip's face and body in the five weeks he had been encased in the tomb. The Flemish attendants who accompanied her began the rumor that she fondled the body and kissed its feet, but this would have been impossible. There were no discernible feet.

Was it because the Flemish did not understand the traditions that surrounded death in Spain? Juana found that the Flemish servants who had prepared the corpse had stolen the royal robes and sold them. They complained that they were not paid enough. There had also been rumors that the Flemish courtiers who had come from Antwerp with the new queen and her consort were trying to steal his body and take it back to Maximilian.

Juana made plans quietly to set out as soon as she could to honor Philip's request to be buried in Granada in the chapel with Isabel. She was in grave danger. She left Burgos and traveled in a funeral train, which was the traditional ritual way of carrying a body—as in *Don Quixote*, when the Don and Sancho Panza meet the priests carrying the body in procession.

Her first stop for the night was in Cabra, only a few miles from Burgos. She seems to have been trying, not to hurry, but to escape her constant fear of the Flemish legation, and the ever-watchful Cardinal Cisneros, who had been appointed regent when the *Cortes* had thrown Ferdinand out of Castile against the dying wish of Isabel.

But here the mystery and the legend entwine. Was her flight brought on by a nervous collapse? Was her refusal to let her husband's body be buried her attempt to prove that he had been poisoned? Who profited from her escape, her legend? Then began—and history, ever the servant of official documents, has taken it as true—the story of *Juana la Loca*, wandering all over Castile with her husband's body.

Ferdinand was one of the few people Juana loved and trusted. She did not trust Cisneros, who was as fanatic a Catholic as Isabel, and who was instrumental in ousting

Ferdinand. He may have been the cardinal who believed Juana was heretical.

Juana's next stop was Torquemada, where she found a small house to live in while she waited for the birth of her daughter and for the winter to pass. She told her entourage that she chose a small house so she could rest and mourn Philip in a place too small for the court to crowd in on her. The legend never took in the fact that a year was the formal length of time for a widow to mourn.

Torquemada is only a few miles from Burgos. This is hardly ranging all around Spain. The small house in Torquemada was, by the way, the first permanent home Juana had ever had in Spain. The children of Ferdinand and Isabel had followed from city to city, army camp to army camp in the long years of *Reconquista*. They had never had a permanent home for reasons of state, since the Castilian cities were passionately independent, and they needed to treat them equally. So it was not unusual for *grandes* to keep local courts open. Juana would, at first, be no exception.

Juana's "wandering" all over Spain consisted of traveling slowly for about a month, and the waiting for the birth of Catalina, who would become the queen consort of Portugal. Even the poor woman's pregnancy was an affair of state. Juana then made a decision. She said she would move again when King Ferdinand came back to Spain. This was far more than a caprice. It was a wise maneuver to get back the one person who she thought would help her rule, the one Isabel had chosen. She held out until he returned. It was in Torquemada, not Tordesillas, that she saw her beloved father again.

There is no doubt that she became a recluse when she returned to Spain and was, so quickly, made a widow. She had longed to be a nun when she was younger. She was certainly a depressive, and as stubborn as a stone. Now that she was the queen of Spain, her father gone, her Spanish court divided, she had reason to try to get away on her own, if for nothing more to do with affairs of state than to mourn a husband she was passionately in love with, and have a quiet time to wait for her last child.

But it was Ferdinand who, three years later, persuaded her to move from Torquemada on to Tordesillas and wait until Castile had become calm under his hand. He was so talented at intrigue that Machiavelli had called him the perfect prince. She was still in Tordesillas eleven years later, peaceful, with her small court around her, when Charles was declared regent of Castile at the age of eighteen, and visited her there. It was the first time she had seen her eldest son since he was seven. Her second son, Ferdinand, had been taken away to be raised in Ferdinand's court. Only Catalina stayed as her companion.

What kind of person was Juana? What of the sixteen-year-old girl who had been sent out of Spain in 1495 to marry in the Low Countries? She was the most intelligent of Isabel's daughters; so long as she had her mother's approval she was her favorite. Isabel had sent with her to Antwerp a small army of attendants, including Moorish slaves, patrician women, and priestly confessors, who were a constant source of intelligence for her.

Juana was said to be the beauty of the family, so fine a dancer that she had entertained the peripatetic Spanish court. She was an accomplished musician. She wrote prose and poetry, which had been praised by her tutors, who gave glowing reports to her family when she was a student. She had been, as were all the children of Isabel, very well but strictly educated. She spoke several languages. One of her tutors had been Torquemada, later the most famous of the Grand Inquisitors.

At the Flemish court, the most open in Europe, the Renaissance was in full flower. The morals and the entertainment, including banned books so freely read, were a shock to the Spanish entourage. Juana was totally unprepared for frivolity or exposure to the new learning of the burgeoning Renaissance, the loose morals of the court, or to Protestant ideas, having come from dour and puritanical Catholic Spain.

This was the sixteen-year-old girl who stood in a room in Antwerp waiting to see for the first time in her life the man she had been trained to marry. Philip the Fair came in at evening. At once there was a *coup de foudre* between them, a love at first sight recognized by every person in the room. He was overwhelmed by her, she by him. He insisted on calling in a priest to marry them at once so they could consummate their marriage that night. They were married in a more seemly grand ceremony two days later.

The sophisticated court was amused by the mountain ways of her Spanish attendants. It was said that she and her ladies wore the new fashions backwards to hide their breasts. They became a laughingstock. Any acceptance on her part of what she saw was reported at once to her mother by the Spanish priests who surrounded her. If she missed confession, heresy was whispered. If she refused to obey her mother, if she ignored her advice, if she lost her hot Spanish temper, all of it was reported.

She made one fatal mistake that obviously disgusted her mother. She broke the royal rules of marriage. Juana did fall deeply in love with her husband. She made scenes. Once she ordered the head of one of his mistresses shaved because he had admired her hair. It was reported that Philip hit her. But gradually, from reading between the lines of the reports sent to Isabel, she seemed to take to the new life, and to dangerous new ideas. Juana certainly joined in the dance, the pleasure of the court.

She danced the night that her second child, the future Holy Roman Emperor, was born, and only stopped when her labor pains began. He was born in a tiring room, in other words, the Ladies' Room, instead of the grand lying-in chamber prepared for royal babies. She bore five children to Philip.

She had been at the Antwerp court for eleven years when they returned to Spain on her mother's death to accept the crown of Castile.

So her mystery was what was taking me along the country road from Avila to Tordesillas in Spain fifty years later. My road went through Medina del Campo, the home of the famous medieval wool fair. Like most of the cities of Castile, Medina del Campo was a center for the manufacture of woolen cloth.

By the sixteenth century, there had been a profound change of population in the country. All over Castile the sheep had replaced the men. The fight of plow against grazing land, herders against farmers was a quarrel the Spanish would bring to the new world, from the wars over water rights to legends of the American Wild West.

Ferdinand, and especially Isabel, had seen the potential of trade. The Honorable Council of the *Mesta* of the Sheepmen of Castile, which was the monopoly of the *grandes* and the sheep farmers, commanded *cañadas*, those hundreds of miles of grazing roads, where twice a year millions of sheep were driven in migrations from the Castilian *meseta* in the north to the south in winter and back again in the spring. There was some poetic justice in the fact that Isabel had died in Medina del Campo, in a small room in the ugly palace of La Mota that hovers over the town.

I began to pass herds of sheep, grazing lands. I was on the eastern edge of the *meseta,* the endless plain that had been the richest property of Castile. In that series of mistakes that are the map of discovery, I had thought Medina del Campo would be a village, maybe even a ruin. I knew that it had been destroyed, razed to the ground, burned, and sacked in the war of the *comuneros,* by mercenaries in the Royal army, its vast wealth in warehouses filled with wool and silk from Seville torched, its citizens slaughtered.

I found instead a lively, prosperous small city. I arrived at a miniature rush hour, and pulled over beside the road to find the best route in the Michelin atlas through the crowded traffic. The cars were too close together for me to break in. I was stuck there beside the road with a view of nothing.

That was when the handsome cop on the motorcycle came up beside the car, and asked me in blessed English if he could help. I followed him through the maze of rush-hour traffic at seventy miles an hour, while drivers honked in angry Spanish. We played with the more temperate cars. We flirted with the stop lights. We arrived at the north side of the city almost panting, as if we had been running a race. My new friend disappeared from my life by waving me goodbye and vooming the motorcycle like a Hell's Angel.

Finally I saw my city, Tordesillas, sculpted out of stone, on the horizon of a high hill above the Duero River, across the bridge which I knew was the last place Juana had smelled and tasted the terrors of freedom. In the fifteenth century

Tordesillas, too, had been numbered among the powerful royal cities of Castile. Ferdinand and Isabel had signed the Treaty of Tordesillas with Portugal there; they had the innocence and arrogance to divide the newly discovered western world between them, aided, abetted, and backed by the Spanish-born Borgia pope, Alexander VI.

The small palace where Juana lived is no longer there, but the grand salon of it is now attached to the Convento de Santa Clara, where she had placed Philip's casket for safety.

On Charles's first arrival in Spain, he met a mother he had not seen since he was five years old. It was said there was much affection between them. Charles was persuaded by his Flemish advisors to be crowned king instead of regent of Castile, and to see that his mother stayed in Tordesillas. Whether mad, or heretical, or just there to be reckoned with, Juana was dangerous. Juana was a nuisance. Juana, in modern terms, was the victim of a hostile takeover. There was nobody to help her.

Carlos went back to Flanders almost at once, when a reluctant *Cortes* had given the money his ambitious followers wanted. Cisneros, the acting governor, had been conveniently poisoned so that the Flemish entourage of the young Prince Charles could carry out their plans for the takeover and the looting of Castile. Once again Juana was the queen on a chess board.

So her son, Charles, became Charles I of Castile. It was the beginning of the Spanish Hapsburg dynasty. He used Spain as a golden, neverending stream of riches to bolster his new realm, the largest empire in the world, Spain, Germany, Flanders, the Netherlands, and Spain's share of newly discovered America. He left his favorite advisor, Monsieur de Chievre, as his sole minister, in total charge of the government of Castile. Chievre made every mistake to rouse the fury of the Spanish, even sinking so low in their eyes as to appoint his own Flemish nephew, who was seventeen years old, to the most important archbishopric in Spain, that of Toledo. It was that appointment as much as the looting of Castile that lit the fire that became the revolt of the *comuneros.*

After Charles's second visit, his quick coronation and exit, he left orders to skim the cream off Castile for the middle European wars begun by his advisors. There were riots and uprisings all over Castile. In Valladolid the Flemish government had to take refuge in one of the *grande* castles. Orders were given to keep Juana in Tordesillas.

I was finding that Tordesillas was not only the last place to cover in my search for Juana. The decision that was made in that small hilltop town across the Duero River affected the succession, the failure of the *comuneros*, the reign of the Hapsburg dynasty, even the Thirty Years' War.

Only once was Juana to be freed of her "retirement." It was in 1520, in the *comuneros* revolt. The first blood may have been in Segovia, and the most memorable conference of leaders of the Spanish cities in Avila, but the revolt reached its greatest success and its most abysmal failure there in Tordesillas.

In Tordesillas the crowd demanded to see their queen. For years the gossip of the town was that she was sane, and kept prisoner there so her unpopular son, considered a foreigner, could rule Castile. Suddenly, after fourteen years, the *comuneros*, made up of the cities' representatives, the new generals, and a patched-up army of militia, arrived in Tordesillas and released her.

She was, at last, recognized as the true queen of Castile. A coronation was held for her. She welcomed the *comuneros* as subjects, and seemed horrified at what had been going on with the Flanders court, and their arrogant behavior. Who should know better than she who had been ignored, treated as a second-class royal, and made the butt of jokes in Flanders? She heard for the first time that her beloved father had been dead for six years, a fact that had been kept from her.

She was, or seemed to be, in full command of her mind and her decisions, and perhaps that was her downfall. She was, after all, a queen in an absolute monarchy, and she had been trained in its laws and its privileges. When the *comuneros*, whom she had welcomed with much sympathy, tried to make her sign an order denying her son Charles's right of kingship, she at first refused, then delayed, demurred, seemed indecisive. All the time Cardinal Adrian, Charles's new governor, was sending secret messages to her confessor to keep her from acting.

The fall deepened. The high plateau with its commanding hills caught the full blast of winter; darkness came, and in the narrow, huddled streets of Tordesillas, the wind clutched at people who in summer had been her friends and little court. The *comuneros* quarreled among themselves. The more conservative *hidalgos* were beginning to withdraw from a *junta* whose new constitution called for much greater reforms than they had reckoned on. They had, after all, only joined in a revolt against a foreign administration, and their main concern was not even the tax burden, from which they were exempt, but the end to the practice of sending Spanish funds abroad rather than using them at home. But when the *comuneros* began to demand a representative monarchy with a permanent, elected *Cortes*, it was, to them, a political obscenity.

Even more ominously, the *grandes* were realizing that they had to make a choice for fear of losing their long-held crown privileges. On their huge tracts of land by royal patent, with their mercenary armies, they were little kings in their own right. They stayed out of the quarrel at first. They considered that they had little to gain from either the crown or the cities, both of which they tended to despise. Finally, they chose to send their private mercenary armies to fight on the side of the crown.

In December the royal army attacked Tordesillas. The commander of the *comuneros,* Don Juan de Padilla, tried to get Juana away. They were captured as they ran across the bridge over the Duero. It was as near as she got to freedom. But it was farther than she had been in fourteen years. Whatever she thought was happening, she was, yet again, a royal pawn. She was back in the hands of the *grandes* and the crown. Silence closed over her.

Finally, in 1522, Charles, in his early twenties and now able to speak Spanish, arrived back in Spain. That was when he had sense enough to bring with him the five thousand German mercenaries.

He went to Tordesillas to see his mother. All that is known of the visit is that he stayed for five days. On leaving, he appointed the Marquis of Denia and his wife to run the royal household of the queen. Then the letters between the king and Denia began. Very little except those letters remains of what happened.

Juana was a danger to Charles as Charles I of Castile; his election as emperor of the Holy Roman Empire depended on Spanish money. A decision of state had to be made. Denia was instructed to keep her as totally isolated as possible, no friends, no talking to servants who might go into town and gossip. She was as near to being in solitary confinement as they could make it. Only a few ladies in waiting were allowed near her, but these she rejected as spies.

There is no doubt that it was Charles who commanded Denia to isolate her. She had been officially crowned queen, so she was dangerous to his sovereignty. She had recognized the *comuneros*, which made their rebellion legitimate, since she could issue royal decrees. For the next thirty-three years she was lost behind the stone walls of her prison palace. She died, an old woman, in 1555 on Good Friday. She was seventy-five years old.

The people of Tordesillas did not forget her. She has lived in communal memory for nearly five hundred years. Her most trusted servant swore she was as sane as her mother. The townspeople had always said she was sane, but their opinion was discounted, both by the court and by historians. The written word was safe, and except for one letter from her daughter smuggled out from Catalina to tell her brother, the emperor, that their mother was a prisoner, ill treated, and isolated, all written word came through the censorship of the Marquis of Denia. He had followed to the letter the orders of Charles.

I crossed the same bridge over the Duero on a sunny day in September. I found a vibrant agricultural town, proud of itself, and on that day, everybody in it was dressed up for its yearly *fiesta*. Where the palace had been were houses. There were apartment windows instead of the palace windows where Juana had kept watch over the *meseta*. The Convento de Santa Clara had survived. The thirteenth-century palace chapel where Philip's body was kept until Charles V moved it and his mother to the grand royal tomb in Granada is still there, attached to the nunnery of a closed order of nuns.

Closed or not, I would bet that the old ladies of Tordesdillas know their every move as they once did that of the queen.

Instead of the sad city I expected there were crowds of young people dressed in white with red sashes, boys and girls, children and their mothers, old men, young men. Young boys and girls strolled together. There were babies in their carriages, always a fine sight in a Spanish town. They wore white, too, with little red scarves around their necks. There were fathers in white trousers and shirts and wide red sashes, pushing them. It was a party, a town-size party.

It was the yearly *fiesta* for the town's patron, *el Toro de la Vega*. The Bull of the Plain. I tried to find out his name but it was impossible. A bullfighter? An athlete? A saint? A king? A Matamoros, a Moor slayer? Or one of those leaders of the revolt of the Castillian cities against a sixteenth-century foreign king who threatened to milk Castile of all its riches to fight a Middle European war? No one could or would tell me the name of the bull of the *vega*, but it could have been any one of them.

I finally found an answer. The bull of the *vega* had no other name. They were celebrating the ancient wild bull of the *meseta* itself. On that one evening of the *fiesta*, in the town bullring, the men would pit themselves against the bull with only the staves and swords their ancestors would have used to hunt the wild bulls for food. It was as if, in our Midwest, in a town on the prairie, the citizens—bank managers, farmers, insurance adjusters, car salesmen—were turned loose once a year to hunt a wild buffalo with native American weapons to honor the bravery of their ancestors and the millions of wild buffalo they had slain.

At noon I followed the slow-moving crowd. The streets were shut off to cars and crowded with people. We came to

the center, the heart of every town, the *plaza mayor*. It was
beautiful, painted in bright colors of red and gold and black.
The ancient stone columns of the colonnade shaded a walkway that went all the way around the square.

The *plaza mayor* was already crowded with people who
had been lucky enough to find seats at the outdoor cafés.
Children ran back and forth. An outdoor stage had been set
up and they climbed up to its wooden floor, dancing with a
rhythmic stomping that sounded like the rhythm of *flamenco*. It echoed against the walls of the houses.

Beside the stage stood a papier-mâché Moor and a
Christian damsel. They were at least twelve feet tall, brightly
painted; obviously their paint was renewed every year for the
fiesta. They were in bright medieval robes, the Moor with a
turban and a scimitar, the lady with a blue cloak and a bright
headdress. Around them were clowns and dwarfs, more children of Tordesillas, with sun faces, moon faces, all larger
than any human faces. In the distance a band began to play,
and the sound of horns and drums echoed against the walls
of the narrow street as they marched toward the *plaza*.

It was a small local band; its spirit and the cheers of the
crowd made up for any primitive sounds they were making.
Slowly the Moor and his lady began to waddle in a stately
pavane, until they were following the band at the head of a
procession of clowns and goblins and all the children who
had been stomping on the outdoor stage.

Those two figures were acting out one of the most familiar
romantic legends found at both ends of the North African
Fertile Crescent, a romance based on the mingling and the
taboos between the Muslims and the Christians, the love
that crosses borders and reconciles enemies, from Romeo
and Juliet, to a Moor twelve feet high in a small town in

Spain, to the Hatfields and the McCoys in the Allegheny Mountains.

Those two figures represented the popular fiction of these meetings and taboos. A Christian woman falls in love with a Muslim warrior, and pines away; sometimes he captures her and they both are killed. In those parts of the world, the story is as familiar as Cinderella. I found a nice variant in a small city in Turkey when a twelve-year-old boy who had learned some English appointed himself the guide to a museum, set on one of the twelfth-century Seljuk *medreses* —religious schools. We came to a room where a funerary statue of a woman leaned sadly on one elbow atop her coffin. The boy rattled off as if it were a historic fact, and as if he had told it many times, the old story that she was a Christian who died of love for a Turk. Our twelve-foot-high papier-mâché lovers of Tordesillas disappeared, swaying along with their clowns and their dwarfs and the children following behind to celebrate the bull of the *vega*.

The word for foreigner and ghost is the same word in Chinese, which shows what they think of foreigners. It is, and this is phonetic spelling, *gweilo*. I felt like a *gweilo*, both foreigner and ghost, transparent in the sun of noon. As I walked between the outdoor tables, no one looked up. I wandered down the hill by a narrow street, where women stood in doorways, on that perpetual watch of old women in villages, missing nothing. They seemed not to look at me except for a brief polite nod. But I had the feeling that they knew the color of my underwear.

There, in one of the ancient stone buildings I had seen from across the river, I found the thirteenth-century Convento de Santa Clara, where Juana had lodged the coffin of her husband, where it had stayed for forty-six years until she died and they both were moved to their grand gilded sepulcher in Granada. The monastery was, as it had always been, frozen in the hot sun in the perpetual silence of a tomb. It is still lived in by a closed order of nuns, hidden away as Queen Juana had been hidden away, to watch the river, year after year after year. The small palace next to it is gone. Only a room of it remains, attached to the convent. To say it was repressive is to beg the issue of that heavy, hot, sunny silence.

I fled back to the *plaza mayor* and the *fiesta*. But I had my answer. I had a sense that these people knew and had known whatever was going on in their town through the centuries, only a yesterday and a today long. Born together, neighbors in those narrow streets, schooled and communed together, married and widowed and hated and loved as only close neighbors can be, they knew everything.

When they said that Juana was sane, they spoke what they knew, and that knowledge made them riot in 1520 and call for their queen to come out where they could see her. Her servants were their cousins, their brothers, their sisters, and her treatment and her person through the years was a part of their town. It is no wonder that her son, Charles V, he of the greatest empire in Christendom, feared their knowledge and their mouths enough to try to keep her away from even the servants in the little palace for the rest of her life. He failed.

It is not the Marquis of Denia who is honored in Tordesillas. There is a street called the *Calle de Padilla,* and one called the *Calle Juan Bravo,* in honor of the two leaders of the *comuneros* who had freed, crowned, and honored her, if only for a little while in her long, dark life.

IN THE *MESETA*

 The *meseta* of Castile was a vast dry sea bottom under a vast sea sky. Where the huge wheat fields had not been harvested, the gold wheat rippled in the wind like waves. The stubble gleamed and then darkened under the shadows of the moving clouds. The small hummocks of hills in the far distance rose as if they had surged up from below the sea floor eons ago and the water had shaped them into underwater dunes.

The only rage of rock and exposed strata of mineral and granite that split the plain was where the little rivers and streams had carved their paths, old, deep, knife cut by water, unlike the surface stones that had been smooth, huge, for all the centuries. In the far distance those mounds of huge rocks, cliffs, or ruins—or castles—slipped out of sight as if they moved and I did not.

For me the mystery of the *meseta* and of Spain began there, where the water-rounded boulders could have been moved by ancient men, or glaciers, or time, or exposure. It was harsh, old, haunted, secret, beautiful. There was a way of knowing that a village was going to rise out of the distance by the etched shadows of lines of black trees long before I saw a house. Oases of trees in formal lines in the distance meant that there was water, the sign of human life on that great high table. There were isolated road signs to small villages, and I wondered what they could look like, and how weighed down they must be under the endless sky and the hot sun.

If it has not happened before, on setting foot in Spain, mystery must begin there at the *meseta*. I thought that Spain's enchantment was in the familiar signs of bandits, sharp mountains where Cervantes put his disheveled wild man of a lover, the legendary ghosts, the *flamenco* dancers, and the brave bulls. But I was wrong, for enchantment depends on surprise, and the surprise, for me, was there in that vast space. At first there seemed to be nothing but a horizon that was so far away that it seemed to be the vision's end of the round earth itself, where things disappear downward, stones, ships, land, the sun.

Dirt roads as straight as arrow flight led to hidden places somewhere between the endless, unfenced, wind moved grain. The fields are such huge tracts of that ancient form of agro-industry the Romans called *latifundios* that the land seems abandoned.

The unplanned, unsought route I was following led from Tordesillas toward Zamora, the northwest corner of my wanderings. The fine modern road was a protection, something familiar against the endless space. It had not been so for the army of the *comuneros* that had been defeated at Tordesillas, and lost the lonely queen.

I had seen in one of the guidebooks I carried that the last battle of the *comuneros* had been fought somewhere in those flat spaces. I watched for the small sign that read *Villalar de los comuneros.* When I saw it, I turned off the main highway onto a narrow, frightening straight dirt road to Villalar that disappeared over the horizon of the *meseta.* The silence and the space were both so endless that I began to feel the panic that comes with loss of direction. I stopped for a while, afraid to go on, afraid to turn around. There was nothing to do but to drive on and on into nothing but the tawny fields, the sky so clear that it went from pale blue to that Spanish clean, windwashed deep blue, toward the black of space. If I have been as alone before or since, I do not want to think of it.

To test my courage I turned off the road at a crossroads exactly like it, drove a few hundred feet, and got out of the car. I stood in that silence as long as I could without panic, then suddenly scuttled back into the car, and carefully, inch by inch, turned the car around on that narrow path, with the awful fear for a second that I would never find my way again.

In a few minutes I was back on the straight road to Villalar. I was following the path of the defeated citizen army, half the size it had been at its zenith. After the defeat at Tordesillas, and the shocking realization that the rank and file of the *comunero* citizen army had sought a representation far beyond the ken of the city fathers, most of the minor nobility and churchmen, who had been the fomenters of the revolt of their *patrias chicas,* had abandoned the militia.

For several months after the defeat at Tordesillas, the little army shrank from desertions to about five thousand men, with no cavalry. They rested and tried to re-form in the little village of Torrelobaton, a few miles north of Tordesillas. The royal army, three miles away, waited for them to move like a fox watching chickens. Finally, on April 23, they marched out of Torrelobaton in a driving spring rain on their way to Toro, the next safe town, eighty miles away, where they hoped for new supplies. They slogged all day for over twenty miles through the downpour that made what gear they had three times its weight.

Instead of the infinite horizon that surrounded me, they could scarcely have seen more than ten feet through rain and fog. They marched all day, and finally the soaked, exhausted *comuneros* straggled into the tiny mud village of Villalar and began to set up a bivouac for the night to wait for the tail end of their army.

They had been followed all day by the royal cavalry, swelled by the *grandes'* mercenary armies and, after them, more slowly, the royal infantry. The cavalry did not wait for the infantry to catch up. They attacked at once when they got to the fields before Villalar. They must have loomed in the air out of the fog, lances pointed, overexhausted, drowsing men. The slaughter was terrible, the drowning of an army in rain and blood. Some of the *comunero* troops got away, hidden by the rain and the coming night. Many were killed. By the time the royal infantry arrived it was over; bodies lay fallen across the mud fences, and around the broken farm buildings.

The three leaders of the army were captured: the greatest firebrand of the three, Francisco Maldonado, the ex-royal *corregidor* of Palencia; the *regidor* and member of the royal guard Juan Bravo; and Juan de Padilla, the bitter aristocrat from Toledo.

The next morning, after a drumhead court-martial, all three of the leaders were beheaded in the tiny green that was the *plaza mayor* of the village. They were granted no mercy except immortality in the hearts of the people of Castile.

On that day when I drove across the *meseta* in the sun I knew none of this. Finally the town of Villalar began to rise up above the horizon like—not a ship but a small flatboat at sea. It was an ancient, tiny, broken village, but in its center is a shrine to the battle of Villalar. The village square is well kept, and carved into a tall, simple stone column are the words A LA MEMORIA DE D. MARÍA PAHECO PADILLA, BRAVO, Y MALDONADO.

When Juan Bravo's body was taken back to Segovia, where I had first run into the traces of the sixteenth-century *comunero* revolt of the Castilian cities, he was given a state funeral. Most of the citizens of the city followed to the church where his funeral took place—Vera Cruz, the round church in memory of the Church of the Holy Sepulcher in Jerusalem, built in the twelfth century by the Knights Templar.

I drove slowly back through that great space toward the main road the way I had come. I fled past Toro, where Isabel's mercenaries had earned her the crown of Castile by defeating the mercenaries of her niece. It was good to get away from that small woman whose shadow still hangs over Spain.

I fled her heavy shadow, and that little city, past safe sign after safe sign toward Zamora, where I had chosen to stay the night, the northernmost city that I would see. I only wanted to rest, to pull my room around me in the safety of what I had been told was one of the most famous *paradores* in Spain.

ZAMORA

 I wanted to get away from war and its sorrows and have a good night's sleep. I have to admit, too, that curiosity, the best guide a traveler can take on the road, drove me to choose Zamora. In one of the guidebooks I had found a mention that more priests had been jailed there during Franco's dictatorship than in all of the countries of the Communist bloc after World War II that made up the Warsaw Pact.

I think I expected an ugly hill town dominated by a prison. I found, instead, a haven. I didn't know why, but for the first time in Spain, and as long as I stayed there, I was at home. There was a familiarity about it which only now I recognize.

It is a small city, aware of a deep, wordless past, defined by a river, behind it the northern mountains, a place for mountaineers. I was born and grew up in a city like it, in a valley where ancestral remains go back to the mound builders. My state, my own American *patria chica,* has a motto that could apply to Zamora, *Montani semper liberi,* mountaineers are always free. Zamora, integrated, isolated, complete, was, like my own city, not on the way to anyplace else. So instead of a night I stayed for three days, but it was not enough.

Zamora is one of the most magical places in Spain. It is pitched on a crag the shape of a ship's prow, high in the air above the Duero, the border river between the Visigothic kingdom and the Moors. This wonderful, historically feisty little city is over two thousand years old. It is absolutely beautiful.

It stands at the northern end of the eighth-century Moorish conquest of the Spanish peninsula, and the beginning of the road south of the Christian *Reconquista*. Within a few years of the Moorish occupation south of the Duero River, its palace was begun on the prow of the great rock where there had been a fortified settlement since long before the Roman invasion a thousand years before.

To call it a living museum for a history of Spanish architecture from 800 A.D. through the thirteenth century is to make it seem as frozen in the past as the walls of Avila. It is not. It is a vibrant working community that might have been the same through centuries, mainly depending for its life on the land around it: in the north the *vega de pan,* in the south across the river, the *vega de vino*—the two valleys of bread and wine. It is one of the most popular hunting and camping places in the country.

The atmosphere is friendly; the people have the easy familiarity of mountaineers, a sense of equality that is deep in its soil, in its mountains and flowing water, and in centuries of isolated self-sufficiency. A political guru once said that there was no use trying to govern people who live at over five thousand feet, and Zamora is proof of this.

No matter how many times it has changed hands, no

matter how many foreign tourists have come through the centuries, or the armies of the Romans, the Moors, the Visigoths, I found it the most independent *patria chica* I visited in Spain.

I drove, almost as if I knew where I was going, up a steep, winding road toward the *Plaza Viriato*, where the *parador* had been marked on my map. When I got out of the car, there in front of me was the most beautiful High Renaissance palace I would see in Spain. Directly across the *plaza*, a large building was half hidden by trees. It had a plain façade, with that look of church buildings everywhere in northern Spain. Near the solemn building, in the open *plaza*, a Roman battering ram carved from stone looked as if it had been abandoned there by invading armies. It was a carving of a ram's head. This rock-carved monster is known as the Roman Terror.

It stood below a bronze figure of Viriathus, Spain's earliest national hero, poised high above it on the kind of huge round stone that is formed by eons of water that I had seen in the *meseta*. But then, I had no idea who Viriathus was, or that I was beginning to discover, before I sought it, the essential quality that defines the Spanish hero. Even before I knew about Viriathus, and Zamora's fighting bishop with his private army, who kept on fighting as a *comunero* long after the army had been defeated at Villalar, I had been drawn to Zamora by priests brave enough to stand up to Franco.

I opened the door into the Renaissance palace. The luxurious, quiet atmosphere of the entry was part of a wide, shaded corridor with a two-story white ceiling crossed with exposed wooden beams the color of old honey. The corridor was enclosed around an open courtyard so large that the tree-size plants in one corner seemed small. There were groups of leather chairs and sofas, coffee tables, lamps, for this was a living room that by evening was filled with people having drinks, talking, the ceiling so high that the laughter seemed soft.

Between Renaissance arches with floor-to-ceiling wood in the courtyard, and beyond encased glass window panes that caught the sun, were classic columns and, above them, portrait medallions of Romans in that resurrection of the deep, lost classic past that was the main impetus of the European Renaissance.

The walls were of local stone naturally tinted from pale coral to gold. Beyond the courtyard, in a large niche surrounded by a curved stone stairway, there was a life-size mounted knight and horse in glittering armor. It was so elegant, so beautiful, so shining, that I seemed to step back into the time of the Count of Alba y Aliste, who built it over the foundations of a Roman ruin in the fifteenth century.

Unlike what I had seen in Castile, it was neither a Gothic monastery nor a castellated fortress, but a palace built as a noble residence without any hint of barracks or fortification. Later, outside of my room, I would find walls with remains of murals of faintly pastel ghosts, not of religious murals, but graceful ancient Greek and Roman deities.

The artists who painted the classic murals, and sculpted the portraits above the columns of the courtyard, were probably local. For it had been their ancestors, of Moorish and Christian descent, who had built a dozen Romanesque churches by the thirteenth century. The superb twelfth-century cathedral with its Byzantine cupola showed the same talent, the same sure hand, the same originality. There has been a long tradition in Zamora of talented local artisans. They had been sculpting the saints and the animals and building the famous churches of Zamora for four hundred years before the *parador*'s original palace was erected.

In the churches, usually hidden, always a treasure when found, were those imps and scenes with the ironic thrust of criticism through the art of comedy that are the mark of ancient untamable Spanish irreverence. Zamora is a wonderful source of these passionately individual, sometimes sunny, sometimes legendary, sculpted capitals. There is a special tour to seek them out among Zamora's churches and examine them, the unicorns, the centaurs, the warriors, the wonderful lively animals, the vines, and, in one of the churches, in every window, small primitive stone figures that are a history of early medieval dress. I noticed, too, that in the windows of these very early churches there were slits for shooting arrows instead of strained glass. The time when these treasures were built was exceedingly dangerous.

I had thought about how to ask the question about the jailed priests which had brought me there, since it might have been an embarrassment to the people of Zamora. I had already noticed that it was not mentioned in the Spanish brochures. So instead of asking directly if it were true, I asked the very polite English-speaking young man at the desk if the *parador* was where the rebel priests had been imprisoned by Franco.

"Oh, no," he said, "That was across the square. The big building," and he took me to the door and pointed across the square to the building beyond the statue of Viriathus. "This," he motioned around him," was a war orphanage."

It was true that Franco had jailed more priests in Spain than those arrested in all the eastern Communist countries. I wonder why I was so relieved. Maybe it shows that there can be a gulf between the princes of the church, those who have climbed the holy ladder of success, in what may be the largest corporation on earth, and those who serve the poor, their countrymen and women, in their villages and their city barrios, who take part in their lives, their hopes, and their disappointments.

The next morning I began a walk quite innocently to discover where I was. That walk was to take me on a path through centuries. I crossed the plaza to look more closely at the battering ram and the statue of Viriathus.

Every Spanish child knows Viriathus, the warrior chief of the Lusitani. In the second century B.C., he had been taken as a slave in one of the wars with the organized Roman army, thought to be invincible, who had already conquered the rest of the peninsula nearly a millennium before the Moors. Viriathus escaped, went back into the country of the Lusitani and the Celtiberian tribes who had lived in the northern and western parts of the peninsula since there were humans there, and raised an army of independent mountain men the Romans considered savages. Viriathus defeated the Roman legions in eight border wars before he was murdered for Roman money by his nearest friends.

All across this war-formed part of Spain, at Segovia with Juan Bravo, at Villalar with the defeated citizen army, and behind the walls of Avila with its saints and its ridiculous war against a dummy king, I found them. Heroic, independent, sometimes saints, sometimes rascals, dignified and graceful, often comic, is the hero who has one talent above all else in common with his fellow heroes. He stands up to his ruler and looks him in the eye. The old oath taken by the ruler of Aragon is the perfect example. He swore that he would rule a people as good as he was, with the understanding that he was no better than they were.

I was beginning to see what the Spanish national hero is made of. From Viriathus, who won eight wars against the Roman invaders, to St. Teresa, who slapped the papal nuncio, all Spanish heroes have this in common: They are passionately independent; they make up their own minds; they stand up to their rulers.

I decided to walk to the castle, starting at the *Plaza Viriato*. In the shady, quiet place under the trees, I was beginning to explore, not buildings, but something else, a sense of illusion and unanswerable questions. So much has been ignored or forgotten by orthodox history. But there is that wonderful grapevine of gossip, known by the Spanish as *teléfono árabe*, in old manuscripts, in letters that were politic and, even better, those that were not. Even what I had thought was a colonnaded building on the left was a façade standing alone. Maybe it had once been a building, I couldn't find out. Maybe it was left there when a building was torn down because it was beautiful. I like to think so.

Beyond it, a road toward the city wall was called *Motín de la Trucha*. I was already learning not to ignore street names, for in Spain they are often memorials to events people want to remember. But the Revolt of the Trout? It conjured up some kind of Disney-like fish war.

On my right, a very small church, *Santa Maria la Nueva*, new St. Mary, looked very old for such a name. My guidebook called it one of the oldest churches in Zamora. It was very simple, a vast relief from the demanding Gothic churches I had seen farther east in Castile. I knew that Zamora bred fighters. I did not yet know that they went to war at the drop not only of a hat but, one time, a trout.

One day in the middle of the twelfth century, a fishmonger brought fresh fish to sell in the market outside the old church. A free citizen of the city chose a trout for his dinner. The servant of one of the nobles grabbed it and said he wanted it for his master, who had precedence. The ensuing argument did not end until there was a full-scale war with Portugal, known ever since as *El Motín de la Trucha,* the mutiny of the trout.

It is one part of that demand for recognition as equals by citizens against the nobles, even if it was only the equality of choosing trout for their dinner. Some say it happened in 1162, some 1168. They still argue. Out of this tangle of the obscure and unexplained, it took me a year to find out what had happened there. The nobles had been chased into the church and the church set afire. When it was rebuilt, only the fragments of the nave were left, with some ancient carvings which must have been so early that the carvings seem unformed cartoons. Maybe age has done that to them.

A narrow lane followed the old city wall past houses with their plain façades that I'm sure hid secret courtyards wild with flowers. I never passed a house when its outer door had been left open that I did not glimpse them, like hidden treasure.

I saw, ahead, a large, modern construction sight behind a wired enclosure. Beyond the barrier of wire that protected it, digging machinery sat in the ruins of the Roman city built after the death of Viriathus. At least six feet below me, newly exposed after over two thousand years, stood a city gate with statues and an emblem that I thought was the insignia of a Roman Legion. There were foundations of Roman houses, or public buildings, or barracks. How could one tell? I was looking down at the city headquarters of the Roman legions, placed at the crossroads that led to the silver and gold mines in the mountains.

Zamora grew from base rock, but the silt of time, of sand and rubble and destruction, had taken centuries to raise the level of the ground to where I stood, six feet above the two-millennia-old fragments of Rome. The modern city, and its eleventh- and twelfth-century churches, sits above the rubble of all that time of wind and rain and battle and death.

I turned away at last and walked on to a narrow street between two churches. On the left side of the street, a semicircle of graceful window frames of stone, was the apse of the chapel of a Gothic monastery. A splendid Romanesque church door was on my right, Santa María Magdalena. I stood there for a long time beginning to learn as I watched how to recognize that last connection with the Rome of Christian Romanesque architecture. The arch over the door was about thirty feet across at its outer semicircle of fine Romanesque carvings of six descending arches, each smaller than the one before it.

I stayed to study it, beginning with the largest. It was a series of recognizably individual portrait heads, some of men with their mouths open in the rictus of death, the rest alive, and carefully portrayed, as if the leading citizens were lined up there to be counted. So I did just that. There were forty-one of them; then I counted again and there were forty-three; so I gave up. In the center of the arch some of them had been defaced.

In the next circle below there were vines twisted into square forms, with a lion's head in the center. The next two semicircles were of leaves or vines, the fifth one with a portrait head in the center above the door. It was a careful portrait of a man. I had no idea who he was, but two stones away to his left was a saint who might have been a bishop, lying on his side with his pastoral staff in his hand.

The arches ended in columns with capitals that seemed at first to be like the classic capitals of Greco-Roman formality, until I looked closer and found that the sculptors had entwined dragons and birds and whatever else they fancied. These capitals were, in church after church, where sculptors had used their own imaginations, and the results are wonderful—some funny, some fearsome, some Bible scenes, some saints, some devils—individual choice run wonderfully riot. I spent much time before such church doors in Spain looking for imps.

The street ended in a spacious plaza garden beyond a wall at the entry to the cathedral. Beyond the cathedral, the castle, begun in the eighth century, crouches, heavy, brutal, and plain, so old, so sunk in time that there is a ramp built down to its entry. A deep, dry moat surrounds it. It stands at the edge of the almost perpendicular rock face studded with descending walls that were said to be completely impenetrable.

Between the cathedral and the castle, a large space that might have been a tilt yard is now a garden. It was the first sight, for me, of one of those oases of Moorish calmness to be found wherever they ruled. Here and there were hints of all the exchanges of rule through the centuries, a delicate marble (alabaster?) Roman column, a small eleventh-century Romanesque church, the fantastic cathedral with its Byzantine cupola, and its carved stone. It was easy just to be there, to lean against the castellated wall and watch the valley and the river. I stood looking over the parapet of the castle keep at the river, and the valley beyond.

The Duero was the first and most fought-over border river of the *Reconquista*. The triumphant *conquista* and settlement of the Iberian peninsula by the Moors in the eighth and ninth centuries had pushed the fleeing local Spanish tribal villagers, the Roman Christian refugees, the Visigoths, into the valleys of the local Celtiberian mountaineers.

For nearly three hundred years they had watched and envied across the Duero, which they called the father of rivers, longing for water, fertile land, and loot. From time to time there had been raids into the richer and more settled Moorish cities and towns. It was not until the tenth century that they launched the first successful reinvasion. It was the crossing of the river I watched beyond the castle walls in Zamora that began the slow and inexorable progress south which is called the *Reconquista*.

These were the people who invented guerrilla warfare, for guerrilla simply means "little war." Their kings were border tribal chieftains who trained by constant war with each other. In the foothills of the Pyrenees the most independent mountain ruler of them all, Wilfred the Hairy, sent word throughout the then kingdoms of Spain that anyone who wanted to come was welcome in his city, no matter what crime he had committed.

In Léon and Castile, from the beginning of the *Reconquista,* there was a series of kings named Sancho, Ferdinand, Alfonso, and Ordoño, among others. They bred, as mountaineers do, fights, feuds, and rebels. The Asturians had wonderful nicknames for people they allowed to be their rulers; Alfonso the Slobberer, Ordoño the Bad, who usurped the throne of Léon from Sancho the Fat, who was so fat and stupid he couldn't rule.

Sancho the Fat's mother took him south to the Spanish medieval version of a famous fat farm in the then Moorish capital of Córdoba, one of the two most civilized cities in

Europe in the Dark Ages. For the first time in his life Sancho saw a great city, and it stunned his eyes. He went back to Léon at the head of a Muslim army which had been lent to him by the ruler of Córdoba, Lean and Mean instead of Fat and Stupid, and ruled Léon for the rest of his life until he was poisoned by a conniving courtier.

It was there, leaning on the parapet above that pitch of rock, that I found the ultimate hero of Spain, El Cid. I saw the small church where he had been knighted, *Santiago de los Caballeros*. It is small, probably tenth century. Its exterior is so simple you might pass it by, but inside are two columns where a tangle of men and animals are intertwined, legs, heads, in a swirl of movement. Later, I was to find many of these capitals. From El Cid's *Santiago de los Caballeros* to *San Claudio de Oliveros*, I found these sculpted capitals that were brilliant, lively, and showed the talent that is essentially Spanish, with its wit, its courage, and its irreverence. I would not see such local genius again until I went deep into the Bronze Age world in the south. They are worth the search, for historic hints and sheer talent.

It was at the siege of Zamora that Rui Díaz de Vivar, a twenty-year-old knight in the service of Sancho II of Castile, earned the title El Cid. Since the word in Spanish comes from the Arabic *said*, pronounced Sa-eed, which means lord, it is one of hundreds of examples of the exchange of language between Spanish Muslims and Christians, who fought each other, made peace, made war, married and gave in marriage, made treaties, broke treaties, traded through it all with each other, for over seven hundred years. So it is even more satisfying that the greatest hero in Spanish history should be known by an Arabic derivative.

In 1065, the great king, Ferdinand I, who had done more than any king before him to unite the petty kingdoms of Castile and Léon in a single rule, had died, after making the mistake of his life. He left his kingdom to his five children in one of those gestures of equality to avoid trouble among his heirs. Sancho, the eldest and the heir to old Castile, decided it was his right and his duty to reunite Ferdinand's kingdom under his rule. He rampaged west through his brothers' and sisters' kingdoms—Léon, Asturia, Galicia, Toro—and defeated them all.

But when Sancho came to Zamora, he ran up against that great forbidding wall, and his sister Urraca. She had inherited the city and the lands around it. She was as spirited as her subjects, and from the castle, between wall and moat, she directed the defense of her inheritance. It was the usual civil war that had raged every time there was a change of rule, in the best Visigothic tradition.

Sancho's commanding general was Rui Díaz de Vivar, the young man who had yet to earn the title of El Cid. The siege went on for seven years. Urraca won by guile, or perhaps innocence and someone else's guile. Who knows? One of her vassal knights pretended to go over to Sancho, whose army was camped below the wall. When he was let into Sancho's presence, he murdered him. So Sancho's brother Alfonso, who had been ousted from Léon and Asturia, hurried back from Toledo, where he had taken refuge with the Moorish king, and claimed the throne, taking by death what Sancho had not taken by conquest, the title of king of Léon, Castile, and the rest of the inheritance. So much for the ever-familiar fight over a will.

Urraca married Alfonso I of Aragon. (Most of the kings in this story seem to have been called Alfonso.) They got on together like two cats in a sack; she divorced him, stayed in Zamora, refused ever to marry again, and, as independent as ever, died in childbirth at the age of forty-six. She was unmarried, and no one knows who the father was.

The story darkens and El Cid is the victim. It is said that he demanded a vow from Urraca's brother Alfonso that he had no part in his brother Sancho's murder before he would swear allegiance to him. He earned the hatred of the new king and, when an excuse was found, was accused of treason and exiled, the finest example in Spanish history of one who became a hero through looking his liege lord in the eye.

El Cid became a freebooter, with a band of three hundred free lances (both of those phrases once meant mercenary soldier.) He proceeded to make a living for his wife and family by raiding, pillaging, working for whatever king paid him. One or more of the kings were Moorish. Finally he "liberated" Valencia and made a Christian fief of it by looting everything that was not nailed down, and killing many of the inhabitants. He ruled the survivors well and happily until his death.

The Poem of the Cid, Spain's first known vernacular poem, of 7,000 lines, is his story, or part of it, written within fifty years of his death, which gives it a validity that other European legends, lays, and romances lack. It is a fairly simple story of a man who sassed his king but was loyal to a ruler who did not deserve it, who loved his wife instead of some unattainable damsel, looked after his daughters, made his living as best he could, and ended up a ruler in his own right.

It shows more than any other contemporary document why the real hero chosen by Spaniards is so unlike, and so much more down to earth than the contemporary King

Arthur's Round Table, or Tristan, or the Song of Roland, or Amadís of Gaul, or any of those too good to be true, too brave to be borne, too beautiful, faithful, and honorable to be believed, that amalgam so attacked by Miguel de Cervantes in *Don Quixote*.

He was more Ulysses than knight in shining armor, tougher, with a living to earn, a man who reminds me of Hamlet's description of his father: ". . . this was a man. Take him for all in all, I shall not look upon his like again."

All of this on one walk in a morning on my first day in Zamora? Yes. Distilled in time, in this small city, I meandered slowly beyond the expected, a place where there is in miniature a visual, hinted, lively history that won't be found in the easy shorthand of guidebooks. The good ones can put you on the road, but they can't lead you.

Somehow, wandering from church to church in Zamora is not like the tourist trudge from grand cathedral to grand cathedral, not to see them so much as to have seen them. They are small enough to be welcoming, unlike some of the Gothic cathedrals that seem to have been built to diminish poor little miserable sinners.

But my favorite church is called the *Iglesia de San Juan,* St. John's Church. I grew comfortable with it when I sat near it to have morning coffee and try to read the local paper, which was, of course, in Spanish, Zamora being far beyond the *Herald Tribune* Belt. I didn't do very well, but my Spanish was getting freer, I mean I had crossed the major barrier to speaking a foreign language by not only looking a word up in the dictionary but letting it come out of my mouth as if I had said it many times, as casual as a nervous child. This great event had happened in the *plaza mayor.*

St. John's Church grew on me. At first I took it for granted, with its fine tower and its always open door. I could hear talking inside, sometimes singing. Once in a while someone would come out of the church and sit down near me for coffee. It was all very casual, very daily, and very pleasing. It made me feel familiar.

It was not the grandest nor the earliest of the churches. But it had a spaciousness about it that was magic, for its high ceiling had only one half-vault, very simple. It soared up from the right lower wall and arched over the interior until, at its apex, at the high ceiling, it ended at the left wall. It made the whole interior asymmetric. It was as if it should have been twice its size, or the rest of the church was only a ghost, for the half vault soared up and disappeared between the wall and the ceiling into the air beyond.

There was a tomb of a robed priest, unnamed, unknown, lying half on his side so that his stone eyes could stare at the choir, which practiced in the evening, their voices sometimes clear, sometime hesitant over a phrase, drifting out over the outdoor cafes and the taxis.

Outside the door two strange statues called the world to order or to prayer. They were black, maybe granite, forms, their faces sculpted as if they were veiled. One blew a silent trumpet, the other beat a silent drum.

It took a long time, months, but I had to find out who they were. Finally I was told that they were the two heralds for the old, old procession for Holy Thursday of the *Semena Santa,* Holy Week. They blew the music of the *merlu* to call the faithful at dawn, and when the procession, marching along to popular marches, was over, they all had traditional garlic soup. There may have been some riot involved, for the cure for a hangover all over the Mediterranean is garlic soup.

As in frontier towns in our own west with their gambling

dens, whores, tough cowboys, outlaws, and lascivious behavior, Zamora once had its own scandal. It was one of the things I liked most about the city. If a city can have an indigenous, unashamed sense of humor, Zamora had it. Even its churches broke the bounds of solemnity. One superb scandal there had repercussions that reached all the way to Rome.

In the choir of the cathedral, visitors peer under the choir stalls. They are not looking for lost passports, money, or wallets. They are finding the erotic bas-reliefs carved on the undersides of the seats of the *misericordias*. They are the most irreverent of the secret Spanish carvings that I found in Spain. No one knew for years (or admitted) why these ironic, funny carvings were there, these fornicating monks and nuns. Was it ridicule on the part of the artist? It could have been, for Spain's other hero can be an anarchic imp who is capable of criticizing the king, the church, and even the Inquisition. Or was it a protest against a church so powerful that only secrecy could be used to criticize?

I think it was, after two centuries, a memorial, and a very detailed one, of the scandal that had brought down a bishop, and almost brought down the powerful Dominican Order of monks. It was used in Rome as a weapon in the neverending quarrels between the mendicant (those who took vows to enter Dominican monasteries) and the episcopal (those who backed the bishops) factions of the thirteenth-century Catholic Church in Zamora.

The *Monasterio de Santa Maria la Real de las Dueñas* is across the Duero River from the cathedral, easy to see from the ramparts. The monastery was started by one of those dissatisfied wives of the gentry, the rich doña Elvira Rodríguez and her sister. In the thirteenth century the only way to get rid of a boring or violent husband was to go into a nunnery, and it was often done. Doña Elvira and her husband agreed to part, he to the Order of St. John, she to her new convent. The order that she and her sister chose was Dominican, and they took the vows of subjection, obedience, and reverence to the Bishop of Zamora up the hill.

It was, from the first, a retreat for doñas who were not married, old, or had, like the foundress, gotten rid of their husbands. They lived well, had their own apartments, some even ate alone, served by the poorer sisters. There were strict rules that anyone entering the convent must undergo a pregnancy test, leave all personal belongings behind, submit to bed checks, compulsory bleedings for health, organized hair washing, half-naked flagellation as punishment, and complete enclosure. Needless to say, doña Elvira and her ladies ignored the rules. When the responsibility for the behavior of the ladies, after a series of fights with the bishop, was taken over by the Dominican monks, things changed radically.

One evening in July in the mid-1270s, watchers along the parapets of the cathedral and the castle were entertained, shocked, dismayed, and fascinated to see the great doors of the convent flung open, the Dominican monks invited in, several of the ladies and their chosen monks making love on the ground outside the convent, general mayhem, frolic, and fornication.

At a trial later it was sworn by the nuns that the monks had been entering the convent, some night after night. They had chosen their lovers, or were chosen by them; it sounded almost like a very pleasant bordello set-up, where the monks brought nice presents to the nuns they loved, and the nuns dressed and undressed them, and did their washing.

It was not all joy and sin, however. Some of the nuns who

had meant their vows hid, terrified, in the great ovens away from the cruising monks. They were suffocated.

For twelve years, accusations went back and forth. For long periods they seemed to settle into some kind of quiet, and then the scandal seems to have been revived and used by the new Pope Boniface VIII, who finally cleared the names of the nuns of Zamora. He described them as the wise virgins who kept their lamps trimmed. He was very partial to the Dominicans.

There was nothing pious or retiring about these thirteenth-century monks. They even had a feud with the Franciscans. At night they would creep out in the dark and scrape the stigmata off the statues of St. Francis.

I found the whole story in *The Ladies of Zamora*, by Peter Linehan, one of the leading historians of medieval Spain. He is a Fellow of St. John's College, Cambridge. The book is superbly researched and catches the same sense of wild humor that I found by being in Zamora. By the way, it is now two years since I was in Zamora and I have just found out that St. John's Church is indeed a half-church. It had been a large church at a place on the bank of the Duero where the Zamorans wanted to build a bridge. There was not room in the *Plaza Mayor* for the whole church, so they moved half of it and shored up the wall exactly in the middle. The Zamorans liked their church and they obviously saw no reason not to have some of it at least.

I went to the young man at the desk at the *parador* and asked how to get to one of the few Visigothic churches left in Spain, somewhere outside of Zamora. He turned from very polite host to delighted Spaniard. "It is my village," he said, "you will go to my village." Here, as always, was the *patria chica*, the pride in it, the pleasure in telling about it. It was quite obvious that even if his job was in one of the finest and most princely *paradores* in northwestern Spain, his heart was in his village. "My village," he said.

It is less than true to say the Visigothic churches and their builders have completely disappeared. Spanish history no longer claims their influence, but it is hidden in their deep past, in their unrecognized genes. Their churches lie, in the north, somewhere under the magnificence of the churches that replaced them, as their stones, in turn, tend to lie above the lost floors of Roman temples. Even those who came as settlers to the empty remains of cities tended to raise their own sacred places where sacred places had been.

I drove out again into the *meseta* and followed my friend's directions to three villages that were bound together as one, by the land that was farmed around them. The Visigothic church had been moved there years before when it was threatened by flooding because of a new dam.

Stone by stone, columns, floor, wonderful simple shape of a cross, it was as solid as it had been in the eighth century when it was built, probably by Arian Visigoths, followers for three hundred years of the long-outlawed Arian heresy, which had been brought to them by a bishop who followed Bishop Arius in the fourth century before he was declared heretical. This would be one of those facts, dull and tarnished by legend, mostly forgotten, had it not been for the fact that the bishop had translated the Bible into the Visigothic language, probably the first translation ever in a common language, for such translations were banned very early on in the official church.

I went into the church. It was simple, almost cozy, obviously well used by the people from the villages. A well-educated local young lady sat as the docent, but she spoke no English and we made the usual signs, one wave taking in the high vault, the transepts, the ancient stone floor. Three words, *Sí, señora, bienvenido,* and she sank back into her chair and her private world, which I am sure was as dignified and tidy as she was.

There was something lonely and sweet about the church. In one corner, a huge stone coffin was in near-darkness, without a plaque saying whose it was. On the heavy, rough stone lid the primitive outline of an enormous sword had been carved, almost the length of the surface. I think the tomb must have been for a very large man, a Visigothic war lord, a local chieftain lying there, once so mighty, waving that huge weapon around his head, his long mustaches waving with fury, doing his job as king or chief or warlord or whatever his men called him.

The capitals of the decorative columns, which were attached to heavy stone stands for the arches, had all obviously been carved by the same sculptor. I hesitate to say they are naïve, for they are not, but primitive and strong as so much primitive art can be. The artist had at least heard his Bible, and he chose what to carve, I think, for the bas-reliefs were not committee work. When the hand of God came down to Abraham sacrificing Isaac, he had carved a large, imposing hand with a finger pointing at Abraham. Maybe he didn't know what a den was, maybe he didn't like that part of the story of Daniel. At any rate, he had carved Daniel standing in the shallow water of a pond, with a lion on either side of him, heads down, as he must have seen animals drink always, lapping the water. All around the plinths and the pediments there were flowers, vegetables, animals, and sometimes heads that were obvious portraits, for they were very different from one another in looks and entirely the same in their concepts.

Beside the nave, in a small chapel, were the font, again heavy rough stone carving, and a modern (maybe) crucifix that had been broken a long time ago and not yet repaired. There was something so true of real neglect in the real life Jesus lived, in the crucifix leaning against that alien Visigothic stone wall, that it brought tears.

I had seen processions at *Semana Santa* with full-sized statues of bleeding, exhausted Christs carrying their crosses, and the Holy Mother decked out in fine robes and jewels with jeweled tears on her carved face, being carried along in towns, led by the priests and the *penitentes* in black robes and hoods that hid their faces. But there was something about the simple Holy Mother in the little Visgothic village church that was more touching, even holier. She was a child-sized doll with a vacuous face and fake flowers in her hair. She sat in what looked like an eighteenth-century sedan chair under a canopy, with poles on both sides so that four men could carry her. She waited there in a corner of the church through mass after mass, all the year, for whatever processions she took part in. I found her so tender, all dressed by local women, that the obscuring velvet and grand pearls of the mourning statues on great floats carried by twenty men hidden under velvet skirts of their platforms seemed somehow carnival.

So there might have been a history of Byzantium and scandal and gold and *Reconquista* at its earliest and most military in Avila and Zamora, but there in the old Visigothic church was the simplicity that had been given to the people of the village from a forgotten time. I had expected nothing of Zamora.

It had only been a choice so I would not fall into the temptation of driving too fast, too far, and missing too much, but when I left I drove slowly down the narrow street and across the Duero on the old bridge. I was heading south, away from that early self-sufficient corner of Castile, loath to leave. Who can resist not only a scandal made immortal in a religious carving, but a city that would go to war over a trout?

SALAMANCA

 I took the *Via de Plata* south. The Silver Road has been the route all the way from the north to the Mediterranean Sea, since centuries before Rome. The two greatest Roman cities are on this road from Zamora, to Salamanca, to Mérida, to Zafra, to the ruins of Itálica and, finally, to Seville. Though it now has the mundane name of Route 630, it is still the way of Julius Caesar, and Scipio, with their unstoppable legions. In centuries I would travel it from prehistoric Tartessos to Rome to the Moorish sultanates, and along the route of the *Reconquista*. It is the road from the silver and gold mines in the north over which there was so much war, to ports in the Mediterranean to enrich the biblical kingdoms.

Parallel to the road, I could see the remains of what once was one of the *cañadas*, the sheep-runs north to south. It was as wide as a farm field, and it was part of a pasture that ran for hundreds of miles. A huge flock of sheep was grazing there, with one shepherd, and it gave me some idea of what it would have been like in the fifteenth and sixteenth centuries to see the animals in millions. Then the *cañadas* would have been filled with flocks driven south in fall and north again in spring, where the sheep munched all before them, and wool money poured into Castile and its newly industrial cities. Some of the *grandes*, who had huge land grants, owned as many as 40,000 sheep. The animals were driven in flocks of a thousand by a population of shepherds, both men and women, who must have had much to do with the centuries of easy familiarity between Christians and Moors.

It was an hour's drive from Zamora to Salamanca—or a millennia, or three centuries—for I was crossing that border of time between the Roman cities, the memory of Roman architecture in Romanesque churches, the ugly Gothic stone barrack-castles, with their scars of the tenth- and eleventh-century *Reconquista*, and the modern era, which began in Spain with the accidental discovery of the new world of America, and the new rich Catholic monarchs.

Salamanca is home to the oldest university in Spain, the pride of kings, in the service of whoever ruled, Inquisition, state, or dictatorship. They all have left their marks. To get to my hotel in the old city, I entered the *Gran Vía*, which seemed to be a deceptive circle with no way out. I had, I thought, memorized my map.

Nothing looked familiar. There were no signs with the names I knew. I was totally lost. There was the awful familiarity of places passed over and over until people on that Sunday morning began to recognize me, smile and wave. I went around and around a merry-go-round of a city.

Finally I decided to be brave, to turn out of the endless circle and search among the little streets for the small hotel I was going to stay in for a week, if I ever found it. I ended up in a cul-de-sac off a quiet street. There was nothing to do but park, sit, and wait for my luck to change. I even got out the deceptive tourist map that had gotten me into trouble. That was when I learned never to use those pretty maps that have little pictures of famous places, only main streets on them, and little else. There was no way of knowing a direction, a north, a south. From Salamanca on I bought the same kinds of detailed street maps used by the Spanish. My nadir of travel into the blind cul-de-sac was teaching me how to be lost.

A pleasant-looking middle-aged couple walked by. She held a small paper bag in her hand, and I guessed that, like people everywhere on a Sunday morning, they had been to the bakery to buy a special Sunday treat. They stopped, spoke to each other, and came back. In Spanish they asked me politely—something. What little Spanish I knew, along with my sense of direction, was gone. I tried to answer in Spanish but all I could think of was Turkish.

I did, finally, mutter the name of the hotel, which had floated up through a pool of confusion to consciousness. The man spoke very carefully and slowly, as one speaks to a foreigner who obviously is stupid and half-deaf. He might as well have been speaking Swahili. He read my face, and turned to his wife. She nodded. He came around to the front seat, got in, and made a circle with his hand. I started the car, and turned it carefully, thanking God that however powerful they are, Spanish cars are small.

In a block or so, he pointed right. We were back in the *Gran Vía*. I felt like I was going to die there. He gestured to the right again, then left for one building, right again, left by an ancient church. There in front of me was my hotel, my home away from home, my street. I had been wandering less than ten minutes from my hotel. He got out of the car. At least I remembered how to say thank you. *Muchas gracias*. Spanish.

He showed that dignified Spanish kindness, not a professional welcome for a tourist. He had taken a few minutes to interrupt his Sunday morning walk, his habits, his life, and take a strange foreign woman he would probably never see again safely to her hotel. It was a small incident on a Sunday morning, but it was my introduction to Salamanca and it colored my stay there. Gestures like it would, over and over, be my introduction to unknown towns in Spain.

My home was a small room looking out on the street leading to the *Plaza Mayor,* and for that week I would walk it often in an illusion that I lived in Salamanca. We began, those who lived there, to recognize each other in the street, in the shops, in the little cheap family restaurants, with red house wine that I could have used for ink. I had left the convents, the castles, the palaces that were *paradores* and had gone to a place where I could live, for a little while, in that street, in that town, among those people.

I had dinner in a little restaurant where Spanish families brought their children early and working couples ate before going home from their jobs. In Spain restaurants are empty until at least nine o'clock in the evening. But that hour gives the lie to visitors who are convinced that, after trudging around all day, they have to starve until nine o'clock at night to have their dinner. My small, unassuming restaurant opened for dinner at the tacky lovely hour of six; by the first meal I knew why the Spanish flocked there. It was very good. By my third visit they knew me and gave me a table where I could see to read. How many scholars had lived in that small hotel while they studied in Salamanca, and eaten at the same table, where there was light? I had become, to them, part of a long procession of students from all over the world.

On the first morning at waking, I walked down toward the

Plaza Mayor to find breakfast, which, too, would become a comforting habit there. I walked through an arched gateway into one of the most glorious squares in Spain, so large that at first I hung back, shy of plunging into that great space. In the past there had been bullfights, religious processions, student riots. Now there are concerts in the evening, and here and there, already at nine in the morning, some students dressed as if it were Halloween, a fool's procession in what I imagined was some sort of comic initiation.

I was also, for the first time since leaving Madrid, back in the Paris *Herald Tribune* Belt. So I sat at a table in the plaza every morning, having breakfast and reading newsprint instead of trying and failing to follow the news in a Spanish paper.

The square had been designed in the eighteenth century by two of Spain's most original architects, Andrés García de Quiñones and Alberto Churriguerra, from whom came the architectural word *churrigueresque*, the Spanish fantasy of flinging whatever could be called to mind at façades, as if the world of the city itself was a fantasy not to be taken too seriously. It is a tradition, if originality and anarchy can be a tradition, that reaches all the way beyond Gaudí, the wild architect who built the cathedral at Barcelona.

Churrigueresque can be a wild delight, an imp of design let loose. From the curlicues carved of stone that seem to be molded of silver, to the fantastic tumbles of carved figures, it seems to draw from deep in the vision of the Spanish artist; it reminded me of some of the twelfth-century capitals on the columns in Zamora. A bad imitation of such fantasy is the Isabelline. The architects of the fifteenth-century churches, where the decoration is named for the queen, tried to achieve that weightless delight by crowding gold on gold, but the result is only a brag of riches compared to the lovely real tradition.

The *Plaza Mayor* of Salamanca has *duende*. A noble *ayuntamiento* like a city palace, grand façades of apartments reaching around the huge square, colonnades of stone where the shops and walkers and those like myself, who gazed in shop windows, thinking of other things, sheltered from the sun. Walks are aligned across the center, benches are set in space, with here and there a streetlight on a baroque metal stand. As evening came, in the late twilight, the square was at its most magic, the *duende* then was light itself reaching out from the restaurants, the shops, to make the stone pure gold in color. The outdoor tables were filled; the talk of the town a huge murmur of bees. The people of Salamanca took their *paseo* in the drifting darkness. In the distance I heard laughter.

In the morning and in the daylight, along the façades above the colonnade, I saw the portrait medallions of kings, of queens, of Miguel de Unamuno, the twentieth century's most famous Spanish writer, and, not yet removed, General Franco. In other cities dictatorial street names have been quietly changed. The statues of Franco's heroes have been removed or shot full of holes on a Saturday night, but not in Salamanca. In the most renowned university town in Spain they haven't gotten around to it yet. These two twentieth-century medallions represent one of the most defining moments of the modern civil war.

For me that moment started at a table in the *Plaza Mayor*. The Spanish have a name for an international habit of hanging out, of meeting like-minded friends in a chosen bar or café or club. It is the *tertulia*, a daily meeting of minds, whether horse race or politics, fishing or philosophy or the *teléfono arábe*, the spreading of rumor.

The long-running, best-known *tertulia* in Salamanca was led by Unamuno, poet, philosopher, novelist, and conversationalist who had started years before as professor of Greek at the university. By the thirties, he had become its rector. He had never been anything less than outspoken, sometimes at the top of his lungs. He sat at the same table year after year. He wore a dark blue suit with a black turtleneck sweater day in, day out. He welcomed foreigners who had come to pay tribute. He knew fifteen languages, including Danish, which he learned in order to read Kierkegaard in the original (he quoted him more often than any other European philosopher in the early twenties, long before existentialism became a philosophic fashion). He called himself, proudly, a liberal, at a time when the priests taught their parishioners that to vote liberal was a mortal sin.

This, through the years, had caused him to be convicted of treason (though never jailed). During the dictatorship of Primo de Rivera in the twenties, he was exiled to one of the Canary Islands. He was rescued in a small boat by his French liberal friends. After seven years of exile, he returned to Spain when the first republic was established in 1931.

Most of the writers, artists, and intellectuals in Spain looked forward to golden years in the republic. Both Unamuno and Ortega y Gasset were the most internationally respected of Spanish writers, Unamuno for *The Tragic Sense of Life* and Ortega for *The Revolt of the Masses*. Both became independent members of the new republican *Cortes*. But when reform degenerated into violence they lost hope.

When Franco began the revolt in 1936 that would turn into the Spanish civil war, the atrocities on both sides forced Ortega to flee the country, and Unamuno to make the tragic mistake of his life. It is generally believed that he backed

Franco, but, as loquacious as he was, I believe that one phrase out of the thousands he used, sitting there in the *Plaza Mayor*, had to be altered for propaganda by Franco. He is supposed to have said that the revolt would "save western civilization." Would the man who lived for the kind of passionate precision that defines the Spanish way of being use so overblown a phrase? He who had written "Neither 'the human' nor 'humanity,' neither the simple adjective nor the abstract substantive, but the concrete substantive—man. The man of flesh and bone; the man who is born, suffers and dies—above all, who dies; the man who eats and drinks and plays and sleeps and thinks and wills; the man who is seen and heard; the brother, the real brother"? I think not.

He defined himself as an incorrigible Spaniard, and this incorrigible Spaniard stayed in Salamanca after the war broke out, and Franco had made the city his headquarters. As rector, Unamuno considered it his duty to protect the university that had been his home for many years. While the German and Italian officers strutted in the *Plaza Mayor,* he stayed on, this stubborn, recalcitrant Basque, this old, brave man.

The arch by the newsstand that leads out of the *Plaza Mayor* past the simple and lovely Church of St. Martin, through the *Plaza del Corrillo,* and down the *Rúa Mayor,* is the walkway to the university. There are bookshops and a place to buy fresh figs, and high-quality schlock stores, all the modern comforts for the visitor.

The first ancient building is the Conch House, which is covered with a disciplined army of stone conch shells, which look very like scallop shells. The street that goes past it to the right is *Rúa Antigua,* and left off the *Rúa Antigua,* past the church of the Visigothic St. Isadore, is the *Calle de Libreros.*

On the front of the main building on the left is the massive seventeenth-century façade of the university. In the college courtyard opposite, a man of bronze stands on a pedestal, watching it forever. It is Salamanca's other Spanish hero, Fray Luis de Léon.

To me the narrow space of the street between the man and the façade holds a history of Spanish thought, a monument to that perpetual Spanish quarrel between extremes, icy reaction and the flow of questing ideas that sometimes becomes anarchic. The street is more arena than alleyway. To see the "famous" façade of the university, it is necessary to stand close to Fray Luis, as if he were a guide. Its carvings cover the centuries, the mistakes, the power.

The lowest level is formal, a discreet design with a large portrait medallion of the Catholic monarchs, Ferdinand and Isabel, one of the greatest administrators Spain had seen up to her time. She ruined her great work by being a religious fanatic. It was principally under her aegis that the Jewish urban minds, so needed by an agrarian people, were burned, forcibly baptized, or banished. Spain lost much of her brains and her urban merchant class. It has taken her up until the twentieth century to recover.

On the second level, with much grand carving, are three coats of arms. In the center, under the Imperial Crown, is that of Charles I of Spain, Charles V of the Holy Roman Empire. On one side is the double eagle of the Holy Roman Empire, on the other the coat of arms of the House of Austria.

Then, having done their duty by the solemn and the powerful, the carvers of the third and highest level of the façade have added their own wonderful, witty goofiness. In the center is a pope being crowned by cardinals (no one seems to know which pope it is). All around them are what purport to be classic figures. A nude of Aphrodite? Or a familiar lady of Salamanca? Who knows? A niche containing Hercules, who is supposed to have opened the Spanish peninsula, viz. the Pillars of Hercules, now called the Straits of Gibraltar.

There are portraits, imps, the whole panoply of stone catcalls at everything below, at power, at solemnity, at death. Much of it is hidden, like the frog who sits on top of one of the skulls. This has all been interpreted officially as sin and redemption. Frog, nude, and Hercules, and probably local portraits of people who wanted the stone seventeenth-century equivalent of their pictures in the paper, have all survived sin.

How can I tell without anger what happened in that building on Columbus Day, 1936? It was in the *Paraninfo,* the central assembly hall of the university. Two men stood, one with the authority to kill the other, in the essential Spanish confrontation, a confrontation that had burst out all over Spain. Military and mind. Authority and rebel.

Franco's army uprising against the elected second Spanish republic was into its third month. There had been little resistance in the north except in the coal fields, and that had been savagely put down. But there had been as much savagery on one side as the other, for hates met that went back through the years, old scores, old passions that fired new political abstractions.

On Columbus Day, as rector, Unamuno was appointed to sit in the place of honor in the great hall of the university in place of General Franco. Señora Franco sat beside him. General Millán Astray, the much lauded commander of the Spanish foreign legion, was two seats from Unamuno. The hall was full of Nationalist soldiers. Outside the hall there had been murder, and on the honey-colored walls of the university and the town since Franco had made it his headquarters, slogans were painted, as in all over the cities taken over by the Nationalists, as they had begun to be called. But their way and their language was fascist.

The most popular slogan was "One state, one country, one chief." *Ein Volk, ein Reich, ein Führer,* the motto of the Nazis. Franco had begun to be called the *Caudillo,* as Hitler had been called *Führer.* Both words mean leader, but *caudillo* is also used for political boss.

Whatever hope that Unamuno may have had for a restoration of a constitutional monarchy must have been long buried in facts. The German and Italian political embassies had moved to Salamanca. A close friend, the Republican mayor of Salamanca, had been shot. Books were being gathered to be burned. Modern young Spain was being destroyed around the old man, while the past that had failed them over and over, the past I had driven through, from Segovia to Zamora, was being revived, which is a failure and a fake, like trying to raise the dead.

In the ceremonial hall of the university that Columbus Day, the day they call in Spain the Day of the Race, Unamuno sat under a large portrait of Franco, which had replaced the traditional medieval and early Renaissance portraits, and listened to one offensive speech after another, one sycophantic praise of Franco and the Nationalists after another from the mouths of his own colleagues, who had chosen to go along to get along.

He had not been put on the program to speak. I suspect he was thought too dangerous, no matter how much he had been used for propaganda.

Fortunately, what happened next had eyewitnesses with long memories. One of them was Vegas Latapie. Unlike his murdered Republican uncle, the mayor of Salamanca, he was a Nationalist, part of the guard of honor that day, and one of those who had arranged the ceremony. He was interviewed years later for the English documentary *The Spanish Civil War*. He said that several speakers, including Millán Astray, had referred to the Basques and the Catalans as "a cancer which should be cut out from the body politic." Then this is the scene Latapie described.

Unamuno began scribbling some notes and ceased to listen to the speeches. According to the program he was not supposed to speak, but when the evening finished he took the floor. Of course nobody could stop him because he was presiding in lieu of the Head of State. He had taken an envelope from his pocket. He stood up and began to speak, and at once I realized that this was something out of the ordinary. "You talk about the Basques and the Catalans, but here is your bishop who is a Catalan and tried to teach you the Christian doctrine you don't want to know while I, a Basque, have spent my life teaching you to read and think in the Spanish language, of which you are ignorant."

Unamuno denounced atrocities on both sides. "Hatred without compassion cannot win minds, to conquer is not to convince," he told the company and the fanatical Millán Astray. Millán Astray jumped up and, "flapping his empty sleeve like a penguin, cried, 'Death to the intellectuals.'" There was an uproar. Don Miguel tried to answer this madman. Those near the two old men said that he told Millán Astray that his motto, *"Arriba o Muerto,"* Hail or arise death, the motto of the foreign legion, was a necrophilic, senseless cry. He said, "I, who have spent my life shaping paradoxes which have aroused the uncomprehending anger of others, I must tell you as an expert authority that this outlandish paradox is repellent to me." He compared the war-crippled Millán Astray to Cervantes, who had lost the use of his arm at Lepanto, and had gone on to write *Don Quixote*, while Millán Astray had only spread hatred.

Then he added, "A cripple who lacks the spiritual greatness of a Cervantes is wont to seek ominous relief in causing mutilation around him."

At this, according to another witness, Millán Astray shouted, "*¡Abajo la inteligencia!*" Down with intelligence! Officers drew their pistols.

Unamuno shouted back, "This is the temple of the intellect. And I am its high priest. It is you who profane its sacred precincts. You will win because you have more than enough brute force. But you will not convince. For to convince you need to persuade. And in order to persuade you will need what you lack. Reason and right in the struggle."

Millán Astray's bodyguard thrust his submachine gun into Unamuno's chest. Doña Carmen (Franco's wife) pushed the gun aside and, signaling to the guard of honor, led don Miguel down the steps while one of the officers supported him on the other side. He could hardly walk. He let himself be carried along a path made by soldiers with their rifle butts at the ready. They put Unamuno into a car.

He was driven to his house, followed by cries of "Traitor" and "Red." He was dismissed from his post as rector. He was not shot but was put under house arrest. It is said that his international reputation saved his life.

But he died only two months later. He was supposed to have been a broken man. I don't believe it. He had done what he had to do, stood up to power, as had El Cid, and the *comuneros,* looked it in the eye and told what he saw. Maybe he had been planning it. Who knows? According to *The Spanish Civil War*, he wrote in his last letters of "a stupid reign of terror" and that the enemy of the Nationalists was "liberalism, not Bolshevism." It was a view of the war that was borne out by George Orwell in his *Homage to Catalonia*.

It is mete and right that Fray Luis de León, the other Spanish hero of Salamanca, should be watching over the place where Unamuno spoke out. He was the university's most famous lecturer in the mid-sixteenth century, poet, a liberal inquirer into biblical texts, which were then, during the Counter-Reformation, dangerous reading. The Vulgate had been declared the official Bible, and Fray Luis, along with other scholars, still studied the ancient Hebrew texts. They found mistakes in the Vulgate translation. In the six-teenth century, pointing this out would have been enough to bring down the Inquisition on one's head. Fray Luis de León was the first to translate the Song of Solomon into Castilian.

He was a descendant of a *converso,* a "new Christian," as was one who was probably his student, St. John of the Cross, and his contemporary, St. Teresa, which made him even more vulnerable.

He lectured in the room next to the ceremonial hall where Unamuno had shown such courage. One day the Inquisition came and arrested him in the middle of a lecture, for his translations, and his general outspokenness, and probably the fact that he was a "dangerous" *converso.* He was kept in prison for five years. Finally he was released, with the warn-ing to avoid controversial issues.

On the morning of his first lecture after his release, he opened with the words, "as I was saying yesterday . . ." Fray

Luis de León's lecture room is as it was that morning, the carved names on the old benches, the lectern in place. There is quiet and a simplicity about the room that must reflect its finest scholar and poet.

I walked in Salamanca until the little shop with the figs became as familiar a stop as the golden buildings. The city is so beautiful a place that I found myself wanting to escape it, and I followed back streets where one-room student houses were still there, nearly ruined, that must have been contemporary with all that grandeur when it was new. Down by the river the Roman bridge is still guarded by a huge prehistoric stone boar or maybe a bull that has lost its head. It is a large, crude, powerful animal of dark stone, like those found in fields in Castile, left there by prehistoric tribes. Most of the sculptures are said to be bulls, and this is probable, for the bull and the mother goddess are the earliest gods known.

But this bull or boar led me to a wonderful new view of a place that was becoming, in my eyes, heavy with grandeur. I could look up again at the façade of the university, and see among the imps and follies the ghost of one with a name. At the corner of that façade that is so grand and where so many secrets are carved, I imagine a corner ripped back from that stern authority. Looking down at the crowd would be the Spanish Lazarillo de Tormes, the rascal survivor in those imperial centuries. He was born to literature long before the American Huckleberry Finn or the English Artful Dodger. He lives on in Salamanca with a real statue of his own. On the wall behind a young bronze boy leading an old blind man, I read, SALAMANCA A LAZARILLO DE TORMES. I had no idea who or what it was, but when I found out, there was another of Spain's immortal rebels that I suspect both Unamuno and Luis de León would welcome into their company.

He is the first *pícaro*, the wandering survivor, the wise innocent who tells what he sees, who survives by trickery. He goes from Salamanca on a journey that takes him through the Spain of Charles V, Holy Roman Emperor. *La vida de Lazarillo de Tormes* is, along with *Don Quixote*, the most familiar of Spanish stories. Every child knows it. Its scenes have been painted by Velazquez, Murillo, Goya, and Gustave Doré. It was published first in 1554 and, with a hiatus of thirty years, when it was forbidden by the Inquisition, has remained one of Spain's favorite and best-known short novels ever since.

Lazarillo starts out in a village near Salamanca, moves to the city where he is hired by a blind man to be his guide, and the first picaresque novel is born. The author is enough of a mystery to have given scholars fodder for opinions ever since, but the first editions were published under the name Diego Hurtado de Mendoza, diplomat, scholar, writer, and famous humanist. The anonymous publications came later, after the Inquisition had demanded the censorship of several chapters that were hilariously critical of the clergy. It was not until the mid-nineteenth century that Spaniards were allowed to read it as it had been written.

It is a picture of survival by an imp in a world of starvation, clerical shenanigans, blind religion, thievery, official stupidity, greed, and violence, an ironic satire of life under the grand reigns of the church and the crown. To me, Lazarillo's gift to Spain is a peep behind that grand façade of official history. He demands of that history which follows the lives of the great, the famous battles, the royal politics, "Me too. Me too!"

It was the bull, or boar, or lump of stone at the beginning

of the Roman bridge over the Tormes, where, as they leave Salamanca, the blind man tells him to put his head against the statue and listen for a mysterious sound within. When he does, the blind man deals him a mighty blow against the stone that leaves him feeling the pain for three days. The blind man then begins to educate him with his first of many pieces of advice. "You fool! A blind man's servant has to be one step ahead of the devil."

I began to see with his eyes that Salamanca was a place for the young, not the dead, filled with students as every university town, and children, wonderful children, one with her *mamá*, who had dressed her in the traditional costume of the town, to go, I suspect, to a party. After her I saw more color, more ease, and I tried no longer to capture the grandeur of the golden stone and the tall towers, the crucifixions and the carved clergy on the great stone doors, and recognized the imps, the animals, the daily life carved on the stairs in the university building, and could walk through history more concerned with ripe figs.

So I had the time and grace to wander. I walked until the narrow paths between the plateresque buildings were part of the cityscape of my mind. I took it for granted. Often I passed, when walking down by the Tormes River, a building up on the hill with the cathedrals and the towers rising behind it. It was as out of place and, at the same time, as totally a part of Salamanca as Lazarillo the rascal.

There was not a stone in its structure. It was a web of steel with magic walls of stained glass that looked in the evening from the street below as if they were made of vines and snow and peacocks. In the front were twin streetlights of the kind seen in American cities in the twenties. The fine stairs behind them led up from both sides to an entrance of light and steel and almost Moorish splendor. On the last day I was there I could resist it no longer. Curiosity more than admiration took me there. It was not even in my guidebook.

I entered my own childhood. I was born in 1918, and my memory is long and fiercely clear: conversations of ladies wondering whether or not to bob their hair, a girl who had come back from Paris, France, who put rouge on her nipples, Lalique vases and orange Coty powder boxes with little white powder puffs printed on them, French dolls flung on beds, Spanish galleons on the piano, my mother's contempt for all of it as tacky, and my longing, which had to be secret, to have it all when I grew up.

It was all there, under a sky-high ceiling of Tiffany glass with colors of blue and green that seemed to move as the sun moved. It was the art deco museum, the *Casa Lis*, one of the finest buildings and collections in Spain of the Art Nouveau period at the beginning of the twentieth century, with Mackintosh, Munsch, Gaudí. That imp who had guided secret Spanish carving for centuries had found its temple; no Ferdinand, no Isabel, no Inquisition, no grandeur, just a beautiful place, not "historic" or "lovely old" or in "good taste." Here were the objects that for half a century, until World War II, we held in our hands, used to put out our cigarettes, gave for Christmas, played with, with no idea they would arrive in time in this lovely place, this hall of mirrors to our past.

There were dolls like the one I had as a child and named Mary Pickford. There were ashtrays with dancers poised on their rims, ladies in fine clothes and cloche hats made of metal, gold and silver plated, painted china bathing beauties, dancers, clowns, and rooms of Lalique and Tiffany.

As I walked out of my last historic building in Salamanca, from a loudspeaker hidden in the ceiling, a soft and nasal voice that sounded like Rudy Vallee was singing,

> On a day like today,
> we passed the time away,
> writing love letters in the sand. . . .

EXTREMADURA

 South across the Tormes where Lazarillo de Tormes was born while his mother washed clothes down at the river, I began a steep ascent up the Silver Road. I was climbing up toward the great central mountain barrier that runs from west to east, from the Atlantic to the Pyrenees, and separates the north of Spain from the south. It has many names.

I was already noticing hints of change, the white houses, the greener mountain fields, and, as it is in mountain valleys, the smallness of things. I drove through little villages where terraced plots had been so carefully cultivated. The ever-present flowering vines hung almost over the road.

I was in the Sierra de Gredos, the western part of the tangle of mountains that have dictated the quarrels and the mutual exchanges of habit, vision, ways of living, and language that have divided Spain all through its history into *patrias chicas*. The roads are hairpin curves, long drops into narrow valleys, circles and angles that can amaze travelers and put their hearts in their throats. I am amused by that, for

I love to drive the mountains, wherever they are. Mountain roads that are terrible to strangers are my joy.

It is one of the reasons I love Spain. If it is true that you cannot govern a people who live at over five thousand feet, the Hapsburgs found that out in Spain. Yet out of all his vast and unwieldy domains, it was to the mountains of Extremadura that Juana's son, Charles I of Spain, Charles V of the Holy Roman Empire, came to die. Maybe he, like people in the mountains of my own birth, had found out that while you may rob a country blind, neglect it, and starve it, you can fall in love with the mountains, their strength, their secrecy.

Extremadura, poor, despised for so long, a no man's land longer than any other part of Spain in the *Reconquista*, was one of the main goals of my search for recognitions. I began, as the road climbed toward the *patria chica* of so many of the *conquistadores*, to find the answer to a question. Why had so many of them come from Extremadura?

It had long been a place of mystery to the Roman Christians and the Visigoths; it was beyond some ancient pale, a land's end, a Finisterre to those who named it after the Duero, that most northern frontier.

As long ago as the tenth century it had been thought of as the land beyond, beyond the expected, beyond the comfort of the known world. For centuries it has been a place of spirits where the unknown and the fearful take ghostly forms. It is haunted and blessed.

At least that was its reputation, a borderland between Christian and Moor for so long, garrisoned for border wars with the Moors and, later, the Portuguese. The *Reconquista* paused there in its southward march long enough for that present to join with Extremadura's deep past. It was too mountainous, the valleys too small, for the *grandes* to be very interested in it. The crown hardly remembered it. So it became a mountain kingdom of its own, a place of vast holdings by the militant Christian orders of knights. They were good landlords. The monastic orders, far away from the intrigues of the church hierarchies, seem to have caught the mountaineers' sense of freedom.

For a long time the Jews escaped from pogroms that were fueled from time to time by the more zealous priests like San Vicente Ferrer in Toledo. They were thrown out of their old homes, their families in danger. The mountains of Extremadura were safer; the Jews hid there and made small towns that prospered, at least enough to keep body and soul together. They taught the mountain tribal descendants their crafts, their laws. When they were finally exiled in 1492, Extremadura suffered more than any other part of Spain from their exile.

After the expulsion the country districts fell into poverty so dire, so deep, that there was no relief until the twentieth century. It became a place to fear, a place of dark mysteries, a place to get lost, forget, go mad—a green mountain desert where travelers disappeared and then were found later, they say, turned into beasts.

Buñuel, the surrealist Spanish filmmaker, made a documentary of it in the twenties. The facts and the images were so shocking that the film was banned in Spain. Alfonso XIII, the last king of Spain before the present Don Juan, went to "inspect it," trundling along the mountain roads with the usual large royal entourage. It contained, by the way, Unamuno, who wrote about Extremadura as a beautiful place. But to his everlasting shame he did not mention that, in a poverty-stricken village when the king wanted milk in his tea, they had to use human milk, for there were no cows or goats.

For most travelers today, it is the boondocks, on the way to other places, far beyond the Paris *Herald Tribune* Belt, *flamenco*, bullfight, and guitar. But to what we Americans became and what we have inherited in habit and land, it is the most important place in Spain. Its haunted cities are so beautiful, so evocative, that I was drawn into their sense of being the strong center of an isolated world. I visited more cities in that mountain kingdom than in any other place in Spain.

It happens, for the simplest of reasons, that so many of the *conquistadores* came from there. By accident, maybe by caprice, probably by ignorance as Charles V and his Flemish advisors were so proudly ignorant of the Spain they ruled, one of the *grandes* of Extremadura was appointed to be the viceroy of the newly discovered world where all dreams came true and survival was too vain a hope for any but the brave and the desperate. Visions were real and for the taking in a new world as wild as the old one they came from.

So they gathered from all over Extremadura, the fighters, the ones who had gone for soldiers, the unemployed, the young and bored, to raise the banners of Castile and the patron saint of Extremadura, the Black Virgin of Guadalupe. And, as one of the *conquistadores* answered when asked why he had gone, "To bring Christ to the savages and make a little money."

I stopped in Plasencia, perched on the side of a steep mountain by a little rushing stream, the Río Jerte. Its fifteenth-century Convent of Santo Domingo had been made into a *parador*, one of the most authentic that I saw. It had the grandeur of true austerity, the stone vaults, the high pitch of the ceilings, and the austere carvings of ancient monks and, maybe, saints. In the dining room that had been the monks' refectory, an attempt to soften the atmosphere into a cosier place had been made, but, thank God, it had failed. The room retained its stern silent dignity.

I came into Medellín where the boy Hernán Cortés had been born. The valley was surrounded by mountains. A huge castle ruin was on the horizon of a hill above me. I climbed a steep narrow path up to it. Its foundations seemed to grow organically from the rocks without human aid, the rocky strength of a stubborn land. I began to see changes in the ways of building left in the fragmented walls. Like stone calendars, they showed their layers of time through more than a thousand years—tribal, Roman, Visigothic, Castilian.

I stood on the hillside beside a small, gnarled tree that could have been old enough for Cortés to lie near in the sun and dream as a boy. It had been tortured by weather and age. Below me, along the curve of the river below, the Guadiana, the small village of Medellín was almost unchanged in size since Cortés's boyhood.

But under the hill I stood on, there were ruins of what had been, in Roman times, a much larger city. A few carved fragments of a Roman theater were exposed in a man-made cave too small to crawl into. But I could glimpse marble fragments imbedded in the cave walls that could have been bits of columns or parts of statues.

A city which had a theater in that six hundred years of Roman rule was an important one. When Rome fell, Medellín was forgotten. As in other cities of fallen Rome, its stones were used to build shelters, its ruins silted over by time. It was a land for a young man like Hernán Cortés to leave to seek his fortune. He had been born to a family without money, but of the minor gentry. He was raised as a *hidalgo* who had been taught from his birth the Gothic scorn of trade and craftsmanship. It was inevitable that his honorable choice was to be a soldier.

In Trujillo I drove into the large *Plaza Mayor*, which was level with the fields around, where the cloud-driven sky at evening seemed more alive than the town itself. I passed a grand statue, the visual center of the town, a man in armor seated on horseback. The bronze plumes on his helmet seemed tossed by the wind. It was Francisco Pizarro, the blood-stained conqueror of Peru, come home in triumph.

He, three illegitimate brothers, and a legitimate one set out together to conquer something, anything, to come home and own the town that scorned them. It is said they left Trujillo "with only a cloak and a sword." Only one of them could read. Pizarro as a boy had been a swineherd, and it was said in the town he had been suckled by a sow. It was he and his brothers, illegitimate, homeless, of no account, who faced and murdered the Peruvian king, Atahualpa, who had tried to buy his life by extending his hand toward the ceiling to show that he would fill the room they stood in with gold. The room was seventeen feet by twelve feet.

The Pizzaro brothers came home and built their palaces. One of them, now called the Palace of the *Conquista*, faces the *Plaza Mayor*. On the morning that I went to see the statue, four boys lounged on its plinth in the sun, ignoring Pizarro, saying very little, maybe thinking of going somewhere, anywhere, to seek their fortunes.

I drove higher, on a narrow road through fields, to find the man who had died there. All around, the mountains were a hiding place, a comfort, a strength. I was in such a peaceful dream that I almost missed the monastery of Yuste, which was the last small home of one who had ruled almost the whole of Europe, Charles V.

If much of the rule by Ferdinand and Isabel had been a series of tragic disasters for Spain, Charles V, the product of a political marriage arranged by them, was himself one of the disasters. He was Spain's first Hapsburg king. His son, Philip II, was father of the Invincible Armada, lost to Sir Francis Drake, the English navy, and the terrible channel storms.

Philip II seems truly to have loved his country, and did his best to rule it well. The other Hapsburgs ranged from lazy to sad to comic, and the dynasty ended with an imbecile, Charles II, the one who in Madrid had been allowed to light the fires of an *auto de fe* as a special honor for his marriage.

The comuneros had been right about Charles V's passion for playing emperor. He had bankrupted Spain. It could almost be said that on one level, the German bankers owned Castile. Castile had paid and paid and paid, for the bribes that bought him the title of Holy Roman Emperor, for the wars that followed. The annual income for Castile had been about a million ducats when that awkward, unattractive, eighteen-year-old boy inherited the throne and was advised by his ministers to keep his mother confined at Tordesillas. Through the years of his reign, the Castilian annual income rose, through American gold and silver, another five hundred thousand ducats, which he spent.

By the time Charles V dragged his worn-out, aching body to Yuste, the monastery that had been prepared to receive him, he had put Castile in hock to the German bankers for over thirty-six million ducats. Imperial Spain never recovered from that terrible drain.

The reign of Charles V had brought the Flemish influence

in thought and in architecture. It was the most progressive in Europe. There was the cathedral in Segovia, and in Granada, the unfinished palace rotunda, and the cathedral where he had buried his grandparents and his parents. The inquiring humanists of central Europe brought Erasmus to Salamanca and the other universities and opened the Spanish inquiring mind, which, alas, later provided much fuel to the conservative Inquisition. Those were the great gifts of the culture that Charles V brought with him. But the reality of daily life in Spain was tragic.

His son, Philip, who would become Philip II, that poor king with the soul of Bartleby the Scrivener, wrote to Charles in May 1545, begging him to come home from his grand wars:

> The common people who have to pay these *servicios* [sales taxes] are reduced to such utter miseries that many of them walk naked. And the misery is so universal that it is even greater among the vassals of the *grandes* than it is among your majesty's vassals, for they are unable to pay their rents, lacking the wherewithal, and the prisons are full.

This letter shines a different light on Philip II. No wonder he worked himself to death.

When Charles inherited Aragon at Ferdinand's death, he inherited more than land. He was left a jewel that is seldom recognized as providing what success he had in the field of battle he so loved. It was the finest army in Europe, designed and trained by Gonzalo Fernández de Córdoba, the man the Italians called "the Great Captain."

He also inherited a boon or curse that was to change Europe forever. On the Feast of All Souls, 1516, a practical, down-to-earth monk, who was a professor of theology, followed the tradition of his university and invited formal debate on a series of theses on which he had given some years of thought. He looked forward to presenting his theses to his colleagues, probably to see how his ideas would stand up to argument.

Such invitations among the faculty had been offered many times before. Open formal debates, posted on the door of the Wittenburg church at the university, were a longtime habit among the faculty, a message board to check in passing. He had no idea that his academic presentation would go beyond the small town of Wittenburg. But it did. The ninety-five theses, meant only for the confines of his university, flew like wildfire over Germany. Written in Latin, they nearly drowned the small university press in demands. Translated into German, they sold edition after edition, and began to shake the foundations of the Vatican.

Opinions are not usually arrived at abstractly, nor by kings in whose name they are made. Often they are voiced by what seems like accident, or simple reactions of love or ambition or disgust. The monk's name was Martin Luther, and he had become disgusted with the bland, open, corrupted sale of indulgences by his Catholic Church. These certificates assured that, according to the amount of money spent, the years in purgatory would be shortened. Church cynicism had gone too far. Luther was not the only one who reacted. That was proved by the wildfire he started. The sale, by the way, helped pay for the great new cathedral of St. Peter at the Vatican.

Charles V's tutor was Adrian of Utrecht, who was the religious dictator of the boy's life, and who would soon become pope. So a lifelong battle was joined for a boy who only liked to joust and dress up in grand armor to cover his ugly, jutting chin until he could grow beard enough to hide it. Instead of learning from the popularity of Luther's work, and trying to find a place for new ideas, as it had done so often through the centuries, the church outlawed Luther.

The factions hardened, and religion became even more political instead of spiritual. The spiritual was left to mystics, poets of their own world apart, St. Teresa, St. John of the Cross, Ignatius Loyola.

The Charles V that is so familiar is that man who seems to rule the world astride a horse and dressed in armor, magnificent, and regal, in the painting by Titian after the Battle of Muhlberg, his most important victory. He was only forty-six. By the time he was in his mid-fifties, he was bounded by wars with France, with the newly Protestant German states, and with Suleiman the Magnificent. Suleiman was sultan of the only other empire to compare in size with his, the Ottoman Empire. The territory Suleiman ruled had once been the Byzantine Empire. His city was Istanbul, once called Constantinople.

By the time Charles came to Yuste, he was an exhausted, beaten, dying man with few friends, terrible regrets, and an agonizing gout which kept him from the only joy he had left, eating. His dearly beloved and most beautiful wife had died early. He seems not to have cared much for his clerkly, fanatically pious son, Philip. He began to give away the largest empire since Rome, larger because America had become its source of wealth after the ruin of Castile.

Along with the unfinished wars, he gave Austria to his brother Ferdinand; Spain, the Low Countries, and the New World was his gift to his son Philip, along with bits and pieces of duchies throughout Europe which needed to be defended. That was when he did one of the few completely sensible things of his life.

He retired to the mountains of Extremadura, to the little monastery I was seeking on the winding road through the mountains, to fish, and listen to music, which he loved, rehearse his funeral over and over, and to die in whatever sanctity could be earned with constant masses said by the monks just beyond his bedroom, where he could see the altar from his deathbed.

I turned into the narrow road through groves of trees toward Yuste. The forest around it was so thick that I was almost on it before I had any warning. A few cars were there, a few people wandered under the huge old trees on either side of a walk leading to a small building. Downhill on the right was a large formal pond in a garden.

The monks have tried to keep it much as it was when the emperor was there. The rooms where he lived were so small that when I went in with a little group of maybe ten people, they were crowded. It was dark in the first room, a receiving room of some kind—the guide spoke Spanish and I had to conjure for myself what the room was used for. There was an old refectory table. Hangings of some dark cloth made the room seem still in mourning. A gout chair that Charles V had been put in to wheel him back and forth as he grew more crippled was the only chair. He had been pushed in it down to the pond to fish, along the walks to take the mountain air, or to watch the many rehearsals for his funeral.

The fine paintings he had brought to Yuste had long since been taken to the Prado or to other royal palaces, but in spirit they still hang there, the Titians, the Flemish tapestries against the dark wall curtains from ceiling to floor that kept the room warm in the mountain winter. It took over a hundred retainers to see to the old man, but that is not obvious.

In this sanctuary, there is loneliness and the peace that comes with it.

I remember only two rooms; maybe there was another one in the emperor's apartments, but it leaves no place for my mind to wander in. His bedroom, with its carved bed, draped in its mourning hangings of black, made the room airless, oppressive, its sound and light muffled. On the wall where he could see them, were once two portraits—his wife, whom he had been deeply in love with always, and of Queen Juana of Castile, the mother he had kept in prison for over forty years.

She survived until the last two years of his life, when, for the first time, he could call himself legally the sole king of León and Castile. For all those years he had, officially, shared "power" with a mother no one ever saw. And if the ones who ordered her permanent solitary incarceration began her imprisonment in his name, later there was letter after letter to her unofficial jailor written by Charles V alone, with orders to isolate her from all outside contact. Did he watch her portrait? Or did she watch the dying emperor from the black curtained wall? They say so.

Yuste was lovely and peaceful. I wanted to stay longer, but I was on the way to one of the most fairytale castles in Spain, one that might have been drawn by a child, or sculpted of sand. Its twin towers, its moated grange, were settings for all of the Gothic romantic dreams of Holy Grails and knights in armor. And this castle, too, was small compared to the great hilltop castellated barracks.

I almost missed it, the *parador* at Jarandilla de la Vera, the name of a small town, where early in the conquest of the new world a then unknown plant was brought back and planted. It grew well in the cup of a valley below the castle that had guarded the town for so long. Today, in the right season, tobacco hangs from wrought-iron balconies. Jarandilla means a little party, a little dance; by its name, it must be a happy place. The town, the few people I had a chance to meet and talk to, reflected it.

That first morning, I was so intent on the town that by mistake I passed the entrance to the castle. I was looking the other way. I found myself climbing a steep, narrow road without any nonsense about guard rails, up and up the mountain with no place to turn. At the only wide place found in the road that seemed to be the top of the world, people came out of the doors of small villas, weekend cottages. They waved, called out by the sound of a motor in that isolated place.

The high crags of the mountains of Extremadura had been discovered again as they had been found, then lost, then found again through the ages. The small houses were well kept, some modern, some traditional. The people who waved from their doors were not mountaineers or poverty-stricken shepherds. The mountains around Jarandilla have been turned into country places for those who, at the weekends or through the summer, escape the Spanish cities within easy driving distance—Madrid or Toledo. The Sierra de Gredos have turned, at least there in the once hard-to-find isolated retreat of the emperor, into a prosperous place.

The castle itself, where once there was pomp, fear, fighting, blood, and power, is a little memory of a time well past and unmissed. The local people use it as a center, a pub in the evening, often an official place for banquets. It is essentially Spanish. I found other *paradores* like it, where, instead of feeling apart from the towns in more luxurious, protected surroundings, I was part of the town itself.

In the drawing room behind the second-floor balcony there are what seem to be eighteenth-century engravings, framed page after page on the wall, of the past kings of Spain, from the ancient tribal leaders, so many as legendary as King Arthur, to the Visigoths, all the way to the last Hapsburg, Charles II, Charles V's great-grandson, the retarded king, the poor forever child, pathetic figurehead, propped up and used, as so many were before and after him, by the ministers who had assumed his power.

GUADALUPE

 She is just under two feet tall. She has great Byzantine eyes. She is probably fifteen hundred years old.

Her sacred robes are painted on her wooden body, and the colors are still bright. The turquoise inner robe is the blue of the waters of Lake Van, in eastern Turkey. Her simple outer garment is painted to represent lace or embroidery. Its color is an ochre that still has faint traces of vermillion. She sits on a chair painted with signs that might be Byzantine crosses. The fingers of the right hand are curled, as if they were carved to hold something, a scepter or an orb. The left hand lies, palm showing, beside a dignified, adult-looking baby Jesus who sits in her lap, his right hand lifted in a sign of blessing. She is carved of dark cedar, maybe chosen for its color, maybe darkened by time that could have stretched from the sixth or seventh century A.D.

She may be called primitive, but she has been made by someone who was inspired. She could have been created somewhere in the foothills of Mount Ararat. What is now eastern Turkey was, for centuries, one of the Christian centers of Byzantium. The other was Cappadocia. In both places there are the huge Byzantine eyes.

She is the Black Virgin of Guadalupe. Her image was taken to the new world as an icon, painted on the banners of the church and the *conquistadores,* one of the two gifts taken to the new world by those brave enough and ruthless enough to go and to stay. She is the Holy Mother of the New World. From her small figure has radiated a vast influence on both the conquerors and the conquered in Mexico, Central America, and South America. In church after church set up by the priests who went with the *conquistadores,* she has been the source of the native vision of a mother figure who looked more like them than the pale, ruthless conquerors. The vision that came to Juan Diego, an Indian bearer, on a hill called Tepeyac was of the Black Virgin of Guadalupe.

In *The Buried Mirror,* Carlos Fuentes wrote,

> In December 1531 on Tepeyac Hill near Mexico City, the Virgin of Guadalupe appeared bearing roses in winter, and choosing a lowly *tameme,* or Indian bearer, Juan Diego, as the object of her love and recognition. . . . From Babylon to Bethlehem, in one flash of political genius, whore became virgin and Malinche became Guadalupe. Nothing has proved as consoling, unifying, and worthy of fierce respect since then as the Virgin of Guadalupe in Mexico. . . . The conquered people now had a mother.

> Any Mexican you stop in the streets of Mexico City could most probably tell you about the vision and how she appeared to Juan Diego with roses in winter, but few could tell you where she came from, these stark mountains in Extremadura, Spain, and who brought her image first to Mexico.

Those who saw her in the thirteenth century when she was found in the lost valley in the mountains of Extremadura in Spain saw her as the embodiment of that most revered part of the Old Testament, the Canticles.

"Nigra sum sed formosa," the Native Americans heard chanted in the new churches of the *conquistadores* and the priests they brought with them. "I am black but comely, O ye daughters of Jerusalem, as the tents of Kedar, as the curtains of Solomon. Look not upon me because I am black, because the sun hath looked upon me." *Sed.* But. The Latin Bible contains this word, which does not exist in Hebrew, which does not use connectives.

So history and legend and change of meaning by translation went with her from a small high valley in that part of the Central Massive on the border of Extremadura known as the Sierra de Tormantos. The valley was so isolated that only the most devout of pilgrims could trudge the mountain miles to pray at her shrine, built on the place where the statue had been found. But they did it. Many of the *conquistadores* prayed there before they left for an unknown and frightening new world that offered hope and violent death as well for those who braved the conquest.

How old she is can be guessed from her face, her eyes, her painted garments. Where she comes from is probably Byzantium. She could have been brought there in the sixth century when the Byzantines ruled the south for seventy years or by monks running north from the invasions of the Moors in the eighth century. She could even have been carved by a refugee from the iconoclastic seventh-century Byzantine state and church, whose sweeps destroyed images, icons, and great murals from Constantinople all through the Byzantine Empire.

Like many of the early icons, she is believed to have been carved by St. Luke. So many of the early icons bear this legend, whenever carbon dating shows them to have been made. But the great eyes that seem so sad lack the formal imperiousness of the royal icons captured from Byzantium, also said to have been painted by St. Luke. Her eyes are so alive that it seems possible to read her thoughts.

I have seen ruined eyes that were once like hers at the half-destroyed Sumela Monastery on a narrow ledge of a steep mountain high above Trabzon on the Turkish coast of the Black Sea, where long ago the armies of the Seljuks captured the city that for two hundred years called itself the capital of the Roman Empire. They have all been scratched out by the new iconoclasts, the Muslim tribes, for they too must have feared the magic of those eyes that seem so alive—*malocchio, nazar, mauvais œil,* the evil eye, the international symbol for fear of the stranger.

But in Spain and Turkey, nothing quite dies. The citizens of Trabzon still take their sick children up the steep path to the cliff to be bathed in the holy well at Sumela, where the ruins of the monastery hang like an eagle's nest. On June 24, the eve of the birthday of St. Eugenios, once the patron saint of Christian Trabzon, they swim in the sea, though they have long since forgotten why. They simply say it is an old custom. Like so much in the two nations today, those unrecognized connections of legends and myths and objects seem as strong as ever. The Arabic derivatives in both Spanish and Turkish have existed so long that their sources have been forgotten, words left in both countries, where wars between Christian and Muslim were fought for so long.

Who buried the Black Virgin in that lost valley in Spain, and when, is unknown. There are as many legends as there are questions about where she came from and how she was found. The stark statement under all of them is that she was found sealed in a leaden casket to protect her by a shepherd called Gil Cordero, who was abiding in that deserted field keeping watch over his flock. So all that is really known is that it was at the beginning of the thirteenth century. Almost at once the machinery of the church gave answers. Now it would be called spin; then it was sacred dogma.

The Virgin Mary had appeared before the poor shepherd in a vision like those found in religious paintings where a mother figure floats in the sky, as she would appear to Juan Diego in Mexico three centuries later. She told Gil Cordero where to find the image; some say it was buried, some say it was down a well. There is a painting of the small statue being lifted from the well by a group of clergy in their grand robes and knights in their armor and cloaks. The myth of their presence is matched by the myth of the image itself, for she is being lifted out of the well, not in her simple painted clothing, but in a fantastic wide skirt and triangular cloak that made her four feet or so tall, the skirt and cloak embroidered with hundreds of pearls, in a crown and halo that made her face small. The baby Jesus is dressed as grandly as she is.

That is the image you still see today. When she is carried in procession she wears a huge imperial crown covered with jewels, and around it is a halo of filigreed gold. In 1928 she joined Santiago Matamoros as a patron saint of all Spain, as she had been for centuries of Extremadura.

She stands in majestic indifference at least thirty feet above the altar of the ancient church at Guadalupe, a tiny, glowing figure in the central niche of the main *retablo* added to the nave of the thirteenth-century church in the seventeenth century.

The valley had been lived in by the Moors since the eighth century. Moorish craftsmen had remained after their own armies were defeated. They were makers of metal work, leather, tiles, jewelry—skills that they learned in the open markets from the Muslim world to China.

At first the two peoples began to learn to live together, the people of Islam, with their little cities, and the hungry warriors from the north, their pride, their flocks, their crude castellated barracks. There was little attempt at conversion. It was not until the conquests of Ferdinand and Isabel centuries later that cities were emptied of their inhabitants when they fell. Gradually the new marriage of town and castle would grow into the typical city of Spain.

I drove from Jarandilla de la Vera south through the wildest mountains I was to see until I found the Sierra Morena in the south of Spain. I could see then that there could be ghosts and hints of the unknown on those high crags and those narrow, hidden valleys. It is a place where you want to glance over your shoulder. Guadalupe was and is far away from anything, or seems to be when you drive the winding roads toward its lost valley. But when I arrived there, it was suddenly the most peaceful place I have ever been. Something of its quietness made me want to give up whatever is given up and stay there forever. It seems to be the most faraway place from anywhere in the world.

One pilgrim who came from so far was the battle-weary Columbus, all the way from the new world, to his port of *Palos de le Frontera* on the *Río Tinto* in the south of Spain, to the mountain shrine. He brought the first two natives from the New World to Guadalupe to be baptized.

The carved stone fountain in front of the church where the records of the monastery say it was done is still there.

Pilgrims could only have come by horse or donkey or mule, or walked. It would have been a journey of several weeks to enter the same narrow gate as I did into a street little changed.

I wondered what those Caribbean island natives thought of the huge, shining basilica that rose higher into the decisive blue of the Spanish sky than any building they could ever have seen. Or what they thought when they were brought to the entrance of the church, where four incredible fourteenth-century bronze doors tell the simple story, new to them, of the life of young Jesus, old Joseph, and the Virgin Mary.

They had been told that these were their new gods. They had worshiped images made to strike fear and awe, fantastic as no living creature they knew, that demanded blood sacrifice. Before them, instead, were images of the kind of people they had seen as they traveled through Spain—a woman, her eyes closed in sleep like the new baby in her arms, traveling on a donkey being led by her older husband; two soldiers hiding from an angry man with a shepherd's crook, its handle a cross; a simple woman in her bed surrounded by weeping men; a group of men, their heads thrown back looking at a dove, afraid; a woman seated on a thronelike chair with what seems to be a doll in her hand. Did they trace the bronze bas-reliefs with their hands to take in the smoothness, they who ate the hearts of their enemies?

When the church was built, the doors were sculpted, according to the monastic records, by Pablo de Colonia, one of the few artists whose names were listed. They have no connection with the prevailing Romanesque or the rising Gothic architecture brought south by the Visigothic Castilian warrior class who had led the *Reconquista*. They are a real vision of a real artist who was inspired by the simple reality of the people he saw every day, to tell, in bas-relief, the New Testament story. Somehow it was right that these simple people should be the entry into the finest architectural marriage between Christian and Moor I had seen.

These bronze doors, with no figures more than a foot high, held, for me, all the true holiness and simplicity of the religion they represent. They tell, quite simply, the story of the birth of Christ, the flight into Egypt, the cleansing of the temple in Jerusalem, the Holy Spirit as the Pentecostal dove descending on the heads of the praying Virgin Mother and the frightened, cringing disciples.

They are a history in themselves of how the human was beginning to be seen by the artist in the thirteenth century, a radical change from figures made formal by medieval eyes and talents. You find such hints of humanity here and there in thirteenth-century religious art. At Guadalupe, the metamorphosis is almost complete. The disciples may be formally grouped, but their fear is palpable. In the bas-relief of the Virgin on the panel of the Annunciation, she is shown as a young women, her hands held up as if she were trying to push away what has come to her. She is awestruck and terrified, mouth open, eyes staring, so afraid that the Indians who saw her for the first time must have felt akin to her strange humanity. The dove of the Holy Spirit holds a cross, the sharp end pointed at her head.

Here is the story told to people who could not read, not of fearsome flying devils, not of hosts of winged angels, not of the lolling mouths and wild square stone faces of the gods who must be fed with human hearts lest the world stop, but the faces of simple people, awestruck or angry or asleep or afraid. To me, of all the grand paintings, the gilded wall carvings, that were influenced by conquest, dogma, and the changes of taste through the centuries when they were added, from the fifteenth to the twentieth century, these four bronze doors, put there at the beginning, are the jewels of Guadalupe.

Extremadura had been in Castilian hands since the battle of Navas de Tolosa in 1212. A territory too vast to rule was opened up, and most of the armies and the forts were moved to the various frontiers, frozen there while the heirs to the monarchies fought among themselves, the new *grandes* fought each other for territory, and so many of the smaller places were left alone, with Moorish people who had lived there for centuries and new Christians who began to filter in where there was better grazing land. Some of the Moors converted to Christianity. Many remained Muslim.

The resulting architecture has been named Mudejar, and it is the most truly Spanish of all the architecture in Spain. I had seen vestiges of it before in the north, but here, in Guadalupe, was a superb building whose walls were obviously built by Moors in the Moorish manner. The arches were Moorish, the scrollwork of the carving above the entries abstract, but here and there a Christian figure of pale rose-colored stone watched over the people walking into the basilica.

But it was in the first huge Mudejar courtyard of the monastery that I stopped, astonished. In the center, there is a *mihrab*, beautifully carved, the kind and size of the small buildings in the center of the *hans,* the country inns in Anatolia, built by the Seljuk Turks as mosques for travelers. The Christians saw them as follies to cover wellheads, but I am sure that, to the Moors who built this *mihrab* under the Christians' direction, it was a memory of a small mosque.

The *paradores* for travelers in Spain were started in the

1920s, spaced a day's automobile journey apart. This speaks for the improvement in roads and automobiles from then until now, for today most of them can be reached within three hours, *parador* to *parador*. They were established for the comfort and safety of travelers, and also as a way of rescuing the valuable monuments to the Spanish past.

The idea was not new. Seven hundred years before, in what is now Turkey, the Seljuk *hans* were built for travelers, too. They protected camel trains in Anatolia from marauders, wild tribes, thieves, and Crusaders. In Spain in the twentieth century they have preserved historic buildings; in Anatolia in the twelfth, they preserved the merchants from the silk road, the wandering Muslim mystics, the *sufis*, and the families moving inexorably east, always east, away from the Christian invasions.

The courtyard of the monastery is, like the courtyards of the Moors, a walled garden, which is what "paradise" means. The colonnades around the balconies surrounding it are arched in the Moorish manner. Mudejar can be said to have been born there in a Christian shrine that through the years and the centuries would become, too, a history of the changes in the church itself.

The simplicity of the bronze doors, then the beginning of the Gothic influence, through the changes in taste, in influences, in the church itself, in the peaks of passionate belief, the depths of cynical power, are all there in the public rooms off the cloister, turned into museums.

There are so many works of art at the monastery, so much jewelry, so much embroidery in gold thread, that to wander through the museums is to be choked with gilt and gold and color and riches. First, the whole history of ecclesiastical vestments can be seen, miles of bright embroidery and gold thread, then the library, both music and text, where the treasures are beyond the reach of gold value.

The seventeenth century of the Counter-Reformation, that time of saints and inquisitions, is there in the spacious decorated gallery where hang the ecclesiastical portraits of the monks of Guadalupe by Zurbáran, the last of the great Spanish religious painters. He painted them in the corridor, as wide as a formal room, where you see them now. Some of the monks demanded of Zurbáran that they be painted as they were seen. Some are in the beginning of those standard ecstasies that you see in mundane painting after mundane painting. One, San Geronimo, is being borne to heaven standing on a pile of cherubs.

To me, the most human, the most alive, is of Fray Gonzalo de Illescas, caught in a pause while working, his hand lifted from his writing, the work he did of helping the maimed and the sick in an inserted study in the upper corner. It is daily, and down to earth, and, to me, nearer to heaven than ecstasy or eyes rolled up toward heaven in the poses that I call plane spotting.

In the formal museum, though, there is one of those surprises that are the *duende* of Spain, not more glitter, more ecstasy, more emaciated, bloody Christs, but a small painting by Goya to remind the world that there was and is a Spain of simple lives and simple horrors. It is a small stone room, half dark; a man stands shackled in the front of the painting, and, behind him, a prisoner lies either dead or asleep, while a priest hears the confession (the last confession?) of another prisoner. Finally, as in that honest and partly hidden country, nothing is denied, nothing is hidden. You simply have to look, and there is the power of belief, the power of the prison cell, and the power of anarchic wit, which is always there, and has survived all efforts through the centuries to destroy it.

No place is that power more evident and more hidden by gold and awe than in the lozenge-shaped central shrine of the Virgin of Guadalupe. The Camarín. It is as if all the threads of time and change have gathered here. At first I saw only a niche with a flat screen in place before her plinth in the Camarín, and on it is the history of the monastery. St. Teresa is there, Cervantes, Columbus, Ferdinand and Isabel, the Battle of Salado, a dead Franco soldier on the steps of the basilica, Pope John Paul, all in painted tiles set into gold. The portraits are about four by five inches in size. The screen is twentieth-century ecclesiastical school.

When the Virgin of Guadalupe is not on her eagle's aerie far above the basilica, this is where she stays. A lever is turned by the monk who is the day's guide. The screen disappears. The plinth revolves, and there she stands, close enough to touch, in full, rich vestment. Nothing, not centuries, not changes of power or taste, inquisition or civil war, can alter her wide, sad Byzantine eyes that look straight at yours.

Around, above, below her the walls have been encrusted with rich bas-relief, gilt, strict ecclesiastical paintings. The ceiling dome is decorated with the coats of arms of Columbus, and of the *conquistadores*, those rough, tough professional soldiers from the small cities of Extremadura who took her with them as their patron saint to the New World.

In niches along the walls are life-sized polychrome statues that reminded me of Meissen or Staffordshire eighteenth-century china figures. They are the women of the Old Testament, Esther, Abigail, Sara, Deborah; they are dressed in brightly colored carnival versions of eastern clothes; they are, in a word that hardly belongs in the rest of the monastery, pretty. One of my favorites is Ruth, standing amid the alien corn, which is a great sheaf beside her, not tear-stained but sweetly melancholy in the sun. Another is Judith, holding the graphic head of Holofernes by his hair and looking as if she had found it and doesn't quite know what to do with it.

But the element I sought and found was in the painted corners above the huge paintings. Nothing can keep out the wily simplicity that in Spain keeps reminding us that it is all, after all, icing of the finest kind. Babies, lots of babies, not cherubs, not angels—babies. They squint; they play; they swim like dolphins in front of one of the ships of those who braved the Atlantic. They grin, they stare, they lounge on the gilt frames. They reminded me that no matter how far from reality into the safety of formality some religious images can go, reality is still there, waiting, whether it is monks and nuns *in flagrante delicto*, Lazarillo the *pícaro*, or tumbling, laughing, staring, implike Spanish babies.

The small town that serves the monastery and the Virgin of Guadalupe is as it was, medieval, with overhanging rooms that shelter walkers from the sun and cascade with flowers and vines, where there is a neighborhood well you drive around, still used by the people who live there. Some of the families who have been there for centuries are known for their metal and gold work. They repair and clean the treasures that have been gathered there for seven centuries. They have learned the history of ecclesiastical art from its local, primitive-inspired beginnings to its modern mixture of the decadence of professional journeymen and, sometimes, a miraculous new spirit.

I drove in a slow procession at the pace of those who have come through the centuries by donkey if they could, by foot, by carriage, under the sun and rain of Spain, and the wind of the Sierra de Tormantos, to worship at the shrine of this small image of cedar. We passed through the shadowed street and broke out of it into the square under the tremendous sun that etched the gold that enchanted the great church, the cloister, the towers of the shrine.

I stood in front of the medieval church, built after 1340, begun by Alfonso XI to honor his victory at the battle at Salado River in 1340. It was farther south than the *Reconquista* had ever been when he defeated the last attempt of the Moors to bring troops from Africa to defend Andalucia. Until he came there to Guadalupe to do homage to her after his victory, she had been housed in a small hermitage. The façade of the royal church he had built, with its superb bronze doors, glowed there in the sun for Columbus and his two awestruck Indians and for me.

The church and the monastery, built by Moors who had lived there for centuries before the *Reconquista*, have grown through the centuries. The Moors were there when Hernán Cortés came for nine days to make a novena on one of his returns home from conquered Mexico. And I think when the local Moors turned Christian so long ago, the ones who stayed, and began to build the new church, they melded into the new population as tin and copper meld into bronze.

Like so many pilgrims who made their slow and hard way to the high valley, Cortés would have stayed where I stayed, in the Gothic cloister, built in the sixteenth century to shelter them. Its courtyard, its carved stones where the local vision is still there, is innocent and simple, the carvings amateur, if amateur means what it should, lover.

When I looked for that early simplicity under all the massive gold and grand corridors and rooms that have been added since, it is there, in the carved bedrock of the shrine. Mary sits with Joseph behind her. The three small kings of Orient seem to dance toward her, and the archangel watches from behind the holy family. It sits there in the courtyard of the Gothic cloister, carved on a trough once used to water animals, now filed with plants. In the center of the courtyard is the well for the ancient pilgrims, the holy and the sick, for it was built also as a hospital. It is now, as it always was, a place for travelers, pilgrims, or the curious, or the quiet, one of the most gentle places to stay in Extremadura, still run by the monastery, still welcoming.

My room was up high, beside one of the Gothic towers. I looked out on mountains. I could see, beyond my window, the little white town, beyond it on the rising hill the first olive groves I had noticed. I walked there, on the hill ground in the Spanish sun, a long way, but when I turned and watched the monastery down below, it, too, seemed small, nestled in the mountain valley, dwarfed by the Sierra de Tormantos. In the distance, beyond the town, the foothills had been long since planted with those gnarled olive trees, their trunks a symbol all over Spain of age and work done long ago by other men. It was in such groves during the Spanish civil war that American boys lay dead, still in their civilian clothes and city shoes. Behind the groves, the Sierra de Tormantos were wild, dark, tier on tier of crags.

There was the center of the kind of peace that has been a part of the little town and its great monastic center for centuries, no radios blaring, few cars, and those at walking pace, and children playing in the afternoon, or doing the kind of chores they must have done once in our small towns, drawing water from the public well, carrying loads of feed and food for their animals and their families. A little girl with six loaves of bread from the market, a woman strolling, dressed as carefully as if she were shopping in Madrid, a slow van. A little boy with a whistle stood on the corner watching the central plaza in front of the church where beyond him rose the high towers.

The Moorish shapes of the windows caught the sun, the walls built by the Moors who remained there when the Christians came, less than a century before they were built. Into the silence a canary sang and it was he, the little boy, blowing his whistle.

I went back to my room and found my dictionary. I looked up canary and whistle. I did this whenever I wanted to communicate, which was so often that, without knowing it, I was learning Spanish, not as an intellectual exercise, but from thing to word to thing, maybe like a child, maybe like a traveler in an antique land. Armed with the words, I went into the street, where townspeople sold leather goods, plates, pitchers of earthenware, and statues of the Virgin of Guadalupe in one of her thousand robes, this one red with gold. She was a few inches high, a foot high, and all the sizes in between for the faithful to take home from Guadalupe as the merchants have forever sold the images of sacred visions, from the temple of Diana in Ephesus, the temple in Jerusalem, worry beads in Mecca, rosaries blessed by the pope in Rome.

I asked for a *pita*. I thought no one understood when they pointed to a basket filled with little terra-cotta pitchers, two inches high, glazed with color and with designs. I was not being understood. I whistled, awkwardly as much like a canary as I could, and used the magic word I had found. I seemed to be receiving only polite indifference, a gesture toward the baskets of souvenirs, closed ears.

Then, away from the sophistication of the souvenir street, I came to a shop. This time the woman picked up one of the little terra-cotta pitchers and disappeared into the back of the store. She came back, blowing through a spout of the pitcher the song of the canary. She had put a little water in the bottom. She smiled when I tried it, and said, "¡Muy bueno!" And when I left I said a heart-felt and secure, "Muchas gracias, señora, adíos," at ease with a few Spanish words for the first time. For it is the opening of the mouth after the opening of the mind that is the beginning of learning a language. So I found out how to blow a *pita como un canario*. And I did, in the street, an eighty-two-year-old grownup among the bird children of Guadalupe.

SHADOWS

 Of all the places I went looking for one thing, and, like Columbus, finding another, Jerez de los Caballeros was the strangest. I was driving toward the town to see another of that nest of small places in Extremadura where *conquistadores* had been born.

It was only a pause on a Sunday morning, a last stop on the way south. I wanted to see the Spanish homes of Hernando de Soto and Vasco Nuñez de Balboa. They had both gone to the new world from this lost mountain town. Hernando de Soto, impoverished *hidalgo,* had set out to capture youth and money. He had discovered as a European the peninsula he called *Florida,* the place of flowers.

And it was not stout Cortés who stood ". . . silent, upon a peak in Darien" in the Keats poem, and gazed upon the ocean he named the *Pacífico,* peaceful, calm. It was Vasco Nuñez de Balboa, the second poor *hidalgo* from Jerez de los Caballeros, who is said to have sailed to Darién, which is a district on the eastern coast of the isthmus of what is now Panama, hidden in a barrel to escape his creditors. According to Peter Martyr, he went to the new world " a rash roisterer" and grew into " a polite and discreet captain."

Statues to both of them were what I expected to find there, and I did, but it was not what stays with me still and haunts me as no other part of Spain. The past is gone, unchangeable, our immortal teacher. We can only learn from it. We suppress it, change its facts, censor it, edit and rewrite it, forget it at our peril. But to face the forgotten or the mis-understood is to find treasure and light in a cave we feared because it was so dark.

I drove into the valley through fine green farmland fed by water from the mountains around it. It was a sunny day like all the sunny days there. The Spanish indifferent sun is the god of terrible strength, a blessing and, too often, a curse. For some reason, an urge or a mild foreboding, which I tried to shake off, I wanted to turn back.

Within a few hundred yards of my driving into the valley, shadows began to drift down around my shoulders like shawls, moving, misted shapes. Large, silent shadow birds hovered around my head, ephemeral as air, dark and heavy. I passed an arroyo. The sign said *Arroyo infierno*. I read it as the ravine of hell.

I was being drawn helplessly toward an unknown town accompanied by the drifting shadows, growing, billowing around my head and shoulders. I knew that this part of Extremadura was said to be haunted. There have been, through the centuries, too many battles, too much hunger and madness born of fear. It was such a beautiful place that I had driven into, out of a normal morning.

I was possessed by a vast, empty sadness. It engulfed me, as the cloak of gray, misty shadows thrown over my shoul-ders. There was no way to turn back. I neither wanted to nor had any choice. I was simply borne along. I passed over an ancient bridge across a small stream. It was called *Río San Lázaro*—the river of St. Lazarus, that dear friend of Jesus, risen from his tomb, the patron saint of lepers, of the sick, the dying.

The valley was physically, like so much of that part of Spain, a little kingdom of its own. But unlike other parts of Spain, where the people who worked the fields gathered in villages or towns by evening, and walked the *paseo*, the people I passed lived on what seemed to be separate small holdings. The land was worked, the animals fed and healthy, the people at that time of the Sunday morning silent. There were tractors, farm machinery, small sheep herds, cattle. For the first time since I had arrived in Spain, at least that I noticed it, nobody smiled or waved.

By the look of their buildings, biers, barns, and corrals, it was a fertile, prosperous valley and had been so for centuries, the houses and the barns sunk by age. We do not see this in America. We sit on top of the ground. These buildings were sunk by time within it. There is a sense of deep taproots, no longer known. When you go to Spain, you realize that the place where we live is still the new world.

The valley ended in foothills. I could not have fended off the shadows that rode me. I had no sense that there was any choice. I was hardly aware of climbing, and yet, after a mile or so, I realized that the valley was far below. There were other cars, other Sunday tourists, not many. They seemed to me less real than the shadows that perched and wavered around my head and shoulders.

I passed the statue of Balboa, one of those twenties modern torsos, all flexing muscles and posed angles, in a neglected looking commercial square that was called *Plaza de*

Balboa, with a bar tavern. Tavern empty. Square empty. Empty pause on a Sunday morning.

Ahead of me there was the ancient gate to the old city, guarded by another statue, this time of Hernando de Soto, in armor of the noble statue school. I paid little attention, drawn upward on the steep, narrow street with its Arab Spanish houses as white as sepulchers, backs turned to the street.

In the center of the square at the top of the hill, a twelfth-century church with a wonderful Romanesque carved door faced another street up a slight hill, watched over by a knight in a niche above the church door, in the place usually reserved for saints.

Duty called. I was, after all, a tourist, and tourists look at churches . . . and churches and churches and churches, a history of Spain in the dates of building of the Romanesque doorways, the pointed Gothic spires, the Mudejar *azulejos* (tiles), the glittering, sun-soaked towers.

Then I walked, as surely as if I were escorted, up that tilted street and into one of the newly restored castle yards of the great Order of Knights Templar, and I knew why I was there. It was completely familiar, even though I knew nothing about the Templars beyond their existence once, long ago. There was one of those well-documented signs that the tourist office puts up, informative and then, to me, completely unimportant.

A flat surface the size of a parade ground was so high above the valley that it seemed to be surrounded by the apexes of distant churches far below. A one-storied single room was built into a castellated waist-high wall. It was the top floor of a high tower that reached down into the valley a hundred feet or so below. There were what for the first time whenever I saw them later I would recognize as the domes of Templar buildings. They were, as so many of the Templar churches and chapels, copied from the seventh-century dome of the Church of the Holy Sepulcher in Jerusalem, honoring who the Templars were, why they were formed.

The domed roof in the distance had been a well cover, the one to my left, a chapel. The whole left side of the space was walled with ancient stone buildings. Along the front of the chapel I walked past formal gardens, cared-for trees, a pool, carefully encased in old pavings, as if someone had honored the water itself, brought up so high above the valley, the pool surfaces shining in that Sunday morning.

The whole place had been restored to look as it might have looked in the thirteenth century, when it was the center of the fortress town. It was as isolated from the rest of the late medieval town as if it had been an oasis in a desert.

The shadows still guided me, but I wouldn't let myself think of that, for I have always been embarrassed by this talent or this curse of picking up what people call the past and what to me is as present as if I stood within a living place and not an empty space on a Sunday morning, a no place.

I walked toward the small room that topped the tower at the left end of the castellated stone wall. It was dim inside, almost intimate: two chairs, a broom, a potted plant, little signs of domestic comfort. The only light came from a narrow window that framed a view of the valley far below, all the way to the horizon.

On the wall front was a sign with the title *Il Torre Sangrienta,* the tower of blood. I could read enough to know that men had died there, within the little, almost cozy, room. Murder? Battle? Trapped? I hardly knew. I only knew there had been death there, and it was the center for me of the awful weightless sadness that I had carried as shadows around my head and shoulders. I waited, not alone, not knowing what to do.

I said a prayer for the memory and the souls of those who had died there, whoever they were, these members of the Order of the Knights Templar, the last, the sign said, to die in Spain.

I walked away, knowing little beyond what I had seen and sensed, toward the sunken well below its fine dome. I was pushed violently down the steps, and I called out, shocked. There was no one there. Only, in the distance behind me, a man had come to stand before *El Torre Sangrienta*, and he, too, was saying a prayer, so intent he didn't hear me call out. Then I realized that, instead of the shadows, I was surrounded with joy and sun and a deep sense of peace. Whoever they were, they had only wanted to be recognized, remembered.

I leaned on the castellated wall, as one so long ago, Christian knight or Moorish guard. Below me, protected and isolated by the surrounding *Sierra Sur*, lay the valley they had guarded. It was the little kingdom I had driven through, that fine cup of grass and water within the hovering mountains.

We see from where we stand. I have brought back from Turkey a small medieval statue carved from what seems to be a kind of tufa. It is of a Crusader, the face a portrait of dumb brutality, the head encased in a helmet, the armored body boxlike and heavy. The figure stands at attention, presenting a sword. On its body armor is a cross. It is ugly, brutish. I have had, until now, no idea why I suddenly bought it. It is the Middle Eastern view of a Crusader, and the name for it, as it was at the time of the Crusades, is *frenk*, a European, a generic Turkish word for foreigner. It is the direct opposite of the noble knights in armor of our western childhood. How long that image has lasted in the minds of those they fought!

Another word in Turkish for stranger, foreigner, is *el*. I went, when I was in Turkey, to a small village to see a Seljuk Turkish *medrese*, a religious school built in the twelfth century. The name of the village was El Bashi, foreigner's head.

The "infidels" were not the only ones who saw the Crusaders as a threat. St. Bernard of Clairvaux, one of the most eloquent of the medieval writers and preachers, called them "an unruly rabble of rogues and impious men, robbers and committers of sacrilege" who went to the Holy Land for loot and pillage. Wherever they stopped on their paths to Jerusalem, the people suffered from violent soldiers, some mercenaries, some knights.

Some had taken the cross as a penance and a religious duty. Such soldiers were never more than a minority of those who went on crusade.

As soon as I could, huddled in a warm room, a New England winter outside, I read and read about the Knights Templar, constantly surprised that they had been so blotted out of our past, and was in their barricades again in the sun of Jerez de los Caballeros, watching the lovely domes. I was trying to find out why the Templars had been murdered in that mountainous, lonely town, named in memory of them the City of the Horsemen.

The twelfth century, that time of chaos and Christian religious fervor, building and visions, was also a time when pilgrims, staff in hand, walked for miles and weeks and months to seek their salvation. As if it were a place. For thousands that place was Palestine, the Holy Land, where Jesus Christ had walked, had spoken, performed miracles. They flocked there, and often died there, victims of Muslim armies or pirates or Muslim sects who were fervently protecting their own domains, religion, and holy places, which were and are all too often the same.

The wandering knights, so parodied in *Don Quixote*, had become a nuisance in the European cities. The solution to this nuisance in Europe could be a blessing in Palestine, where so many stories had come back of pilgrims slaughtered. The pope and the nobles found a way to harness the pillaging and violence of the so-called Knights Errant, put them to work, get them off the streets. The pope announced a holy war—a crusade. The word "crusade" can be understood in the terms of the Muslim holy war, or *jihad*, familiar to us now in Palestine and in Afghanistan. A crusade had to be declared by the Christian clergy, as *jihad* was and is by the Muslim.

The First Crusade, at the beginning of the millennium that has just passed, was called by the pope and preached in the pulpits, religious passion harnessed into a vast directional flow of people and hope toward the Holy Land. Some died along the way. Others, the more belligerent armies, skimmed the towns they passed through for food and loot. Think of a river of people, fed by the creeks of small towns, those who seemed touched by God, hungry and hopeful, sick and well, dissolute and holy, pouring toward a dangerous, violent passage across countries where they were not wanted. They were feared for their demands and their diseases, swept on by the wild preaching of the monks and the priests who shepherded them. They died by thousands.

On July 15, 1087, Jerusalem fell to the Crusaders and was looted. Victory was celebrated by the murder of so many of its people that witnesses wrote that the Crusaders splashed their horses through streams of blood up to their fetlocks to pray at the Church of the Holy Sepulcher, the center, to them, of Christendom. Jerusalem was declared a Christian kingdom.

After much political wrangling, Baldwin became the first king of Jerusalem, which was called in Europe *Outremer,* simply Overseas. He built his palace on the twenty-acre walled rectangle of the Dome of the Rock near the mosque, Al-Aksa, one of the holiest sites for Islam. This is believed to be the rock Abraham had lain Isaac's head on to sacrifice him to his God, who sent the ram in the thicket to take Isaac's place.

Before its capture by the passionate converts to the new religion of Islam, it had been the sight of Solomon's temple, ruined in war and then rebuilt by Herod the Great. His temple had been totally destroyed and plowed under by the legions of Hadrian. It was, and has remained, a Holy of Holies for three religions, akin to each other, who all claim Abraham as their ancestor. It is one of the most fought-over places in the world. The Crusaders called the mosque, reconsecrated as a Christian church, the Temple of Solomon.

Some of the holy places were well beyond the walls of Jerusalem—Bethlehem, the Jordan River, Nazareth, Galilee. Every place where Jesus could have rested on a wall, or given water, or healed, or preached, had been long since identified by the Orthodox Byzantine Church of the Eastern Roman Empire, established in Constantinople by the Emperor Constantine in the fourth century. Even after the Crusaders had taken Jerusalem, Saracen raiders attacked pilgrims when they went beyond the city.

In 1119 eight hundred pilgrims were walking the six miles across the desert to the river Jordan to be baptized in the water where Jesus had been baptized by John the Baptist.

They were attacked by Saracen raiders. Three hundred were killed, and the rest taken as slaves. It was only one of the many times such attacks had happened.

One day near Christmas, 1119, the French knight, Hugh of Payns, and Godfrey de St. Omar, his second in command, went to Baldwin with a proposal. Both of them had taken the cross as a penance, leaving large estates in France. They suggested to the new king that they form a group of knights who would take vows as monks after the Order of St. Benedict, the strictest of all the holy orders, and would as soldiers guard the holy places and escort the pilgrims.

It caught the passions of the king and the church. A few knights took vows on Christmas of 1119, of chastity, obedience, and poverty. They swore to welcome into their ranks all those renegades who were outside the law and who had come to *Outremer* to be absolved and take home some loot— blasphemers, schismatics, thieves, even murderers. They welcomed them all to take the strict and holy vows of monks, and guard the pilgrims. That was how it began.

Though they swore the vows of monks, they kept their arms and skills as warriors. It was the first time outside of the local orders in Spain, formed against the Moors in the *Reconquista*, that there was a well-ordered and cohesive army since the Roman Empire.

Bernard of Clairvaux, who had so denigrated the Crusaders, was a friend and cousin of Hugh of Payns, who begged him to welcome the idea. He did, with a letter called *De laude novae militiae*, which would, from that time until the end, be the motto and guide of the men who at first called themselves the Poor Knights of Jesus Christ, then the Knights of the Holy Sepulcher, then the Poor Knights of Jesus Christ of the Temple of Solomon, and finally the

Knights Templar. They were a foreign legion, known and honored beyond all others who took the cross for the Holy Land.

As well as his letter, Bernard of Clairvaux wrote a long set of instructions about their task, their behavior, and the holy places they would go to as guides. His instructions were well beyond the original idea of protection. Think of knowledge-able museum guides, or guides to European churches today, armed with weapons, riding horses, great red crosses on the backs of their white cloaks.

They gave up all comfort, all ease, and, above all, all loot-ing, in the name of Christ and St. Benedict. They lived, at first, on the leavings given them as alms, fodder for their horses, food, old clothes. Knights who had swept in glittering armor through Jerusalem appeared anew in tatters, old armor, whatever they had been given. For a few years they were like that; then, as all the convents and monasteries that were popular, they were fated to become rich from alms.

By 1127 grateful pilgrims, monarchs, great noble houses had showered the new order with gifts, no longer an old cloak, a horse, some food, but the beginning of vast territo-ries, great houses, estates, all given as benefices to the holy knights.

But all the time they kept to their vows, poverty, obedi-ence, and chastity; they rose at three in the morning to begin their holy days, matins, thirteen paternosters in a Latin few of them could understand, and on through the strict and harsh day to nones at eight o'clock when they slept in dormi-tories, in their clothes, lights on.

Anyone who has been in an army knows the drill, and it was the same with them. Same was the word, rise, drill, eat, march, drill, obey, keep vigil; and with it all the prayers.

These were simple men. Three deviations from holy orders were theirs. They did not have to be able to read and write, know Latin, think. They had only to obey, pray, live simply, and fight. They were excused from fasting since too great austerity weakened them for their essential task of battling to protect the pilgrims.

Change came as it does, almost without notice, as habits change, erode, or reform under the cover of daily life. To protection of the pilgrims was added through the years protection of the royal government of *Outremer* and later the fight to expand the Christian kingdoms of the Holy Land.

In two hundred years the group of illiterate thugs who formed a holy boot camp after the Order of St. Benedict, the strictest of all monastic orders, had become the richest corporate entity in Christendom. By the second century of their being, their leaders were a powerful directive for political change. The wealth they had accumulated they did not spend; the land they administered between Crusades was fruitful. They had entered the most central tug of war of the thirteenth century, that between the evolving strength of the national monarchs and the greatest power in Europe, the pope, who were fighting to retain their precedence over the secular powers.

It was the pope who set in motion the Crusades, the pope who could excommunicate monarch or serf, the pope who held the reigns on the sometimes untamed, sometimes battle-weary countries, nobles, kings. The center of papal passions and hopes for two hundred years was the Holy Land.

The Templars were under the pope's sole command. They could be borrowed for local fighting between Christians, but only with papal permission. Within their barracks, their farms, their estates, they lived as they always had, by the rule of St. Benedict, morning, afternoon, and night, prayer, drill, and sleep, simple food, clothes reissued twice a year, for winter and for summer. But only the knights wore the white cloak with the great red cross on their backs; the other ranks and the *sirvientes* wore black or brown habits, and, as all Templars, the large red cross.

The Christians lost Jerusalem. They lost most of the Christian ports. Damascus, Tyre, Sidon fell. Then came the last of their cities—Acre. At the fall of Acre, people fought in the water for places on the boats that would get them away to safety on the Templar island of Cyprus. Palestine belonged once again to its indigenous population, Muslim Arabs, Jews, and a few ancient orders of Byzantine Christians who had been there for so many centuries they drew little attention.

What of the Templars? Most of those on Middle Eastern duty were killed at Acre. The few who got away did so as their duty, to guide and protect the fleeing Christians. Apart from these few, there were those who had been posted in Europe. They were often given lifetime postings, to the estates and castles all over Europe. They had the gifts of buildings, fiefs, estates to administer, while they still lived their austere lives in the midst of riches. The estates, the villages, the castles, the retreats that had been showered on them were vast, and produced a steady income and responsibility, which had been invested in crusades in *Outremer*. They did much that was useful outside of income. They raised and bred prize animals, kept houses and castles for those too old, too sick, or too young to fight, for to join the Templars was to serve and then to be cared for until death. The Templars by then were known as the foremost bankers in the Christian world, lending money to kings. Their banking grew into a vast financial empire.

After 1292 there was no Christian holy land. The knights, the sergeants, the *sirveintes*—farmers, farriers, blacksmiths, nurses, scribes—and the rank and file, the aged, the wounded and the sick were posted to properties around France, England, Ireland, Germany.

In Spain it was and had been for years otherwise. The Spanish Templars were the most important and powerful legions in the *Reconquista*, since the pope recognized the border between Christian Spain and the Moorish kingdoms as a Crusade against the infidel.

Jerez de los Caballeros could only have been a Templar stronghold since the *Reconquista* under Ferdinand II, which had recovered more territory than any conquest before it, from the Tagus River to the Guadalquivir, a huge section of the peninsula. The moves south of the Christian armies can be dated by the crossing of rivers in Spain—in tenth century, the Duero, in the eleventh century, the Tagus. Sometime between 1230 and 1235, with the capture by the Christian Castilian king of Mérida, the Guadiana. Then, in 1248, the Christian armies crossed the Guadalquivir. They finally controlled all of Extremadura. Seville and Córdoba fell.

After 1248, the *Reconquista* halted. The border would stay at the Guadalquivir for over two hundred years, at least four generations of people, living in their towns and their villages, first under Moorish and then under Christian rule, often changing from Christian to Muslim and back again. There seems to have been little attempt at conversion of the people until the reigns of Ferdinand and Isabel.

There were wars of succession, border conflicts between Christian Spanish kingdoms, and too many local troubles.

Not the least was the long process of learning to govern the vast spaces of Spain that had been taken so quickly by the Castilian and Aragonese armies.

The Templars would have found themselves far behind the frontier by 1300, in peacetime barracks, administering estates, waiting, as peacetime armies have done for ages, to be recalled to arms. In whatever year the site was given to the Templars, and their occupation began, they did there what they had done in so many of their domains for a hundred years. They built their small replica, as nearly as they could, of the Church of the Holy Sepulcher, their spiritual center in Jerusalem, now long lost to Crusaders. Their wellhead was a dome, too, and they looked out, on guard, drilled, kept their rule of St. Benedict as they always had, and went on administering their valley and their tenants.

They were mostly, if not all of them, Spanish. There were only a few of them on permanent watch. A few knights too old to fight, a priest, perhaps two or three sergeants who were in charge of maintenance of the corps, of military discipline and drill, and the *sirveintes*.

Day in, day out, year in, year out, as in monasteries today, they kept their vigil, did their daily work, spent almost nothing, ate sparingly as the rules demanded. But, unlike the other castle-barracks in Castile, there may have been other Templars as well, and the only clue to them is the river that I crossed, the Río Lázaro, on the way up the valley.

The hospitals for lepers were called Lazarettes, and because of the Templar exposure to the disease in Palestine, many of them were affected. There was no cure, only isolation, for it was understood that leprosy was a communicable disease. Hospitals run by the Order of St. Lazarus were often built near Templar strongholds. That morning when I crossed the St. Lazarus river, that tiny stream, I remember that my back chilled, but then I did not know why.

On the night of Friday, October 13, 1307, every Templar in France was arrested by order of Philip, king of France, who needed money. For several years before, a vast conspiracy had been at work. Rumors were carefully planted about the secret practices of the Templars, so that the public was prepared for the arrests when they came. The Templars were thrown into prison and tortured to obtain the needed confessions of heresy, sexual deviation, and worship of idols, all of which were the accepted sins of the time. Several thousand of them were burned at the stake.

The methods used were the medieval equivalent of the Moscow trials in the twentieth century, where the "heresy" was a trumped-up charge of treason against the communist state, or a hostile takeover in our own time when the methods of secrecy, falsehood, and surprise are used. Thousands of ignorant, simple men were victims. One of the greatest of modern medieval scholars said, "If I were to name a day in the whole history of the world, which appears to me in the truest sense as a *dies nefastus,* I should be able to name no other than the 13th of October, 1307."

In Castile, when the Templars were accused, they, too were thrown into prison, but after a council at the University of Salamanca, they were acquitted. The trials and papal bulls went on until 1312. It was then that the pope, who had been pressured for years by the king of France, issued a dissolution of the Order.

In Spain, some of the members were received into other Orders, some escaped to the Moors. Some held on to their strongholds and fought back when the royal armies besieged their castles to evict them. In many cases the townspeople

fought beside them, for they had been popular and just landlords, sometimes for years. Those defeated were arrested and
imprisoned. I could find only one case when the Templars
were killed to a man, boy, servant, and knight. Jerez de los
Caballeros. Why this one? Was it the greed of some powerful
local *grande* with a mercenary army? Was it the royal government who considered the castle too important as a border
stronghold with Portugal? Or could it have been because
many of them were lepers? All we know is that the last of
them were driven into the Tower of Blood and killed.

But on that Sunday morning I knew none of this. I only
knew that the shadows lifted from my shoulders after I had
recognized whoever had been killed there and prayed for
them; that a silent city came alive for me. People nodded and
smiled, farmers in the country as I drove away waved from
their fields and their houses. I crossed the bridge on the little
river, St. Lazarus, and when I passed the sign for the arroyo,
it read, innocently, *Arroyo del invierno,* the winter ravine,
where they must have kept their livestock in the coldest
weather to protect them.

MÉRIDA

 There was a sensuous swing as the road curved into a new landscape. I was out of the mountains to where isolated high hills had been rounded by time. Dark rows of olive trees disappeared across the crests, dipping down into valleys where there must never have been anyone living, ever, only sheep. I was taking a little while, on the way to wherever I was going, to visit the Roman Empire before I tumbled happily into Andalucia.

It was one of those stops that we think we ought to make when we travel, not to see, but to have seen. After all, Mérida was a World Heritage Sight, and I was passing it. I even dawdled, crawling toward Mérida by stopping in Caceres for lunch. It was one o'clock. Old Caceres, one of the most famous and perfect small medieval cities in Spain, was poised and still, completely isolated from the living city below it. I parked in a huge *plaza mayor* full of cars. All around the square were those shops that gather where the rich live, the smell and softness of "taste" and luxury.

I had decided to walk up the steep hill to the old city

through the narrow streets to the *parador*. I got as far as a long flight of stone steps up into the sky, that unforgiving sky, beating down on me at midday, and decided, sensibly, to drive. I turned back to the car, and began to labor up and up under a splendid Roman or not Roman arch, through streets narrower than any I had seen yet in Castile or Extremadura.

Everything had its back to the city below, and to me. The doorways were the grandest I had yet seen; the plain façades of houses hinted at hidden mansions within. Caceres was so perfect an early medieval stronghold that I had doubts, not of its authenticity, but almost its existence. Dreamlike, deserted, the large empty plazas, the square Romanesque churches, the ecclesiastical buildings, the barricaded mansions were totally silent in the sun.

There was nobody to ask, and so I found the *parador* for myself. It, too, had its back to the street. But inside, the first room was an enclosed atrium painted the most beautiful, strong, Pompeian red. There were arched colonnades with their delicate Roman columns. The sun, tamed by a veil of glass, drifted down. The empty armor of some long-dead knight, a reminder of what I had left, posed against the red wall.

Through a wide, bright corridor, I was escorted, not led, to lunch in the open garden in the center of the house. I was welcomed as if they hadn't seen a living person for a while. Courtesy and color and wine and a shaded table in the sun; I was seduced by the scent, the quiet.

A perfectly appointed table under a bright Saracen canopy—I had truly rubbed the lamp. The djinn who seated me looked very like a handsome young Spaniard. Almost within touching was an orange tree in full fruit. I was the only person there. I have no idea how long I stayed, for the whole lunch, the place, the plants, the beauty, seemed suspended in what is now a timeless memory.

What had been a dead medieval museum had become quietly hospitable, splendid and expensive and perfectly ordained. Money, money, money, old, old ecclesiastical and *grande* money! I finally made myself get the hell out of that fearsomely enchanted place. I almost ran though the empty plaza to my car to get away to Rome and Mérida as soon as possible.

In a plaza that seemed to have been born empty, with its harsh, almost undecorated churches, and its faceless mansions, almost every building seemed to advertise its claim to nobility with a large stone escutcheon; here what looked like a carved Hapsburg eagle, there an ecclesiastical shield over a door on a blank, unforgiving wall. Because I wanted to get away before I found out that everybody was dead, I panicked, and made the mistake of taking the first of those narrow streets downhill.

On one side of the street was a church wall, on the other a short row of small houses, and beyond the last house my only way out was a sharp right-angle turn. I was stuck. When I moved forward or backward, I could hear great stone claws tearing at the paint on my poor car. And frankly I was not surprised. I had finally found a tourist trap.

From Caceres on south I came to a world of white houses of the kind that I would see all the way to the Mediterranean. Cacti bloomed, vineyards were huge, the ever present olive trees marched out of sight beyond the horizon. These were the endless fields, cultivated for miles without fences, still providing grain, olive oil, and wine as they had for the Roman Empire. I had come to the beginning of the southern *latifundios*, the huge estates that seemed to be unfenced all the way to Mérida. These estates had been inherited from Rome; it was the Roman Empire that depended on provincial agro-industry. Little has changed since. The *latifundios* have haunted Spain with the power of a minority of land owners since they were granted as prizes from the Roman invasions of the second century B.C. to the *Reconquista*. These divisions were kept up through the time of the Visigoths, and, later, the Spanish *grandes*. One heiress in the eighteenth century was said to be able to walk all the way across Spain on her own land.

It had taken the Roman Legions two hundred years to subdue the Celtiberians, the wild Lusitanians, the Carthaginians in the Punic Wars. It had made a Spanish hero of Viriathus, a Roman hero of Julius Caesar—two hundred years to make Spain behave, and tap the minerals and the gold and silver, enslave the wild tribes who wouldn't bend to Roman will and efficiency. The country became the center for vast mining operations and agro-industry that would serve the Roman Empire for another four hundred years.

The Roman military camps grew into new cities, with efficient planning and more impressive architecture than most of the local tribes had ever seen. But they brought more than physical architecture. They brought education, citizenship, Roman gods, and a Roman culture where irony had replaced the Greek idea of love, where satire and obscenity replaced comedy. And we have inherited it all—class distinction, agro-industry, and, above all, the Latin language, the father tongue of English, French, Italian, and Spanish.

The people were divided legally into patricians and plebeians. Since *pater* is father in Latin I have always wondered if patrician simply meant in the beginning that you knew who your father was. Caesar, Emperator. Tsar. Kaiser, Emperor. A title for the pope is *pater patriae*. Professors are *emeritus*, when they get too old to teach; it comes from the word that Augustus used, too, when he built a city for retired soldiers—*emerita* means retired. The surviving city built for retired soldiers of the Roman legions is now called Mérida.

We have used the Roman grid system, their columns, their concrete and their stucco ever since. We have inherited their lust for power and their scorn for enchantment. What is left of Rome does not and never has had the essential *duende* of Spain.

Rome is a presence—not a haunting, for that would fly—and this presence walks with the heavy lockstep of Roman legions, stolid, controlling, planned. To study the rise and fall of the Empire, go to its far reaches, where the new Roman cities represented strength, were imported complete, instead of growing, as most cities do, in an organic process as their functions and their populations change. Go to Antalya on the coast of eastern Turkey. Go to Mérida.

I have seen Rome in a crude tower in Catalonia, in a small entrance to an abandoned digging into the hill that covers a whole huge theater underground in Medellín. Rome is still there in the tumbled, newly exposed marble stones in Zamora, five feet below the rocky surface of the medieval city, in the carved battering ram in the plaza where the bronze Viriathus stands.

Rome is in the deepest layer of cut stone at the base of the tall towers in city walls that still stand, once as grand, as overwhelming, as useless in the long run as the fortresses on the old Maginot Line between France and Belgium. It is in the superb sky-high aqueduct at Segovia. We go to see these things and learn from them a powerful sanitized past. They are Rome, what is left of it, and their straight military roads all too often have become the modern highways that take us there. The concrete they invented paves our streets, and their stucco covers our walls.

How could it have happened, this bullying passion for expansion that spread the Roman Empire over most of the known world? The first man to assume the title of emperor was Julius Caesar's nephew, Octavius. He won the battle of Actium in 31 B.C., and lost the personal immortality, for it was there that he defeated Anthony and Cleopatra for the mastery of Rome. He imposed an empire on a culture that prided itself on its republican roots. As Caesar Augustus, he proceeded to spread it all the way to the Atlantic Ocean, then the dropping-off place of the known world. A huge marble billboard in the east, in Ankara, Turkey, lists the imperial feats of Augustus in carved Latin. None of it made Rome love Anthony less and Octavius more.

The last major Roman battle on Spanish earth was Augustus's Cantabrian victory in 26–25 B.C. To celebrate it he decided to build a city, and impose it on an empty hill. It was to be a little bit of Rome for retired veterans of the Cantabrian War, Roman, grand, and civilized to remind them of home.

The sight was chosen where there was fine farmland for those who wanted to farm, a hot springs for health, a rolling hill with plenty of room for a circus, an amphitheater, and a theater. There were fine patrician homes, administration and religious centers. The whole plan was advised by Vitruvius, Augustus's architect, who was a Grecophile, and tried to revive the architecture of Greece. His monumental treatise, *De Architectura libri Decem, Ten Books on Architecture*, was the most influential voice not only in contemporary Rome but also during the Renaissance and the eighteenth-century Roman Revival, which has lasted all the way to the Supreme Court building in Washington. All that the imitators had to copy came from discovered, faded fragments, and a few rain-leached buildings; so that white became the norm for the revivals. It is ironic that ancient Rome was almost gaudy with bright colors. As Vitruvius made Roman buildings look Greek, the modern public buildings are meant to be Roman and are, instead, twentieth-century Bank Building classic.

This Rome from Rome was a prize for the retiring legionnaires, four thousand of them, and twenty thousand still on active duty. Think of our own far-flung Americas, the PX and the USO. And then think of them as whole cities with married quarters for homesick American soldiers and their families, and there is some idea of what this city, at the ends of the western earth from Rome, was like. Think, too, of the villagers all that imposed spaciousness replaced. Many were enslaved, for this was a society completely run on slave labor. The slaves were drawn from the defeated in war, the conquered civilians. They were often the highly educated backbone of the administrations. Many of them were the visual artists, the doctors, the educators, the actors. Most expensive of all were the successful gladiators and charioteers. They were considered good investments.

Augustus wanted the best for his legions, and the best is preserved in Mérida better than in almost any of the old Roman provinces anyplace else in the world. The religious center was built to worship Augustus as a god, the beginning of emperor worship. The administration center faced the temple on the other side of a huge forum, so that the temple commanded the center of the city. From its grand columns in the rear of the building, it must have seemed to tower against the horizon of miles of rolling farmland. From afar it was always the reminder, a shining white temple on a hill outlined against the sky looking down on an alien world. It is still there, and its half-ruined condition makes it far more graceful than it must have been when the busy people in the forum bustled around it. It was, at one point, incorporated in a town palace. Only one palace wall stands, its windows looking nowhere.

Its forum has been the pattern for the way Spanish *plazas mayores* have been built ever since: a church, an *ayun-tamiento* (town hall), and a large space, like the Roman forums, for a market, gatherings, strolling, gossip, and the Roman version of the *paseo*.

Other cities had grown from more ancient Spanish roots in the two hundred years of conquest, but Mérida was the first, the grandest, and the largest of the new cities that were to spread Roman culture, efficiency, law, and language to the benighted others. Many Spaniards had already been assimilated into the Roman legions. Soldiering beat slavery. They earned citizenship by serving in the legions, whose supplying and comfort, such as it was, were the most important tasks of the Roman administrations.

The legions' power was to make and break emperor after emperor. After the empire had grown to its greatest size, very few emperors came from Italy. They came mostly from the far reaches of the Empire, where the legions were in control. Spain was to provide three of the most honored, Trajan, Hadrian, and Theodorus.

Romans were efficient and unsentimental. Officially they were sensible; they took into citizenship at once most of the leaders in the areas they conquered and made them a proud part of the empire. Even St. Paul of Tarsus, which was as far east of Rome as Mérida was in the west, who embraced the religion of pure equality, bragged, "I am a citizen of no mean city." It is said to have earned him the privilege of being beheaded instead of crucified.

The lower-brain practicality of the Roman mind, brooking no argument, has always frightened me, and it does here, in Spain, in the fine uncovered city of Emerita Augusta, now Mérida. The streets I wandered are not those of the Roman city, but almost every time the underground power lines are repaired, or a foundation is dug, or the modern sewers have to be exposed, there is Rome, with its two fine forums and the grid of streets paved with large stones, where people strolled through the center of a town. Within the town limits only walking was allowed. Of course the patricians, officers, and charioteers of the legions could thunder past driving their chariots as they cared to, which accounts for the deep ruts on the paving stones.

Gardens, sewers, colonnades, the fragments of the forums in front of the Temple of Augustus, the remains of the second forum in front of the *parador*, have been uncovered. Modern archeological techniques expose more of the Roman city every year.

The second forum's entrance was once the Arch of Trajan, naked to its rough stones after the marble of the façade, the statues, the inscriptions were taken off, or fell, or were stolen. Imagine the massive raw stone arch which still stands covered with gleaming marble, statues to gods and emperors, triumphs of armies of legionaries in miniature, shining in the sun.

This city, like so many over the once-Roman world, is what is left of the terrible power of Augustus Caesar, that world dictator who appointed himself a god, and bred one of the most unattractive families in the centuries of Roman imperial government, the Claudians. And whatever was happening in Rome affected the far west, where the Roman Empire was finally lapped by the Atlantic Ocean, and the east, where the emperor was master of Jerusalem and the Black Sea region.

Roman engineers, architects, administrators, those who were the genius of Rome, made buildings and cities that you see now and can recognize by their sameness, whether in Mérida, the Roman city of Ephesus on the Aegean, or Londinium, where the Roman Tower of London stands on the Thames. Their differences can be judged, not by the modern country they are in, but by the time when they were built.

How big the empire was! We take that fact for granted until it becomes meaningless. The Roman Empire stretched at its largest, from the north of England to the Sahara Desert, from the western sea, the Atlantic, to beyond the eastern sea, the Black Sea. It contained what have become Spain, France, England, Belgium, Holland, Italy, Romania (hence its name), the Balkans, Greece, Turkey, Syria, Israel, Palestine, Egypt, the whole of North Africa.

On the way to Mérida I saw a lake that seemed to be airborne in the shimmering heat; at first I thought it was a mirage. Suddenly, what lay ahead of me was all too real. There was Mérida, on the hill across the river Guadiana, a prosperous, well-built modern town, center for the huge *latifundios* I had passed in the country around it, this place that had once been the capital of Lusitania, the *ultima thule* of the Roman far west.

There in front of me, reflecting each other as the water reflected them both, were two bridges over the Guadiana. I had to stop the car to take in what I was seeing. In the distance, downriver, was the longest and most famous Roman bridge of the many still being used in Spain. But this one by now is for strolling. Its center rests on an island, now returned to its primal shape. This was the island that had controlled the Guadiana; there had been a high wall around it, pointed at the upriver end, to increase the channel flow of water, and deepen the river through time, so that the spring rises were contained and the fields around Mérida were safe from flood.

The modern bridge I was about to drive across was as beautiful as I have ever seen, a fine-drawn silver half-circle in the sky, so strong it held up a modern roadway, so seemingly frail that it was like a rainbow of silver light framing the Roman bridge downriver beyond it. This, to me, is one of the sights that is the genius of Spain today.

The modern Spanish engineers are as accomplished as ever the Romans were. They have to be. The land, the mountains, demand it—beautiful roads, beautiful bridges, and the reservoirs which in Roman times tilted from the heights, flowing on those stone lace aqueducts high above the cities they served, some as much as four or five miles away in the mountains.

Here on the Guadiana, added to the fine engineering that may well have been inherited from four hundred years of Roman schooling in waterways, in pipes, in plumbing, in military engineering, is new Spain, the contemporary bridge that contains all of that in efficiency, with a beautiful imaginative design. A rainbow-shaped bridge. The two bridges are a visual marriage of the past and the present that I was beginning to see wherever I went in Spain.

Because I had hesitated and did not know enough Spanish to explain to the cop that I was admiring the bridges, the past in the present, the town, I simply said, slowly, "*¿Dónde está el parador, por favor?*" to the policeman who came up to the car to see if I was loitering. I think the Spanish who helped me so much must have thought of me as Señora Dónde y Está. But when you go without a guide and without a plan, *dónde,* where, is the most useful word you can learn.

I followed his motorcycle up the steep street, past a large, elegant *plaza mayor* that was to become so familiar, into a small, well-planted *plaza* on the sight of the second forum, where the trees seemed older than the buildings, their heavy shade palpable. I was to get used to handsome, hippie Spanish teenagers lounging there at all hours of the day. The pure white *parador* that faced the *plaza* garden had been a monastery, built on the foundations of the Temple of Mars. It had also been a jail, an insane asylum, and, for a while, the first museum of Roman finds in Mérida.

Needless to say, the day I planned to stay stretched to a week. I began to take for granted that if the weather was warm in the evening I would have my drink in the open eighteenth-century cloister with its reused ancient Roman columns. When it was too cool, sometimes I sat, with a book, in a stunning room, pure white, constructed from an old church and a formal meeting room together. Its ceiling was so high that it contained the cupola of the old building. It was large, full of comfort and antiques, and, except for me, usually totally empty.

The bar of the *parador,* like so many in the less tourist-crowded towns of Spain, was a local meeting place for an attractive group of people, there for an hour or so, the children well behaved, the parents obviously in from the country where once at the beginning of the Roman city there had been small farms allotted to legionaries who farmed them and sold their produce to the army. *Tertulias* of small groups of men, a table of women who had come from offices, gathered every evening. Here and there was a very old lady, one so grand in body and stare that she made a space around herself, sitting bolt upright, seeing nobody. They were patients taken to the baths at Alange each morning. The spa is Roman, and had been used all through the centuries. The baths are the original Roman ones. They are famous for cures for nervous states.

I did at first what you do in Mérida, trudged uphill through walking streets toward the famous ruins that have made Mérida a World Heritage treasure of UNESCO, with its fame and its protection. The theater is still being used or, better, used again after the centuries of burial and neglect. Here, where obscene mimes from Rome had once entertained the troops, Plácido Domingo had sung.

The semicircular seating cut into a hill was much the same size as those I had seen at the eastern end of the Empire, in Ephesus and Antalya in Turkey. This one had a capacity for six thousand. It had been built on the lines suggested by Vitruvius, with baffles under the stone seats placed so that the acoustics were perfect, and a low voice, almost a whisper, could be heard high in the semicircle. The theater in Mérida had been built around 16 B.C. as part of Augustus's city, the stage rebuilt in the time of Hadrian, during a Greek revival in Roman architecture, its columns graceful and simple, its two-story stage delicate against the sky.

A large statue of the goddess Ceres sits in the peristyle behind the stage, ample-bosomed, and intrusively calm, the backstage centerpoint for the performers. The peristyle was built in the time and by the orders of Hadrian, one of the four emperors who had been born in the Roman/Spanish colony at Itálica and who, like Vitruvius, was a Grecophile.

It is wonderful to imagine it in Roman times, not the

white marble of the statues and the columns we think of as Roman, but a theater painted red and ochre, touched with gilt, and silver, and gods and goddesses with their faces made up, their eyes brightly colored so that they must have seemed to stare down even on Caesar. What now seems delicate and graceful was full of color, and noisy, bawdy—crowds of older veterans, the young legionaries on leave, whores, bawds, and families all together.

Beside it, less than a hundred yards away, is the amphitheater, almost entirely preserved as few others are, either in the east or west. Here, as in the theater, was segregated seating: the patricians in the lowest seats, safely on a level above the arena, the plebeians higher in the stands. The highest tier of seats, which no longer survives, was for slaves, natives, and women.

It is easy to say it has a hateful atmosphere because we know as part of both folklore and history what happened there, day after day, year after year, century after century. It was a killing field, a popular entertainment. It satisfied a cultural passion for bravery, and a bloodlust that was considered to be a training for war. There were, of course, Christians martyred there, but they were usually fed to the animals at the beginning of the games; these acts were less popular, like the executions of upstart slaves.

The famous acts were the fights between trained slaves fighting wild animals or each other in scenery that made the arena into a forest, an inland sea, a battlefield. There was heavy betting. Unless the slave was a known and profitable fighter, the animals were often more valuable, since they came roaring and furious all the way from Africa, raging and half starved from the underground cells that you can see in the center of the arena, now roofless. These men went into the arena alone, unprotected, against wild animals they had never faced before. Sometimes the human fighters earned not only their lives, but their freedom, by their elegant and graceful fighting.

The mixture of grace and courage is a trait more deeply admired by the descendants of warring tribes and warring Roman legions than any other. Bullfights, no matter what we think of them, can be understood as part of the vicarious experience by an audience of honor, courage, and bloodlust. The modern bullfight may come from these games, but there is a difference. Today the bull is bloodied and half dead from the darts of the picadors placed where the neck muscles meet the spine, so that the animal cannot raise its head, before the toreador comes into the ring.

Beyond the ancient city walls, the circus was the largest of all the public entertainments for the citizens. It seated thirty thousand people, which would have been almost the whole population of Emerita Augusta. Now, where the city of Mérida has long since grown around and beyond it, there is only an indent left in the ground like the print of an enormous foot.

In the days of the Empire, walls enclosed the circus. The spectacle was grand, the parade of the charioteers past the royal box, where a representative of the faraway emperor and his friends sat. Heard across the city was the noise, the trumpets, the betting, the races. The most authentic chariot races ever filmed were those in the movie of *Ben-Hur*, advertised as completely true to the most valid research. I once met the producer of that epic, which seemed so dangerous to the thousands of extras who were the Roman throngs. I asked him if there had been any accidents. "We didn't lose a single horse," he replied. I thought it a very Roman remark.

Then there were the others, what we call now the majority. Little has been told of their daily life, their survival, their living and dying. There are hints, but in an atmosphere of slightly amused contempt. They were seen as cute, magic, mysterious, and comic. We find them in Apuleius, the North African satirist and in the *Satyricon* of Petronius Arbiter, the Roman. They were the ignored, the forgotten, those who did the work of Empire, those who were garnered by St. Paul like ripe fruit for the taking. Jesus, the rabbi from Nazareth, spoke to them in a language of love and recognition that they had never heard before. It was these people, led by the educated vestiges of Roman Spain, who suffered the cataclysm and the invasions of the barbarians from the east. They were the survivors, who would assimilate the barbarians to become in time, the French, the Italians, or the Spanish.

In Spain they kept within themselves the capacity for anarchy, for rebellion, that has stayed in the Spanish soul and is one of its heroic attributes. But one of the strongest weapons for survival must have been pure, silent stubbornness.

I found out what I already knew, what happened in the amphitheater, what was popular among those who made up the Roman military population, in Mérida 's marvel of a modern museum of Roman art and history. It is, with the archeological museum in Madrid, a place that should be as important to see in Spain as the already familiar Prado.

It has taken nearly four hundred years of care, collecting, saving of the Roman discoveries in Mérida, to make this place what it is today. The building itself was finished in 1980. When the foundations for the building were dug, a section of the Roman city was uncovered: houses, shops, a Roman street. Instead of moving it, they left it intact. In a quiet semidarkness, you walk a Roman street and peer into the broken walls of houses where generations have lived.

Between the foyer and the main exhibition room, you pass through a glass corridor high over a Roman street, and when you study it, you see how carefully the pitch of the pavement was made so that water did not rest on it. There is a sense of being there as much as you can be after so long and so much violence and loss.

The central exhibition room is about five stories high, open to natural light from the glass roof, the modern equivalent of an atrium. A series of arches divide the space into sections. The scale of the place, and of the great temple of Augustus, now called the temple of Diana, is emphasized by a single column from the temple that reaches almost to the roof. It was that temple which was built for the worship of Augustus, but through the centuries Diana became its goddess in popular memory.

There is the best balance between scholarship and aesthetics I have ever seen. You can learn the difference between the sculpture and even the religion from the first century B.C., when Mérida was built, to the fourth century A.D., when it was destroyed. There are paintings, mosaics, and sculptures of a whole way of country and urban life, from a tombstone showing a vintner at work, to the hunters, the fine horses, the performances at the amphitheatre of the gladiators and the animals.

In the mosaic murals of the charioteers, the horses toss their heads; the charioteers are dressed in shining armor. These were the popular heroes of that military Roman population that through the years was gradually becoming more and more Spanish. There was Marcianus, one of the greatest of local champions, and you can see on the mosaic the words *niche,* victor, and *Iluminator,* Inner Light, which may have been the name of his lead horse.

There was Paulus *nica,* the word for victory in more classic Latin, perhaps first century. Though the human figure is missing, the mosaic is more delicate, the horses portraits rather than cartoons, and over the missing charioteer, the delicate frond of a victory garland waves. This mosaic is earlier, for the delicacy was of the time of Augustus; it would take another three hundred years, till the fourth century, before the local Spanish spirit would show in the mosaics, the hunters, the animals, the sportsmen, the philosophers. There is a freer and more individual surge of talent, the breakup of rules, the movement of figures.

Change was slow, and through the centuries, as it was in the rest of what later would be Spain, the land became part of the larger and larger *latifundios* until by the fifth century, individual farmers had almost ceased to exist. You can see it now if you drive to neighboring Medellín, or to the spa at Alange, the wide fertile *vega,* and the empty small roads between what seem to be miles of fields.

By the fourth century the once-small farms had been combined into huge estates with their grand houses, and their outbuildings and slaves who did the work, their mercenary soldiers who guarded them, a small village to serve their houses.

The estates had hundreds of slaves, but it was the gathering into villagelike estates by the freemen farmers who had to give up their independence for protection in the countryside that changed the face of the country around Mérida through the late Roman occupation. It makes the urbanity of the white and gleaming city seem somehow imposed on what was still a dangerous and rebellious countryside.

Through the years the Roman administration kept the illusion of stability, then the patricians moved to the country out of what they considered a stinking and dangerous city of mobs, theft, and violence, cut themselves off from all but the civilized illusion of a classical world. There was only the Catholic Church to give any semblance of education and culture to the urban people.

On December 31, 406, the Rhine River, which had protected Rome from the German tribes, and the German tribes from the Roman legions, froze over. It was one of the accidents of weather that make momentous change. Thousands of starving refugee people crossed the river into the Roman Empire. They had been chased from their own homes by the invasions of the Huns under Attila.

The tribes ate, raided, killed across Gaul, destroying a civilization that rejected them. They must have seemed like a plague of locusts, and everything before them, except for a few *latifundios* where they were welcomed as tenants, was thrown down, broken, wasted. It took three years for them to eat their way across what is now France. On Tuesday, September 28, in 410 A.D., a pass was found across the Pyrenees. The invasion of the much-favored Spanish colony of the Roman Empire began.

The barbarians began to flood the Iberian peninsula. There was no semblance of cooperation to stop them between the patricians of the countryside and the plebes and slaves of the city. Buildings, once so proud, had become grass- and weed-covered spaces where there had been fine streets. The towns had been allowed to go to seed. The powerful did not give a damn, secure on their village estates, protected by mercenary free booters. It was not only the wild, violent savages who destroyed a six-hundred-year-old imposed culture in what is now Spain. It was patrician neglect.

One of the tribes was the Sueve. They were savages. When one of their warriors was arrested for killing a man in the street, they protested. There had never been a law against killing a human any more than there had against killing animals. They swarmed into Mérida, killed most of the men, and made slaves of what was left. They pulled down the statues, infested the public buildings by squatting in mud huts on their floors. What they could not eat or use or rape, they knocked down. In Mérida, Rome did not fall; it was destroyed, and under the rubble were many of the buildings you see reconstructed today.

If there is any doubt of the savagery of these people, hungry, shaggy, dirty, vicious, they were everything our wildest dreams conjure up, and more. What they did to Mérida sets the record straight. What they did not understand they burned; books, documents went up in their campfires.

Having laid waste to the city, the Sueves, in what seems like a miraculous turnabout, proceeded to establish the first kingdom since Rome within the boundaries of the Spanish peninsula. It only lasted about thirty years, but it was there, and it was documented, while so much of what is so rightly called the Dark Ages remained in darkness. It is due to a bishop called Hydatius, who carefully set down all he knew, saw, or was told.

The invasions by the Sueves are summed up by the historian E. A. Thompson with these words:

> The devastation caused by the Sueves was so implacable, so unremitting, that it is something of a wonder that they . . .

managed to survive the 5th century at all. In these dark and desperate conditions was founded the first independent kingdom of western Europe.

The Visigoths, in the pay of what was left of the Roman Empire, finally got rid of them, and set up a kingdom of their own, which lasted until the invasions of the Moors in 711. In 1230 the city was wasted again, this time by the aggressive, hungry Christians from the north. The country was beginning, unofficially, to be called Spain. Since the defeat of the Moors, the people have lived through yet another culture, one that has not yet ended. Great stretches of time, survival, a return to daily living, as it has happened for so long in this world where we attack and decimate, or try to, one another.

In the centuries when the empire was literally underground, its reality was replaced by legend, a Golden Age. The Renaissance uncovered an ideal Rome, with its white columns and its white statues, its tame gods and goddesses. Now, in Mérida, I had at least seen an always disappearing shadow of what Rome might truly have been, by the day, among conquered people, an imposed and shining monument. The Renaissance had been a dream of what was known and admired of ancient Greece and Rome. How much of the learning that survived the so-called Dark Ages refueled and changed the view of the ancient world. Instead of slaves, and circuses, and harsh government, it became a place made up of philosophers, orators, great architects, and trouble for schoolboys who had to relearn a Latin their own ancestors had assimilated—melded with their own language and changed into tongues called French, English, Spanish, and all the rest of ex-Roman patois.

There is what is to me a magic center of Mérida, and it was a forecast, a hint, a seduction toward what I hoped to see farther south. It is not an outdoor museum so much as an outdoor attic to wander in, investigate, discover as if it were newly uncovered from the past, for it looks still like an archeological dig, and I hope it will be left that way. There is a feeling that no one has told you what is valuable, made it easy, tidy, "over-found."

This looks like the Roman finds must have looked, picked up, set aside for more digging when the theater, the amphitheater, and the circus first were uncovered. I had a sense when I first saw this space of ruins and color by the river, that if I just stayed long enough, looked hard enough, something would be found there that would make the dead ground tell more secrets, and maybe more lies.

It is the *alcazaba* built by the Moors when they conquered as far north as the Guadiana river in the eighth century, and it was the next level of discovery of Spain as surely as the ancient DNA of the people. Here, touched by ancient hands, thrown down by ancient fury, recovered by archeologists, were the piles of priceless rubble. Large fragments of Roman mosaic floors still cling to their concrete underfloors. There is the entrance to a cistern with Visigothic lintel to the doors, left from three hundred years of a now lost kingdom. Down on the river side is a part of the surviving Roman wall that once went all the way around the large city, with its breakwaters to control flooding.

But the most beautiful and the most mysterious fragment is the small façade of a delicately constructed porch made of such objects as still litter the ground, sometime before or after the seven hundred years of Moorish civilization. It is made of unmatched Corinthian capitals and plain columns with faint color, made delicate by time, and, inserted over the arches, an ancient plaque. Of all the surviving buildings it is the only one that retains the faded color that was once Mérida, when the theater was painted Pompeian red and ochre, blue and gilded, and the piles of marble mosaics still show the kind of color they loved. When I go back to Mérida, I will go first to the *alcazaba*, as we go first to a favorite memory.

I was finally poised to enter Andalucia, where southern Spain was rescued from the Dark Ages by Byzantines and Muslims from Africa and a dynasty from the Middle East that had ruled since the death of Mohammed. There, on the edge of Andalucia, I saw myself standing with the semi-primitive Sancho the Fat, whose mother was taking him to a more civilized place to lose weight, in a civilized Muslim world that had been there for five hundred years.

ISLAM

 I went again to Córdoba, drawn there by the fascination of one daylong past visit which had haunted me ever since. Then I was seeing without understanding, and I had left immersed in fairytales instead of reality. So I yearned to go again, and learn, and be there, if even for a few days, as one who lived, ate, slept, made habits as structures for my stay, however short. I think that it is the only way of beginning to know a place, instead of seeing from outside, like a perpetual stare through a window.

So I want to stop now on the border of this new country, one of the oldest civilized places in Europe. But I cannot go beyond this moment into a search for Andalucia, or the land of the Vandals, Al-Andalus, without facing my ignorance.

Islam is one of the most widespread religions on earth. It has billions of followers, more than Christianity. I cannot remember Andalucia without trying to understand. It is impossible to follow the history of the changes and the barriers in Spain through the centuries without that attempt.

This is what I have learned; I know it to be superficial, but I must try. Even now, when we are faced with direct confrontation and invasion into our daily lives by the more fanatic of its followers, we refuse to learn. We don't even know what the word Islam means, and how its worshipers live. Our worst ignorance is that we think we do.

Islam, the word chosen by the prophet Mohammed, simply means submission to the will of God. It is the name he chose for the revelations which, for him, came from God, and which he dictated to followers, who wrote them down as the Koran. The Koran and the New Testament, both written after the events they describe, rest upon the Old Testament, which they both recognize. There is one essential difference between the two. The Christian testament is based on the life, teaching, and miracles of Jesus. Islam recognizes Jesus as the last prophet before Mohammed, five hundred years later. He is not *recognized* as the Son of God. "One in being with the Father." There is no God, but God, *La Illaha Illallah,* the Muslim answer, is heard from every mosque every day all over the world. Both religions are the children of the revelatory changes in the lives of Abraham and Isaac and Jacob. Islam recognizes another ancestor, Ishmael, the first son of Abraham. What seems a simple difference is so profound that it has changed and cost millions of lives.

The New Testament is literally a testament of belief in Jesus as the Messiah, and Jesus as the *logos,* the Word. The Koran calls itself a guidebook to a way of life ordained by God as revealed to the Prophet Mohammed, which tells how to live, on a daily basis, how to pray, how to wash, how to start a war, everything from the use of a towel to the use of weapons, to what a Muslim can eat, what he or she can drink—a list that controls the daily choices of a Muslim, the manners and habits that oil the wheels.

In short, it, unlike the New Testament, contains a list of

daily rules. In this, it is like the Talmud, which is also the setting down of rules for Orthodox Jews to live by—concerning food, ritual, cleaning, what day to dress, what day to rest, what day to fast, what day to feast—still followed throughout the world. Change is anathema to the extreme fundamentalists of both Judaism and Islam. They also exist on the same plots of land, one the negated child of the other as Ishmael was to Abraham.

Islam, in the calendar of revelations that have changed and restated religious and political orthodoxy, is the youngest of the three main western religions. Mohammed was born in Mecca on April 20, 571, half a millennium after Jesus. He was, as was the custom, taken with a foster mother to the desert for his first few years. So it was to the desert he went when he began to have the revelations which are the basis for Islam.

In Spain it was the time of the Visigothic kingdom, which had grown slowly from the time when the Visigoths had been hired to cleanse the Iberian colony of the more violent barbarians by what was left of the Roman Empire in the west. They had already been converted, to a Christianity later called Arianism, while they were still in Germany. The name came from Bishop Arius, who was the main political rival of the Orthodox Christian bishops at the fourth-century Council of Nicea, which had met to agree on dogma. This was not a private ecumenical council. It was dead center in most of the riot, trouble, and factional hatreds of the early Christian church, which had just been declared the official religion of the Roman Empire. There were riots in the streets of Alexandria and Constantinople. There were murders, more political than religious.

Arianism taught that the teachings of Jesus were holy

truth; they believed that he was the first among the saints, but not that he was an uncreated part of God. Erudite? Certainly. But the people of the late empire were passionate partisans. It was a joke in the large cities that if you asked a man in the street for directions, he would answer by telling you that Christ was begotten, not made. The next man would answer that Jesus was not one with God. After the Council of Nicea finally agreed on the Nicene Creed, anything other than acceptance of the orthodox creed was considered heresy.

Of course beliefs so passionately held cannot be entirely erased in a day. The new revelations of Mohammed spoke to the old arguments among the descendants of the same people, on the same lands. It was a rich field to harvest; many of them had been Byzantine Christian by law only.

The tribes of Arabia were the first receivers of the new revelations of Mohammed. They had been desert animists; a religion of djinns and goblins, angels and spirits.

Islam spread not only by persuasion but by *jihad*, holy war led by Mohammed, who became one of the greatest Muslim warrior leaders. Yet the message he brought by war was tolerance. What the new Muslims went through in their early years was almost a replica of the Christian tortures, wars, and final acceptance that had happened five centuries before. But in the seventh century Islam was new, and Christianity already had its schisms, its quarrels, its political passions, which threatened to obscure the message of Jesus. It had long since become political, with the fights for power, the internal quarrels, the official acceptance, the convenient miracles.

Islam was, in the next two centuries, to travel much the same hard road before it became more widespread than the official animist religion of Arabia Felix, and the vast red sands of Arabia Deserta and the countries that bordered it. Mohammed succeeded in changing the habits and the attitudes of the desert Arabs. He brought them in out of the desert. He stopped the age-old feuds, which had tended to start over water rights and go on for generations. He taught the wild desert tribes cleanliness, and a brotherhood across the borders of the millennia of quarreling tribes, even to wash their feet before entering the mosques, since the mosques had dirt floors covered with mats and beautiful rugs.

And it brought, for the first years, a new and urgent attitude of man to man—tolerance. This was one of the most powerful reasons, as the recognition of the dispossessed had been in early Christianity, for its spread. Slavery and serfdom were abolished for Muslims. A Muslim was equal to any other Muslim in a world of slavery and social condemnation of birth, both in the Roman separation of classes and its Visigothic inheritance, and in the Visigothic persecution of the Jews, who had been in Spain since the first century.

Mohammed made them pray together, toward the *Ka'aba*, the stone cube in Mecca, which had been a center for pilgrimage for thousands of years, long before either Christianity or Islam. It was one of his wisest moves to spread his revelation. All over the known world, then and now, Muslims bow toward the center said to have been built by Adam and rebuilt by Abraham. Whatever he said was revelation. It was religiously democratic. King knelt with subject on a totally equal basis in the far-flung mosques of what we now call the Middle East. No Muslim could be a slave.

Islam surged across the Fertile Crescent among the forgotten North African tribes. Like Christianity it paid attention to the poor and the suppressed. Like Christianity it was to forget much of its original teaching. And like Christianity, through the years, it was to change, with the entry of authoritarian clergy, the recurring surges of reform movements that tried to take it back to some purity lost in a deep past, and, all too often, in the hands of those whose religious zeal was poisoned by hate. In both religions, there was destruction of cities, terrible slaughter of the unorthodox, terrible slaughter of the orthodox.

Christianity and Islam had and have much in common, both in their strengths and their weaknesses. They are both a balance between ritual and revelation, and when that balance is lost to fanaticism on either side, the lack of balance often brings terror. Witness the time when Geneva, under the leadership of John Calvin, followed to the letter the Ten Commandments. Among other deaths for sin, four-year-old children were said to have been killed for breaking the third commandment by striking their parents. The City of God is said to have lasted only six weeks.

We are suffering worldwide from that loss of balance in religion today, when fanatics who, seeking an inhuman perfection from their fellow men, have destroyed so much. This has happened over and over again in the history of Christianity and Islam, the constant threat of judgmental certainty that has upset the balance not only of Islamic tolerance, but Christian compassion.

It was Islam in its early, purer stage that was brought to Spain, and was, in a few years, organized by a refugee who had fled for his life from the palace revolution that changed the caliphs from the Ummayad Arabs to the Abbasid Arabs, and the caliphate from Damascus to Baghdad. In a hundred years after the death of Mohammed, Islam in the East had already entered its phase of power seeking, betrayal, and murder.

When Mohammed died, the religious structure he had set

up required that he have a representative; the heir to Mohammed was called the caliph. He was the ruler over all Muslims; below him were Emirastes, governed by an emir. The caliphate had been taken over by the powerful tribe of the Ummayads in the Persian city of Damascus thirty years after the death of Mohammed in 632 A.D. The Ummayads won the never-ceasing civil strife to chose the representative of Mohammed, the caliph. They seized the power to provide the caliphs, the leaders, through eternity, with headquarters in Damascus.

Eternity is short when ecclesiastical politics enters. The Ummayads were overthrown and murdered by the Abbasids, who captured the caliphate and moved it to Baghdad. Only one member of the ruling family escaped the slaughter, which happened at a dinner party, known to history as "the fatal dinner." It was Abd ar-Rahman I, the only direct Ummayad heir. His mother had been of the Berber tribe in North Africa, and so it was there he went for refuge. He went on to the frontier town of Córdoba, which had only been in Muslim hands for a few years.

At first Córdoba was an emirate, with Abd ar-Rahman I as its emir. He was the great-great-grandfather of Abd ar-Rahman III. It was Abd ar-Rahman III who turned the emirate into a caliphate, as his ancestors had been after the death of Mohammed. It was under Abd ar-Rahman III's rule as caliph that the best and the brightest, not only from the Muslim countries but from Europe began to flock to Córdoba from the east, Arabia, Syria, Palestine. Abd ar-Rahman III began to make the attractive Spanish city you go to today into the powerful international capital for the only time in the Muslim reign over the polyglot tribal kingdoms that would become Spain.

Spanish Islam was to survive its earlier phase, and build a great city, which grew into the most civilized center of learning in Europe. But it, too, was finally brought down, the victim of rigid fundamentalism that can grow in all religions when they become an arm of the state. So I went to Córdoba, where much of the glory remains, but also the ruin left by the destructive fanatical armies of both Spanish religions.

CALIPHATE

 As the lands changed to the south there were more and more olive groves in endless formal black lines, unfenced fields to the horizon, sharper cliffs. From the road below, I could see that thinner and higher watchtowers, dark against the sky, were more like minarets than the castles of Castile. They were not minarets, and the castles in the air above Spain had not turned out to be castles. In their difference they were alike, one sharp and graceful, one heavy and brutal, both for protection, one against the other for seven hundred years; two countries that had become one, with their histories and their ways of building still intact.

I crossed into the foothills on the southern, the Andalucian, side of the Sierra Morena. I was expecting magic, beauty, and violence where the Muslims had once built a civilization so grand and so rich. I had known about this magic world, the stories of Aladdin and Haroun el Rachid, since I was five years old, and learned to read secretly by stealing *Stories from the Thousand and One Nights*, from the Harvard Classics edition that had a place of honor on the bookshelves in Pineville, Kentucky. I lay across an overstuffed chair in the living room, legs over one arm and head against the other, totally lost in a world of djinns and wonderful lamps. Now, these too short years later, I wonder if I learned then that I must keep on telling stories or die.

New trees looked as if they had been flayed. They had. These were the cork trees, providing their bark to make corks for a wine industry that had served the ancestors of the modern wines, sherries, and ports in the Roman Empire. There were hundreds of hairpin curves, like those I had been used to all my life, opening into valleys below.

Wide places for turning and for resting were fenced against the steep, harsh hillsides that sloped toward the valleys. I got out of my car. All around me in the mountain meadows, cattle grazed. Then I looked up the hill at the last mountain I had crossed. Against the sky, black as a Spanish shadow, was the concise outline of an enormous and terrifying fighting bull.

I ran back toward my car, and as I opened the door I looked up again to see if the huge animal had moved toward me. I leaned against the car, slack with relief. It hadn't moved. It was not going to. This huge black bull against the clean blue sky of Andalucia was a statue, or a silhouette. I thought it might be an ancient religious symbol, like the white horse etched into the chalk bedrock of a hillside meadow in the west of England. There was not a word to read, not a sign to explain, only the black shape. I photographed it, as I am sure thousands of tourists have, seeing it for the first time, almost to prove it was real.

It turned out to be a billboard, or what had once been a billboard, advertising Osborne sherry. But there was no word, no Osborne, no sherry. There were only the bulls. I was to see them many times, always against the sky, always stunning, the new symbol of this oldest civilized part of Spain.

The story of its survival in Andalucia has to do with a law passed in the *Cortes* in Madrid, during the general cleanup of Spain in 1976 after Franco's death. The law banned all outdoor advertising signs. The Andalucians refused to obey. The rest of the aesthetically offending signs could go, but not the bulls. When the law declared they should be removed from the roads along with all the other billboards defacing the landscape, there was a public outcry—a torrent of letters to the press, protests, meetings dedicated to saving the fifty-ton iron symbols of the Spanish fighting bull.

The *Junta*, the legislature of Andalucia, passed a resolution making the bull signs in their province into national monuments. There are over thirty of them on the hills in Andalucia, and they are there for a reason. The Andalucians like them.

The bull is one of the oldest religious symbols in the Mediterranean world, as far back as the bull's horns on a wall of the eight-thousand-year-old town of Catal Huyuk in Anatolia, in Turkey. Bulls are on the ceilings of the caves at Altamira, the walls of Minos in Crete. The heavy bulls of Guisando, whose shapes were only partly released from the stone from which they were carved, have been in northern Spain since they were set, in prehistoric times in the fields near Avila. They stand in a line abreast, as if they are waiting. The carved marble bulls' heads in the museum in Mérida show all the grand brutality of Rome. The beautiful bronze Tartessan bulls' heads are some of the earliest works of art that are essentially Spanish, that elegant, concise art which has marked a work as Spanish from the earliest known kingdoms in the south to the bullfight painted in swirling movement by Goya.

The bullfights. They cannot be avoided in any understanding of Spain. They are on the television in most of the bars in Spain around five o'clock. *A las cinco de la tarde.* At five o'clock in the afternoon. The hour of the bulls. The faces of the sometimes bored, sometimes ecstatic crowds reflect that poised second of blood, elegance, and *duende,* the kill. It is Spanish, which no foreigner can ever truly experience.

I think it was while standing there, resting against the fence, that I tried to understand, as everyone probably does who travels in Spain, what is to us, the strange survival of the bullfight. The first poem I read of Lorca's was the "Lament for Ignacio Sánchez Mejías," which begins, *"A las cinco de la tarde."* In the recording of Germaine Montero reading it, I hear that phrase as a Greek threnody, a choral lament.

Without choosing to watch on the television in Madrid, I had already been caught, as I flipped the dial, by the images of a confused, dying animal and the cold, bored faces of *aficionados* watching from the stands of the bullring. They disapproved of the animal's way of dying. Once again when I was changing channels in a hotel room, the animal's tongue was hanging out in its death throes. It was gushing blood while a pretty *torero* danced around it trying, with passes of his cape, to rouse it out of its death. The last glimpse had been when I was waiting for dinner, and was seated in the bar next to the dining room, waiting to be called to my table. I could see the bullfight. I turned my back, but was swung around by the music of the band in time to see men covering the body of the dead bull with what looked like red capes, while a band played "Amazing Grace." It was too much for me. I began to cry and hid my face so I could get out of the bar without being seen. I agree with Gary Cooper, who, when asked if he liked the bullfight, said, "No." When asked why, he is supposed to have answered, "The bulls lost, six to nothing."

But what about the legend? What about Lorca's tragic poem about the dead bullfighter as a heroic figure? What about the love of the Andalucians for a great iron silhouette? I think it goes back to the essential legend of intelligence and courage against might—to Viriathus in Zamora, whom the Romans could only defeat by trickery, to the wall painting in Mérida of the gladiator who is charging a snarling lion with a small spear, to El Cid, who stood up to his king, to Numancia, where the besieged people starved to death rather than give up to the Roman legions.

I think the Spanish do not see, as I see, a professional actor dancing around a dying animal, sometimes flirting with wounding or death to give the audience an extra thrill, for they have come to see death, one way or another. I think the Spanish, and the foreigners like Hemingway, who used the legend in his ever-failing search for a definition of courage, see instead a small figure, brave in a "suit of lights," a David against Goliath, that represents themselves against the odds, personal or national, they have had to suffer through so much of their past. For Lorca it was not the moment of the kill, it was the courage and grace of the *duende* in the pause of the *torero*, poised on the rim of the moment.

Down out of the mountains, and into the last valley, I began to see among the industrial wrecks of the modern city, the white houses, the bright tiles, those signs of strange familiarity that I had known since I was a child. I was entering the outskirts of Córdoba; I knew it was, along with

Constantinople, the only city in Europe where there had been no Dark Ages, and where culture and beauty had never been entirely destroyed.

I took with me, from the polyglot reading we tend to do before we go to a new country, a favorite story that would guide me. Events in the reign of Abd ar-Rahman III had been recorded by Muhyiddin Ibn Arabi, the foremost Spanish Moorish *sufi* of the twelfth century. He wrote the story a hundred years after it happened, and legend and the editing that is memory had made his story glow with jewels and power. His words are translated in the book *Moorish Culture in Spain*, by Titus Burckhardt.

Muhyiddin Ibn Arabi was born in Murcia. He traveled the Muslim world, preaching, writing, studying. Only Jellaludin Rumi, the Turkish mystic poet, the *Mevlana* whose followers in Konya began the cult of the Whirling Dervishes, was as famous and influential in the *sufi* movement. Jellaludin Rumi's warning to his disciples is chilling: "What is wine to the pilgrim is poison to his disciples."

Arabi's story was part of the legendary history of the first caliph in Spain. It began at the gates of the richest, most superbly decorated Moorish caliphate in Muslim Spain's history. It had happened in the tenth century, during the reign of the fourth heir to the emirate of Córdoba to come from the Arabic Umayyads. It was he who had changed Córdoba from an emirate to a caliphate, and had become the first caliph of Córdoba, Abd ar-Rahman III.

Christian ambassadors, soldier diplomats of the Visigothic kingdom, arrived at the gates of Córdoba to sue for peace in one of the early outbreaks in the seven hundred years of intermittent war, the *Reconquista*. They, born into war, their homes walled fortresses, were welcomed with a staggering

display of wealth. They were escorted through the labyrinthine streets to the largest mosque in the Muslim world, a
constructed oasis of treelike columns that disappeared into
an infinity of marble and color. In the center of the city,
close around the mosque, they passed some of the thousands
of shops that sold silks and satins, jewels and gold, book-
stores with the gilded leather covers of book after book, in a
city famous for its teachers, its philosophers, its poets, its
scientists.

They were stunned by glimpse after glimpse of private
courtyards paved with bright tiles, their white walls tumbling
with flowers, fine houses, parks, *medreses* for Muslim religious students, and hospitals, unknown in the north.

The caliph had just built the palace of Madinat az-Zahra,
named after a favorite Christian slave girl in his harem. The
palace was about twelve miles from Córdoba. The ambassadors were led along a royal road past fields rich with grain
and grapes, enough to feed a city, and along creeks of fresh
water, all the luxuries of a natural garden, mile after mile.

A double line of soldiers in bright armor that glistened in
the sun held high their naked swords, touching the tips to
make a roof of steel over the ambassadors, all the way from
the city to the palace, a long, awe-inspiring stroll.

They arrived at the superb main gate of the palace. It
was the largest of a line of gates in the outer wall of the
palace, all crowned with huge semicircles of stone. The
wide doors below were big enough for teams of horses, for
chariots, for marching armies. The circles were decorated
like the arches of the great mosque they had been shown,
red and white stripes that seemed to meet in the empty
center, an imagined geometry of lines.

They were stunned by the magnificence of the new building. It spread out on a hillside far into the distance, a royal city. The sun fell on gold mosaics, on silver doorways, on walls encrusted with gems. They walked on *azulejos* in green and blue designs, past shining white walls of marble. Great trees had been brought full grown to shade the royal city. Scented fountains tossed cascades of water into the air. A wall of falling water cooled one of the public rooms. If there was an Aladdin's castle in the world of Islam, it was Madinat az-Zahra.

A carpet of brocade stretched for a quarter of a mile from the great gate to the Hall of the Ambassadors. The outdoor passage was full of courtiers, dressed in red velvets, rare silks, jeweled turbans, gem-graced scabbards and handles for their swords and daggers.

They were led into the great reception room, not fortified, but open to the air and sun so that the hangings breathed and the marble columns with their lacelike stucco capitals were touched with sunlight. There was no one there to receive them. They were led further into a smaller, almost empty room.

A man sat alone on a sand floor. He was dressed in rags. He tended a small fire in a brazier, cooking a meager meal. There were only the Koran, a sword, and the fire itself in the otherwise empty room. It was Abd ar-Rahman III, the first caliph and the greatest leader of the Spanish Muslim caliphate since the illiterate North African Berbers had arrived as mercenaries in Spain two hundred years before, the man known in both Christian and Muslim Spain as "the glittering ornament of the world."

When the ambassadors had prostrated themselves before him, he held up the Koran, and said, "This, not I, is the ruler of the caliphate of Córdoba. God has chosen us to call upon you to submit to this." Then he raised the sword: "If you refuse we shall compel you with this." And he pointed to the fire: "If we kill you, you will go thither."

The scene was protocol, not a warning at conversion to the Christians. The caliph was dressed as a *sufi,* the Muslim version of a Christian monk, not as a beggar. And his caliphate, following the basic rules of the Koran, did not attempt to convert Christians and Jews, "the people of the Book." He ruled a caliphate where both were tolerated and, at least during his lifetime, were protected by law. There would be outbreaks of intolerance, as there are in most radical fundamental forms of religion, but they were not blessed by the state until the fall of the caliphate. For the most part Jews and Christians were left in peace. One of the reasons the Muslim rulers did not force conversion on the conquered, as the Christians would do later, was a practical one. They paid higher taxes than the Muslim citizens.

Córdoba was the twin city to the only other place in what was left intact after the fall of the western Roman Empire. They were the only two places in Europe, besides a few obscure, hidden monasteries, where there were no Dark Ages. In the east Constantinople, a Christian city, was almost surrounded by Muslim tribes. In the west, Muslim Córdoba would be threatened not only by the warrior Christians from the north of Spain but by the constant raiding warfare of its own more primitive tribesmen. Córdoba as the seat of the caliphate held Moorish Spain together as one country for over two hundred years.

Córdoba reached its zenith in the reign of Abd ar-Rahman III. It was not only the most enlightened but the most beautiful city in Europe. Who were they, these people of Córdoba who were able to reach such fame, such open debate, and such love of learning? Why, all through the otherwise Dark Ages, was it so known as a center of philosophy that it was visited by pilgrims, not for religion, but for open knowledge?

From a thousand years B.C., Phoenicians, Carthaginians, and Greeks had been settling there as armed merchants, and joining the other Bronze Age people who were natives to the peninsula to become, as they became, *cordobanos*. The rich proud country of Tarsus, Tartessos, whose proud ships were known to Isaiah and Jonah, had left their mark on it. When the Romans had arrived as conquerors in the second century B.C., they found an ancient, worldly, civilized city that already overlay an even more ancient, half-forgotten city.

In the sixth century Belasarius, the most famous general of the reign of Justinian, the Byzantine emperor who ruled the eastern Roman Empire in Constantinople, won the fight against the Vandals, who had laid waste to the south, and chased them into Africa. Córdoba became a Byzantine Roman city for seventy more years, the only civilized city in a quagmire of barbarian invasions.

It had grown, in the two hundred years since Abd ar-Rahman's great-great-grandfather had become its ruler, into the capital of the most famous center of scientific research in the known world, a Muslim city on the border between the mostly illiterate Christians of the north and Al-Andalus, the Muslim south of the Spanish peninsula. For the first time, there were native converts, whose new religion demanded that they practice the tolerance that was the revolutionary gift of Islam.

There had been no Moorish invasion in the beginning. This tends to be forgotten in the protective legends about wild Berber invasions into a peaceful Spain. There had been some minor inroads across the straits between Spain and

North Africa, but it was not until they were invited onto the Iberian peninsula in one of those habitual wars for succession to the Visigothic crown that they came in any force.

The brother of the reigning monarch hired some mercenaries from North Africa, a few Christians, some Muslims from Syria, to help him usurp the throne. The Berber mercenaries had lately converted to Islam from their animist tribal religions. The small battle that followed grew monstrous in importance for Spanish history because the Berbers did not go home afterward as mercenaries were supposed to. When they saw the fertile valleys of Andalucia, they stayed.

Eighteen thousand or so of them, mostly from across the narrow slip of ocean at Gibraltar, settled around Córdoba, in what was left of the old Roman city. Since they had brought no women with them, they married locally. This marriage of past and present was to happen all over Spain where the Muslims took control.

By the time the Muslims arrived, the *cordobanos* had been a community for seventeen hundred years. They outnumbered the Berber tribesmen by thousands. So the extraordinary reputation for learning and for open-minded questioning had been among these people since the days of the Roman *cordobanos*, Seneca and Lucan, if not long before.

The legend that Islam was simply an overlay on the Christian inhabitants is misleading. It has fed the illusions of political and racial self-protection that have often led to prejudice. The marriage of Islam, Christianity, and Judaism was part of the fertile loam of Córdoba's ancient culture and love of learning.

The first great gift to Córdoba by Islam, surprising in view of its later brutal intolerance, was the tolerance that was so new to the world. The second gift was a surprising passion for poetry, music, and storytelling that the desert tribes had brought to Islam.

By the time of the caliphate in the late tenth century, Córdoba was a city of nearly half a million people. Thirty-five thousand streetlamps glowed at night. London and Paris were to stay dark for another seven centuries. Roman ingenuity was copied to make huge water wheels to harness the river's current and bring clear water to thousands of gardens. Today when you walk through the old city, with its courtyard after courtyard with white walls that are covered with a luxury of flowers and vines, you are seeing what the Christian ambassadors saw in the eleventh century, a way of life that was started there by the Muslims with their desert memories. They simply fell in love with water, and greenery and blossoms were their luxuries.

These flower-rich courtyards are still the pride of Córdoba, covered to the tops of the white walls with hanging, trailing vines and pots of plants ablaze with color. Every year there is a festival to celebrate that love of color and floral blessing, and a prize given to the most beautiful courtyard.

When I had been in Córdoba before, that first glimpse served only to make me promise myself that I was coming back. I remember that day, almost hour by hour. It had started at the mosque, one of the most famous in the world, and the most beautiful Muslim religious architecture in Spain. I had strolled through the main gate beside the church tower that had once been the minaret into a huge open courtyard of stone with shelters of orange trees in the Spanish southern sun. People wandered in a way I hoped to do, treating it as an open city square, taking it for granted, living there. I longed to join them. The mosque was a mystery, the narrow streets, the delicate doorways, the glimpses of courtyards so filled with flowers that they seemed to over-flow with color as magic as they must have been for the ambassadors who came to treat with Abd ar-Rahman III.

The mosque seemed to me to be a neverending forest, the human copy of an oasis. Once the interior was open through arches that let the sun pour in, it was as if one passed gradu-ally from sunlight into a wooded place.The sunlight dimmed into twilight. The *mihrab* in the Great Mosque of Córdoba was given to the caliphate by the emperor of Byzantium, who sent tons of gold, tiles, precious stones, and the Persian workmen to put it up.

Already, by the end of the ninth century, the new mosque was too small for the thousands of citizens of Córdoba who had come from all over the Mediterranean world to learn, to trade, or simply, as tourists today, to stare. As it was added to, it became the largest in the Muslim world. Abd ar-Rahman II added to it in 848, Al-Hakam II from 962 to 965, and finally it became its present size under the fearsome dictator Al-Mansur from 981 to 1008 A.D.

When the mosque was the center of Muslim worship, sun-light had poured through inner arches to touch the red and white of the high double arches and bring them to life, so that there seemed to be little difference between the interi-ors and the garden of the oranges in the huge open court where the ablutions were. The sun streamed within, under the high roof of wood instead of leaves.

What a center of life it had been. Judges, lawyers, philoso-phers, all found their places on the rugs that once covered the bare ground under a roof so high it is hard to see the del-icate carving on every inch of the old wooden beams. Its double arches seem to reach to the sky, held up above Roman columns that were gathered from all over the broken

Roman city of Córdoba, where both the Senecas had been born and lived long before a mosque or Mohammed had entered into history.

The mosque represents the whole Muslim civilization of Córdoba, and its fall. For in the center, glittering with gold from the Indies, rises a complete cathedral, built over two hundred years after the Christians from the north finally took Córdoba in 1236. Now there are only glimpses of the true colors, when an outside door is opened The open arches around the whole of the mosque have long since been closed and chapels made of them where minor saints stand over their altars.

The little shrines to these mostly unknown saints, neglected, unlooked at, and badly carved, now shut out a sunlight that was part of the design, the brilliance of this building. It seems almost an attempt to make it drab, not holy, not a great work of man but a perpetual twilight So the light must be imagined, and the Muslim world of the caliphate conjured up out of shadows. The mosque has been desecrated by these closed walls. From the fifteenth century on, that one pure quality has been denied it. Light.

It had been built to be open, a sheltering roof over a stone and stucco forest, a vast ceilinged space of alabaster and marble columns, red and white horseshoe circles, stucco doorways brightly painted to look like colored polished stone, a million tiny mosaics to catch the light and return it to the spaces and the fretted arches and the carved wooden ceiling in prisms, and shafts that picked out one magic color and then another as the day passed around the forest of black and white and painted columns into night.

Surely by now, over six centuries later, the people of Córdoba no longer need to prove their faith by such dimming destruction. It would be a greater act of faith to fill those places that were once open with glass so that at least the color of that magic forest would shine out.

It costs money to go into the mosque. Why not glass to keep control of the crowds? Why not honor both religions by flinging the missing shining light into the darkest parts that were not meant to be hidden? Maybe the original builders of the mosque were following the same Bible as the Christians and the Jews when God said, Let there be light.

When I first walked into the mosque and began to wander, lost in a forest of columns, in the half-dark, where doubled arches rose into gloom above my head, I had no idea a thirteenth-century cathedral had been built in the center of it. It gives some measure of the size of the huge mosque that a full-sized cathedral can lie unnoticed there. I must have wandered for an hour without running into it, for I certainly was not looking for a full-sized glittering Christian church. I recognized how large it was when I stood high by a window in the Roman-Muslim tower, which was once a royal palace and remains today a guard for the still-used Roman bridge across the Guadalquivir. From the other side of the river, I could see the church rising up beyond the roof of the mosque in the middle of the building like a setting hen.

That was the city I had taken away with me, a mystery and a beauty. I wanted go again and to live there, if only for a few days, until I could take it all for granted. I promised myself that one day I, too, would stroll as familiar as the local people seemed to be, on my way to the market for oranges, wine, bread, and cheese. So this time I wandered in the back streets and the narrow lanes, a modern ghost in a medieval Muslim world. I found, of course, that it would have taken a lifetime.

It is, to me, miraculous that tolerance and compassion still linger in the mosque—an atmosphere, an acceptance. I found a new and gentle quality there which was hidden at first because I was blinded by the awe with which I saw its size. Huge as it is, the mosque can be an intimate place, as when in a forest you might find a tree, spread out your picnic, put up your tent, and make a circle of familiarity in the small space around you, so that the forest is forgotten for the intimacy of your space, your picnic, your own trees. Early Moslems called these buildings forest mosques.

The mosque was not only a place of worship but a courtroom, a university, a *plaza mayor*. An advocate could find there, sitting by his chosen column in the forest of columns, a *cadí*, or judge. A religious seeker could find an *imám*, a teacher of the Koran, sitting on rugs by his column. Students from all over Europe sought out teachers, waiting at their own familiar columns, surrounded by students under the high roof in the shade of the mosque of Córdoba.

I stayed in a hotel named for one of the greatest of Jewish thinkers and physicians in medieval Judaic history, Moses Maimonides. He had been born in Córdoba's Judería and educated both in the synagogue and the mosque in one of those periods of tolerance, Muslim and Jewish alike, in the twelfth century, long after the caliphate had been destroyed. For the intellectual center stayed long after the political center had disappeared and been forgotten. My window looked out directly across the cobbled street from the church tower. I knew it covered the ancient minaret that I could see in my mind's eye, not the fairly pedestrian tower it is now, like so many of the towers of Christian churches that once were mosques. But under the architectural desecration, I could see, in my mind's eye, the slender column of the minaret and hear, as a whisper, the call to prayer by the *muessin* that had awakened me at five in the morning from the minaret of the Blue Mosque in Istanbul. The Koran says that the first prayer should be when the black thread can be seen as separate from the white thread at first dawn.

Sancta Sophia, the fifth century church of Justinian, had been made from church to mosque, as the mosque I looked out on in Córdoba had been made from mosque to church. Both changes had failed. Even Catholics in Córdoba talk of going "to the mosque" to mass, and in Istanbul, there are only the huge calligraphic signs near the dome to show that it is officially a mosque. There is no prayer there, no rows of hundreds of prostrate Muslim men, but only the fragments of a time, a time when the Venetians destroyed and looted the great city when it was still Christian, and then when Mehmet II rode his horse into the most famous church in Byzantine Christendom, through the blood of its defenders, and declared it a mosque. Both miraculous buildings mirror each other in my mind, how they changed and how they failed.

It is ironic that it was the Christian armies of the Republic of Venice who destroyed the orthodox Christian city of Constantinople. It was the Muslim Berber mercenaries who laid waste to the caliphate of Córdoba.

The library collected by the second caliph, Hiram, had been second to none in the enlightened world at the time. The first caliph had allowed the Malecite clergy to grow strong for political expediency, since they represented the conservative mullahs, whose authority came from the most conservative reading of the Koran, and who controlled those of the illiterate and still seminomadic public who despised any kind of free thought.

It was one of the few shortsighted mistakes that political genius made, simply so they would not bother him. The strict and rigid construction has always been the weakness of Islam, a shadow that haunts the great periods of Islamic thought. To the fundamentalists, then and now, tolerance is heresy. Anyone who questioned; anyone who experimented; anyone who thought beyond the letter of the Koran, was *zendik,* heretical. Scientific discovery, humanist reading, the liberal thought that had made a culture that attracted philosophers, poets, jurists, and religious thinker from all the Muslim world, began to be forbidden.

All of the religious and humanist thinkers could flourish in Córdoba in their different centuries, and all of them were victims of autocratic ignorance, first from the Roman government, then from the barbarians, and then from the half-civilized unlettered men of the deserts of Arabia and North Africa. Seneca was forced to commit suicide on the orders of the Emperor Nero. Lucan, the poet, was executed for treason. Maimonides had to leave Córdoba when he was fifteen years old and take shelter in the Fatimid caliphate of Egypt, where he became physician to Saladin. Averroes escaped to Africa to keep from being murdered by the fanatic orthodox clergy aided by the dictatorial powers of a single ruler without hope of tolerance, which had become an orthodox sin punishable by death.

Yet what they stood for has survived. There is a conversation in Michener's fine book about Spain, trammeled as he was by the dictatorship when he wrote it. Michener had asked a Spanish doctor about the place of his profession in Spain (this in the early sixties). The answer:

> There is no analogy between the role of the doctor in Spain and the doctor in any other country. Our tradition

stems from the great Jew Maimonides and the Muslim Averroes. . . . A man is sick, cure him. We set a high pragmatic standard and this gets to be known in the community. From Maimonides and Averroes we also inherit the high position enjoyed by the doctor. This was never a Spanish trait. It was a Jewish and Muslim trait, and fortunately for us, it was adopted by our society.

Then the doctor added something that explained how he, a liberal, could have gone on living in Spain during Franco's dictatorship: "We are able to espouse liberal causes where others would be afraid to do so, because we have a prepared position to which we can retreat . . . because doctors are needed."

I was crowned with luck and change. The Spain where I traveled in the year 2000, as ancient as it is, is young and new and old and, as of now, unsuppressed for one of the rare times in its history.

It saddens me that Michener had to be fettered by the deadening dictatorship of Franco. He wrote his book about Spain before Franco died, clutching a relic, the little dead dried hand of poor hard-working St. Teresa, in 1975. But it adds to the value of his book, for the stunning difference is documented.

Reading Michener's book gave me yet another reason to marvel at the burst of energy since Franco's death that has quietly revived that beautiful city. I was saddened by the fact that as late as the sixties, Michener found Córdoba under Franco dirty and neglected, the old city, which has now been so beautifully revived, was a slum.

There was one building in Córdoba which I hated. It was the old Muslim palace built before Madinat az-Zahra. Heavy, dark, square, squat, built long before the caliphate on the foundations of the old emirate palace *alcázar* it became a palace for the Christian monarchs when Córdoba was captured by Ferdinand III of Castile and became a Christian Castilian city in 1236.

This building was the headquarters of Ferdinand and Isabel in the last push in the *Reconquista* to make the peninsula into a Christian country. They are said to have lived there for eight years, 1484 to 1492, and to have directed the siege of the last of all the Muslim states, Granada, which finally fell in 1492. For the first time the great water wheel in the Guadalquivir River, which kept the gardens alive with precious water, was stilled forever when Isabel ordered it stopped because the noise bothered her.

In 1492—the year of Columbus, the fall of Granada, and the expulsion of the Jews from their thousand-year home in Córdoba in the city's Judería—the monarchs gave the building to the Holy Inquisition, and there it sat for three hundred years sniffing out heresy, ruling the souls of what would be left of Córdoba.

The first thing, and thing it was, that I saw, was the statue of Ferdinand, all knight in armor of the modern-medieval school of ecclesiastical art, a Visigothic battle sword before him. The statue is a blush pink marble hunk of knightly righteousness without expression or personality. Inside the rooms were some fine surviving objects from both Muslim and Roman culture.

Then I went into the gardens. The contrast between the interior fortress and the garden was almost overwhelming. There, laid out as a Muslim paradise, or walled garden, was one of the most beautiful formal gardens I have ever seen. Water was its center. Ever since the wars over oases in the prehistoric desert past of the Arabs, water had been, beyond gold or precious stones, their most valuable and necessary luxury. The two pools are oblong. They flow into the distance between a series of fine jets that keep the water fresh and clear, like the design of the gardens at the Generalife higher on the hill above the Alhambra in Granada. The gardens on either side of the pools are wide, spacious, and there are fine walks.

The air is cooled by the veils of water, and the flowers and shrubs are not a riot but a dream of color. The water comes not from the scoop wheel in the river but by the modern water system. It feeds the flowers, the shrubs; it drifts in the air around statues, one of a Muslim poet, others of Ferdinand, Isabel, and Columbus, who had to follow the court for so long before they paid any attention to him. I remember nymphs, classic figures, as I remember, and will always, that there are now statues in the old city of Córdoba of Maimonides (this one of the finest in Spain), of Averroes, and Seneca.

Michener was disappointed that there were no statues of Averroes when he was in Córdoba. I wonder if his remark fostered a move to have a sculptor make one? It is very good. It sits on a plinth also near the gate into the Judería. Only this. Alas, the abyss of ignorance and malice in the world had reached there as well, and someone thinking that the bust is of Maimonides, had scrawled a swastika on it when I saw it the first time.

I wish that Michener, who loved Spain so well, as I do, had been able to see the new youth of the country, the cleanup of the public buildings, the welcome that seems never to be professional but to have kept the ancient manners of Spanish dignity and grace, which seems to have replaced the old fashion of Spanish haughtiness and pride. And I wish it had not been raining when he went to Madinat az-Zahra.

I had saved it until last, for fear, maybe, of disappointment. I did not know that ruin and grace, the haunting, the sadness, somehow made a once royal city/palace that covered more earth than any before it in the Muslim world tender and small.

Of course there were no soldiers with their scimitars along the road to it, no gilded minaret, no childlike illustration to an old fairytale. I followed the small sign I had passed on the main road a few miles outside of Córdoba, and drove slowly across what seemed to be a vast, unfenced field where the green weeds had grown so high that I could hardly see beyond them. The road was narrow—an old farm road? It had no shape that told me it led to imperial splendor instead of wheat or pasturage. The patient grass, the centuries of farming, the forgetfulness of what had happened had buried all that. It was somehow nerve-wracking. It would have been better had I not known what happened there.

At the crest of a hill, I stopped the car. I was able to see the city/palace in the distance for the first time. How small it looked under the vast Spanish sky. It could have been a shelter for a cattle herd, a random heap of stones left by earthquake or storms, or neglect. There was no royal city. From a distance the ruins of the buildings had left only a ghost, a hint, a shape of what has sunk into the past and now is only a skeleton to show where it has been.

I stood where any visitor would first see the city of stones below, on the balcony of a neat government building, shady with vines, a peaceful place as there should be for visiting a cemetery. The rediscovered rectangle, hints of streets, hints of rooms, a little city of foundations was spread out below me, part of it on the hillside, and the rest down on the level fields that could have been, once, a forest, a huge parade.

The little map given me showed a palace, but what I saw was only more squares, more stone. I went down the long stairs under a relief of trees, for where there was no shade the sun beat down as if to drive the rock back into the ground. Why do such places buzz? They do. Ruins have a sound of their own, the buzz of dead silence.

A careful walk had been provided; away down below a few people walked, strolled, for the Spanish can stroll even in such a sun. Here and there were attendants, or at least I took them to be until I went nearer and saw that they were helping with the revival of Madinat az-Zahra, treating it with care as if they were poised to find jewels just below the next rock, in the next dry runnel, the next fallen wall. From the tiny fragments they are finding they have taken on the task of putting the palace together again like a vast jigsaw puzzle.

For some years now there has been an impressive effort to make what was only a field of stones, what I saw before I really saw the little city, into itself again; the archeological workers were tender, using brushes instead of shovels, and when four of them walked by carrying a stretcher carefully with a large fragment of marble on it, they were as gentle as if it were a body. Student volunteers do much of the work.

One thing had not changed, the labyrinth that is a part of all medieval Muslim buildings, and so, of course, in trying to find what my map said was the main entrance, I got lost, and one wrong turn took me into the depths of the palace itself. A horseshoe arch, naked stone of walls that had once been marble, a stillness that once would have been brushed away by the wind that moved a curtain, a door opened and closed in the distance. All of those sounds and movements of life we take for granted as stillness were gone, leaving true stillness, dead, that buzz of silence.

But I wanted to enter as the ambassadors had done in the story I had brought there, and when I found it, there it was as I had expected it to be, the great horseshoe gates of red and white revived, the largest in the center, massive enough for carriages, for cavalry, for pomp, but now, instead of a huge wall that would have been part of the maze of entrance, there was only the remnant of a stone wall, with steps that looked diminished.

I walked toward the Hall of the Ambassadors marked on the map on an imaginary carpet of brocade instead of dusty stone. There was the scent of jasmine as there should have been, then a copse of tall rich trees, then a formal garden, and the place was coming alive again. Here and there young people sat gossiping, little bouts of laughter, some flirtation, fragments of the gestures and the ways that would have been part of the place when it was alive.

The jasmine scent grew stronger. What bright keeper of the palace had thought to put it there? It was perfect, and the garden was perfect. Ahead of me I could see the finest reconstruction of all; the entrance to the hall where the Christian ambassadors had been received, and had seen so grand an assembly of silks and turbans, and veils and jewels, that they had thought this vizier, then that one, a joke played on the barbarians from the north, was the caliph himself.

It was the memory of one of the most beautiful rooms that had been. Much had been found, which was a miracle in itself, a frail design of stucco lace uncovered by a brush to be copied and replaced where it had been once, the pink and green marble columns, the fine capitals, all of it still to be finished, or never finished. They were trying to revive a city.

Which of the rooms off the great hall had been the one the caliph knelt in, tending the brazier in his rags, the greatest of all the rulers of the Spanish caliphate?

It was in these rooms, along these corridors, in these revived gardens, that was played out in terror the whole symbolic scene of the end of the caliphate. The Christians did not destroy the caliphate. It was done by fellow Muslims, many of them fanatic believers who gleaned from the Koran and from charismatic preachers that such places were evil, too luxurious, that innovation was a crime, that too much questioning was heresy.

What had been built by Abd ar-Rahman III and his scholarly son Hisham, who collected a library of four hundred thousand volumes, written in the Arabic calligraphy by scribes, and bound with the famous leather of Córdoba, tooled in gold, had been inherited by Hisham II when he was only ten years old. His mother's lover, a scribe, was made his guardian, and rose to be the most fearsome dictator Muslim Spain had ever known. He was the man known as Al-Mansur, the conqueror. In his short reign he destroyed by cruelty and avarice the trust that the other small city-states had put into the hands of the caliphate. Like so many power-mad generals and dictators since, his talent as a general was overshadowed by his cruelty and greed. By the time he died, he ruled the rest of Muslim Andalucia by terror, armies of mercenaries, made up of fanatic North African Berbers who had embraced a tyrannically rigid form of Islam, by Syrians on the prowl, and by Christian freebooters from the north. It was only after the short-lived reign of his son, while the true caliph still sat at Madinat az-Zahra, a semiprisoner, that the rest of the states revolted and broke up into individual *taifas,* or petty kingdoms, vulnerable to the northern Visigothic invasions. One after another they were picked off by the Christian armies. It would take them three hundred more years to conquer.

This field of stones, these hints of decoration of a palace, did not fall into ruin from neglect or time or being forgotten. Madinat az-Zahra was beaten down, set afire, sacked, and destroyed by the mercenaries who roamed the country after the fall of Al-Mansur's dictatorship. For centuries it acted as an open grave where robbers could come and take what they pleased. It is said that much of the Mudejar *alcázar* built by Moorish artisans for Pedro the Cruel in Seville came from the ruins of Madinat az-Zahra.

THE END OF THE
RECONQUISTA

 So far my voyage of discovery had been mostly by chance, whipping along the highways and the mountain trails in a tough little European car with a manual shift, leaving Columbus, Magellan, and the rest of those to whom the unknown held less treachery than the known in my dust. I had only chosen ahead of time three people to see. I wanted to visit two women, and I did—the "mad" queen of Spain, and lovely, tough St. Teresa. The third was taking me toward Granada at last.

Otherwise, like Columbus, I had indeed sought something undefined, a direction that happened to be from north to south in a part of a country I did not know, and finding what I had not set out to discover.

I had crossed the Castilian *meseta* and found a sixteenth-century civil war; stopped in Zamora, where the earliest raids of the *Reconquista* had taken place, and found rowdy nuns and a war over a fish; stayed in the golden university city of Salamanca, haunted by Erasmus, Unamuno, and the Spanish civil war, and heard "Love Letters in the Sand." I had searched for the first home of the Lady of Guadalupe and found a three-thousand-year-old whistle; stopped at a beautiful Roman city and found that, once again, I disliked the whole of the Roman Empire, with its exported brutality.

The unplanned stops were on the way to Granada, my lovely city that I had known for years but never had seen. I was at last going for the first time to the city that had formed Federico García Lorca, the finest Spanish poet of the twentieth century.

On the way I had sought out the ancestors who had fought in South America and the south and the west of my own country. The maligned and honored *conquistadores,* like our own English-speaking invaders, had had to be the kind of men who for riches or for freedom were tough enough to face the great unknown. I had driven toward the south, on and on until, like the Christian Castilians, like their kings and their Goths and their soldiers, I had crossed three of the four great rivers that make up the map of the *Reconquista*— the Duero, the Tagus, the Guadiana, the Guadalquivir.

I was on the road from Córdoba east to Granada that had been a main trading road for the Carthaginians, the Romans, and was a main road of the caliphate. It was one of those finely cared-for minor roads of modern Spain. On every mountain crest, sky high above me in the distance, there was a fortress, a castle, a watchtower. It was a war zone. I felt as watched as the armies of Ferdinand and Isabel, the Catholic monarchs, who had come this way.

Even before I ever saw Granada, I sensed that I was going home over a familiar living and ancient landscape. Even though I went again and, God willing, will go again, the first time was the most innocent, the most ignorant, and so the most impassioned discovery.

I stopped at the most ancient place I saw in Spain,

Antequera, in Andalucia, "the old city," called ancient even by the Romans when they went there in the second century B.C., and found, on a hill on the outskirts of Antequera, three dolmans, prehistoric, maybe three or four thousand years old. Who knows? We only guess, as I am guessing now, standing again in the doorway of the largest burial chamber made of cleanly cut, smoothed walls of stone.

I was looking toward the mountains to the east, where the central peaks formed a sacred vision. It was the head in profile of a giant, a ragged profile, a man or a god, the size of the mountain crest, asleep. He seemed to be on guard over the barrier of the Puerto de los Alhazores mountains between Antequera and Granada.

When the last war of the *Reconquista* began in 1481, these were the mountains that the *caballeros* of Castile had to cross. They waited in the border city of Antequera for orders to attack, at last, the Moorish kingdom of Granada, the final stronghold of Islam in Spain.

They blamed Ferdinand for their delay. After all, Córdoba had been a Castilian city since 1236. They began to see his patience as weakness. Finally, like quail breaking cover, they decided to go on anyway. They pranced along the street through Antequera, under the intense sky of Andalucia, their banners waving, their flags alive as birds, their armor shining, some of it silver, some trimmed with gold, in a parade to war, so bright and so fine that they say in Antequera that people have seen them, the ghostly columns, ever since. They were followed by another army of camp followers and merchants, so sure that they were invincible that they were eager to be on hand to bargain with the soldiers for the treasure and the loot, the jewels of Granada, the gold of Málaga.

I followed their wild paths through sharp mountains, where

every crag seems still to have at its horizon a watchtower, an ancient castle, as if the Moors were still on watch all the way along the road to Granada. They had watched from the peaks that were passing far above me, as they had been when they saw the knightly banners, their gold and silver catching the sun and throwing it up to the watchers like signals. They had waited until the guides took the invaders into a nightmare of twisted roads, loose rocks, steep hillsides, sharp, incisive peaks. The Castilian army was caught there by the black, moonless night, watched always from the mountain towers, where the signal fires as far away as stars flared their coming.

They struggled in the enemy dark. They tried to escape in a blackness that had no direction, only the night fires circling above them. Some forced their mounts along the narrow paths and lost them and were found by Moorish watchmen familiar with their own land. Some tried to climb the steep mountainsides of rolling shale, loose rock, and sliding sand. The horses stumbled and fell far down the mountainsides. The knights lost footholds, crashed into the narrow defiles below. Finally the survivors found a valley that was flat enough for them to gather with what horses were left, but it was a trap, the Moors thought, sent by Allah.

The defenders of Granada threw down such a barrage of great stones on the struggling horses and their riders that the grand company was almost entirely wiped out. Those left, the few not killed or captured, limped back to Antequera, haunted and broken. For centuries afterwards, the crushed helmets, the breastplates of steel, the skeletons were found among the crags of these haunted mountains, guarded by the sleeping giant. A thousand prisoners were taken to be sold as slaves, or ransomed by their Spanish families.

A few escaped. One of them was the most talented fighter

in the armies of King Ferdinand and Queen Isabel, Rodrigo Ponce de León, of the family of our own *conquistador*. His nephew, Juan Ponce de León, was one of the few *caballeros* who would go beyond the unknown western ocean. He sailed with Columbus on his first voyage, and later discovered Florida.

I looked for the road south to the spa at Alhama de Granada. I wanted to go there because it was the place of the Lament of Boabdil, a folksong arranged by several composers from the old tune sung by countrymen and gypsies. The attack on Alhama in the winter of 1482 had been the most decisive battle for the city of Granada.

I wanted to find out why Alhama, not Granada, was mourned by Boabdil, the last king of Granada. It had been the strongest fortress protecting the city, and had fallen in one of the first major battles. It was only thirty miles to the west from Granada. It would be another ten years before those last miles were conquered.

The road crossed a deceptively high, hilly plateau with its endless precision of olive groves, a great chessboard of trees stretching over hills with spaces of golden crops. Here and there were small villages. They were old, and gleaming white in the sun, isolated like abandoned ships in a sea of spacious fields, sometimes vines, in a luxuriant landscape that seemed to go on forever.

At the turn to Alhama, the road dipped down a steep hill, over a small bridge at the bottom. A cliff-lined dirt road led to the small town of Alhama. I was astonished that I found so little there. I did not yet know that, in 1481, what had been a rich city had been almost totally destroyed by the Christian armies under Rodrigo Ponce de León, and that it has never recovered as the large commercial center it had been.

It has been a historic mystery that the soldiers would destroy and loot it so viciously. The food that they destroyed was needed for survival, since they were so far into the treacherous mountains. There is a report to King Ferdinand by Fernando del Pulgar, secretary and official historian to the Catholic monarchs, that gives a reason for some of what seemed mad destruction. L. P. Harvey, the historian who quoted it, comments that Pulgar was not a crazed ascetic!

The Christian soldiers found what was to their eyes a den of sin and luscious iniquity evil enough to be wiped off the face of the earth. Those alien people, the Moors of Alhama, which was a resort for the royal family and the rich Granadans, washed their bodies!

Pulgar was trying to find a reason why the assault was so devastating:

> . . . it had pleased God to show his wrath so suddenly and cruelly against them [the Alhaman townsfolk]. We discovered that very close [to Alhama] there are baths in a beautiful building where there is a natural hot spring. Thither men and women used to resort, both from the town itself and from the surrounding region in order to bathe. These baths were the cause of a certain softness in their bodies, and of excessive pleasure (*deleites*) from which there proceeded idleness (*ocios*) and other deceits and evil dealings which they inflicted on one another in order to sustain the ease to which they were accustomed.

The Christians took the castle and held it through one of the most violent Moorish assaults in the whole of the ten-year war for Granada. What is left of the city, which had been a major fortification along the protected border of Granada, and the favorite retreat of the king, known to history and more to song and legend as Boabdil, still seems empty.

Back at the bridge across the little Alhama River, there had been a sign pointing the way to the spa. I turned onto the country road through a deep, narrow gorge, its sides so high they darkened the sky. The gorge was a deep, secret wound in the high savannah I had driven over through the calm empty fields of the olive trees, the vines, the sun-drenched crops.

Just beyond the gorge, a few cars were parked in one of those places where in memory there is no time and you are simply there and then not there. It was a cool, green, leaf-canopied little valley where a river ran shallow. In what time past had it been a raging torrent that tore at the earth above us and carved the narrow gorge? Now it was quiet, an oasis, a dream place.

I walked to the center of another little bridge, shaded by old trees. I stopped to watch upstream, where fishermen cast their lines among the water-shaped rocks. Below me, down-stream, there must have been fifteen or twenty people, some playing on the rocks, some wading, but most of them quite still, with their feet and legs soaking in the rushing water of a spring that fell into a half-ruined small marble pool that must have been there in Roman times or before. One woman sat up to her waist, her shirt floating out around her. Another, a large, sick woman, was being carried by what must have been her relatives, maybe her sons, to the water. People who seemed to know her moved aside so they could lay her fully clothed body into the tumbling water, with her head resting on one of the stone sides of the pool. They were the local people of the town and, I suspect, for miles around who, from time immemorial had come to the hot spring for relief from the creaking of rheumatic limbs, the aches and pains of age or accident.

Across the bridge old trees shaded an earthen plaza, the trees' trunks huge and virgin, their shade a canopy the sun came through in frail rays of light. All around the plaza and along the road were buildings. Some looked nineteenth century, some ages older. There was no way to tell. But here was the place that had been made immortal by Boabdil's lament.

I made my way down among the rocks below the bridge. The men standing there gave me their hands to help me, and the women made room for me to sit down. I had fallen on a pebbled plaza at night and hurt my knee, which was swollen. I was limping. It seemed to make me one of them. I sat down in the place they had made for me, my Pool of Bethesda, and tried to answer their murmurs in Spanish with smiles and murmurs of my own. I put my legs into the hottest natural spring I had ever felt.

The quiet, the hospitality, the warmth of people and of water—no wonder Boabdil mourned it more than he did Granada itself, and his song was the song of timeless loss. No wonder that for so long modern composers have revived it. As a folk memory can do, it distills the story of the fall of Granada, and every stanza of the story ends with the voice of Boadbil singing, ¡Ay de mi Alhama!

It tells of a messenger arriving at the Gate of the Bib-Rambla in Moorish Granada to report the loss of Alhama to Boadbil's father, the emir, and of his killing the messenger for bringing terrible news. It tells of the call to arms and the rallying of the Moorish knights of the country of Granada when they heard of the fall, and blames the loss on the murder of one of the most honored clans of the kingdom, the Bencerrajes, "the flower of Granada."

No one in this new millennium should ignore what happened in Granada in 1492. Al-Andalus. Andalucia. Spain. It was one of the first places mentioned as having been stolen from the Muslims in an early televised Osama bin Laden tirade of bitterness and intent. Few in this country knew where it was or what he was talking about. He was using ancient hurts, ancient trials, ancient brutalities, to fuel his own modern hatred.

In the city of Granada, within one year, the weathervane of the world turned, and the lives of all of us in what was once called Christendom were thrust into a new direction. It was then that the final sword of the *Reconquista* was plunged into the earth of Spain, the triumphant end of over seven hundred years of the retaking of the Iberian peninsula.

Perhaps there should be an unnamed, unexplained, and unhallowed shrine to wonder and mistakes, that put us all here instead of there. A new westward tribal flow began, not across the frozen Rhine but across the North and South Atlantic Ocean. Decisions were made in 1492 that have taken Spain centuries of rigidity and civil war to face, and from which it is finally recovering. It was in 1492 that the final acts of conquest took place, not only of the Moors but of the Spanish people themselves. A whole section of what is now Spain lost a tolerance in religion and in law and set religious fear in its place.

The fall of the last Muslim emirate on the Iberian peninsula, the planned and carried-out persecution and expulsion of the Jews, the official discovery of America, which opened up the most revolutionary new scope for the tribes of Europe to find land, and dispossess the native tribes of an unknown continent—all of it began within that one year in that city, Granada.

The Battle of Las Navas de Tolosa in 1212, when vast Muslim lands fell to the Christian north and when loot and land made the Christians drunk with new power, was the last of the major battles from 1212 to the reign of Ferdinand and Isabel, which began in 1474. The border raids never stopped, but for two hundred and fifty years after Tolosa, north and the south lived officially in some kind of amity. There was trade between them, and recognitions of local sovereignty seesawing with attempts to starve out the towns, but there had been more peace than at any other time in the seven hundred years of the *Reconquista.*

One small *taifa* or local tribal kingdom after another which had grown up after the end of the caliphate of Córdoba was occupied by the Castilians and their allies. Córdoba itself in 1236, Seville in 1248. That was the year that finally the last great river of the *Reconquista,* the Guadalquivir, was crossed.

The Mudejars were left to worship as they pleased. They went on working the land as they had done for nearly a millennium, only for new masters of the *latifundios* granted by the Christian kings to favorite *grandes,* most of whom had been rewarded as border raiders. It was during this long time that the three religions, Christianity, Judaism, and Islam, lived side by side in some measure of amity. There seemed to be little interest in conversion, forced or otherwise. There was intermarriage among the "old" Christians, and among the Jewish and Muslim families and especially the early *conversos.*

It seems inevitable among the most ferocious animals in the world, humans, that the conqueror should look down with contempt on the conquered. The Muslims became known as Mudejars in the newly acquired parts of Andalucia. Their talents and their skills were used to build churches, houses, and monasteries all through the conquered lands. I had seen this in Zamora, and even more in Guadalupe.

The western part of Andalucia was good for grazing, so that the Castilians who immigrated there, and who were given the great grants of land, knew how to use land as pasture. It was a kind of farming they had used for centuries in the *meseta* and the valleys of Castile. There, today, the fine Spanish/Arab horses, the fighting bulls, still graze the fields.

The still unconquered Granada and its surrounding *vega* was a garden. It was the most fertile, lush, and beautiful in all of Andalucia. Pure water ran out of the thirteen-thousand-foot-high mountains that surrounded its capital, the white city of Granada. Snow lay on the crests of the Sierra Nevada, which protected its lush green *vega*. In the conquered parts of Andalucia, there was an ever-growing minority who chose to emigrate to the emirate of Granada instead of staying in the newly Christian cities.

The city of Granada was so beautiful that it was famous throughout Europe. In 1350, Ibn Battuta, the medieval Muslim traveler, reached Spain. He described Granada as "the capital of Al-Andalus and the bride of its cities . . . it is surrounded on all sides by orchards, gardens, meadows, palaces and vineyards."

The city became, through the last two centuries of Moorish rule, a distillation of all that Al-Andalus had stood for at its best, through over seven hundred years. It had long been a center for artists in metal, gold and silver, weapons, the silk industry, the home of a revived Arabic, of poets, philosophers. It was, for the rest of the world, a jewel, until it, too, by the mid-fifteenth century, was tipped on the edge of disaster by family quarrels.

The emirate of Granada had been formed by the first emir of the Nasrid tribe, Muhammed I, who had been a local farmer but who claimed ancestry in the ancient caliphate. For protection against the various Christian kingdoms who were nibbling at the borders of Al-Andalus, he put it under the protection of Ferdinand VII, the king of Castile, the conqueror of the *taifa* of Córdoba.

By 1480, the border had moved to the east of Seville; Gibraltar, Ronda, Antequera in the center of what had been Al-Andalus had been conquered by Christian armies. These last moves of the *Reconquista* prepared the way for the final tragedy, which was not primarily the conquest but the despotism that came after it. It was a war waiting to begin and had been ever since the accession of the combined rulers of Castile and Aragon, Ferdinand of Aragon and Isabel of Castile.

Isabel was extremely intelligent, wary as a street urchin, and soon to show that she was one of the most practical housekeepers of a kingdom in Europe. She had chosen borders rather than people to marry, both for herself and her children—England, Portugal, and, instead of France, the inherited enemy, she skipped over to the Low Countries to contain France both from the east and the west, and made a marital alliance with the Holy Roman Empire. Her decisions were made on a map.

When Ferdinand finally inherited the crown of the kingdom of Aragon in 1479, they ruled jointly. Isabel the Catholic became, in the hands of her spiritual advisors, a religious fanatic. It was a devastating weakness.

The joint kingdoms of Aragon and Castile were poised on

the frontier of Granada, which, for so long had paid tribute to Castile to keep the peace. But in 1481, on the first of April, the old emir of Granada, Abu'l Hassan, a man in love with war since his childhood, refused to pay his tribute to the Catholic monarchs, and surprised the unwary castle of Zahara, in the mountains of the Sierra Margarita, less than sixty miles from Seville.

Because there had been so little major action on the frontier for so long, he was completely successful, and he woke the war that would destroy the Moors in Spain. It would take ten more years of rough and killing warfare in the mountains where the land took as many lives as the enemy.

The old man had made so many enemies in Granada that it was said he went to war—as so many other heads of state have done before and since—to consolidate his power.

The Christian armies besieged Granada for so long that they were able to build a city, made up of material from villages they had taken and laid waste. They named the city Santa Fe, holy faith. It was only eight miles from Granada. There Ferdinand and Isabel held their court during the last of the long years of their seige of the city.

The petitioners who always followed where the court led gathered at Santa Fe. One of them was a Genoese who had tried to sell a plan in Italy, Portugal, wherever he could, and whose last hope was to interest Ferdinand and Isabel in what most people around the court laughed at as a cockamamy scheme to sail west to reach the east in a more economical and safer route to the Indies. Of course he was refused by the monarchs, that is, when he could get close enough in the crowds of courtiers, soldiers, whores, and priests to speak to them. He so lost hope that he finally gave up and started back to the west of Spain, where he had left his son. It was, of course, a disappointed and bedraggled Christopher Columbus who rode slowly back to the west on an old mule.

When the campaign had begun, ten years before, and Ferdinand and Isabel were keeping their court in Córdoba, it was rumored that Isabel took a vow not to change her underwear until Granada fell. That was the word among the ladies of Granada, so when she rode in state into the city ten years later, it was said the ladies giggled at her from behind the wooden harem grills of their windows. Of course this is only one of the legends that have long since replaced little naked facts about the end of the *Reconquista*. But sometimes, like the editor advised in John Huston's movie about Judge Roy Bean, if you have to make a choice between the facts and the legend it is better to print the legend.

It was finally Boabdil who surrendered the last jewel of Spanish Islam to Ferdinand and Isabel. In the ten years of war, the fields had been burned, the villages uprooted, and the beloved green *vega* had become a deserted, brown no-man's-land. The people of Granada were starving when he finally surrendered the city.

No pomp and grandiose entry into a city has been so documented, minute by minute, as the royal Christian entry into Granada, trumpets blowing, the flags of Castile and Aragon whipping in the wind, the shining armor, the crossing of the *vega*. The procession stopped while the whole army and the court knelt on the wasted earth in prayer and the singing of the "Te Deum" was heard all the way into the city, where a great silver cross caught the sun above the highest tower of the Alhambra, the Vela. Yet another of the political wars for water and grass and power, that used Christianity and Islam as excuses, had ended at last.

Boabdil slipped out of a gate in the Alhambra that has

been closed ever since. With a few retainers, he rode east into the mountains to meet his household and his family, who had gone ahead to wait for him to hand over of the keys to the city.

When he heard the artillery roar in celebration of victory, he began to cry, and his warlike mother said, "You may well weep like a woman for what you could not defend as a man." His life was tragic. The mountain pass where he stopped to look back is still known as "the Sigh of the Moor." Isabel had finally captured enough loot to take a chance on Christopher Columbus.

When she heard that he had left the court she sent a messenger after him to tell him that she had decided to back his scheme. Ever the most practical of rulers, she also is said to have sent money and word that he should buy a new mule and some clothes so he would not cut such a drab figure at the triumphant court.

Ferdinand and Isabel moved into the Alhambra, the most beautiful palace in Spain, and one that today brings people from all over the world to see it. How it has survived over the years from the time of the Christian takeover to now is one of the miracles of both rescue and care.

The first thing that the monks who were preparing the palace for the king and queen did was cover the offending scrolls, tiles, and decorations with whitewash in every room in the Alhambra. The intention was to conceal any Muslim calligraphy and sinful symbolism there might be. The fine *azulejos* had been introduced into Granada from what is now Turkey by the Seljuk Turks, who had brought the way of making them from China, which is why china is called china.

The surrender agreements between Boabdil and the Catholic monarchs were fair to both sides. The combined troops of Aragon and Castile would occupy the cities, both Alhama and Granada. A triumvirate was left to govern Granada: the Count of Tendilla, one of the Mendoza family, was the civilian governor; Hernando de Talavera was made first archbishop of Granada—he knew Arabic and had an interest in studying Islam; Hernando de Zafra was the royal secretary. One of the earliest acts of the new rulers was to close the sinful public baths and make washing the body unlawful. St. Ignatius Loyola once punished a young monk for using soap to wash his hands.

Under the Capitulations, which was the name given to the surrender document, the Muslims of Granada were to remain Muslim, with their own laws and their own clergy. Some loot by the Christian armies was to be returned. It was, on the whole, a fair and tolerant compromise. The Granadan Muslims had made sure that the Jews, of whom there were many in Granada, were included in the dispensations. These choices, both of governors and compromises, showed that at first the monarchs intended to keep their pledges.

It was not so with the Jews. The Cardinal Archbishop Francisco Jiménez de Cisneros was the most powerful man in Spain, outside of the rulers themselves. Otherwise an intellectual, tolerant man, he was an almost insane religious fanatic, one who today would be called an extreme right-wing fundamentalist. Of course such fanaticism was completely accepted by the fanatic queen.

The combined monarchs had acquired an unprecedented power in the church; they had persuaded the pope to put the Holy Inquisition in Spain under their command. It became their strongest asset, their bank, their mode of punishment that could not be questioned. For the first time European monarchs controlled the Catholic Church in their own domains. There had been *autos de fe* against the *conversos* for a long time—anti-Semitic riots, especially in Toledo. But there never had been an absolute order to convert or leave Spain until 1492, when, at Santa Fe, in the same month of the surrender, Cardinal Jiménez demanded that the monarchs force conversion on the Jews. It was the beginning of the end for the three religions to live side by side as they had for the centuries of the Middle Ages.

There is a famous Spanish painting of Ferdinand and Isabel receiving a delegation from the Granadan Jews offering to help back the peaceful takeover of Granada, where Jews were a strong and wealthy minority in the community. To this offer they added a contribution of thirty-thousand *maravedís* to help rebuild the decimated city. The meeting was interrupted by Cardinal Jiménez, who, in the painting, is seen at the moment he is supposed to have shouted that Judas betrayed Christ for thirty pieces of silver and the Catholic monarchs were about to betray Him again for thirty-thousand.

Jiménez became the voice and power of the Spanish monarchs in Granada. His fanaticism and impatience was let loose; ten years of careful and tolerant work by the triumvirate who had ruled Granada was replaced by the jackboot of Cardinal Jiménez. The treaty was overturned.

In the Bibrambla, then the *plaza mayor* of Granada, the punishment center was set up, and the killings and the tortures began. Jiménez insisted not only that the Muslims convert to orthodox Catholic Christianity or leave the country but that Muslims whose ancestors had been Christian seven hundred years before when the Moors won Al-Andalus were to go back to their ancestors' religion, or leave for exile from the place that had been their *patria chica* for centuries. There had been thousands of them through the centuries of Islam. Agree or leave or be punished. Once again, as it has in totalitarian regimes for centuries, and would, as we know too well, be the only choice for centuries more, religious orthodoxy was the only law, and any deviation was heresy and punishable.

The deaths took place in the Bibrambla. So did the burning of books in Arabic, copies of the Koran, any vestige of Moorish culture. Some of their dyed leather covers were chased in gold with beautiful designs. Many of them were illuminated manuscripts, so many heirlooms in families, as the family Bible would be. The flames of the book burnings and the *auto da fe* destroyed most of the ancient libraries. Only a few of the books on science were left, and those were put under lock and key. It was not the Imperial army but the religious madness of the Spanish Inquisition that cleaned up nonconformists as if they were termites.

One of the misapprehensions about democracy is that it is the rule of the majority, leaving out its other and more revolutionary premise, the protection of the minority. Overkill had replaced tolerance. The ten years' work of the tolerant Count of Tendilla, the archbishop, and King Ferdinand lay in ruins. Instead of a governed populace, there was a sullen minority who felt betrayed. But they were patient people. Many of them who had the means to do so exiled themselves to Morocco and Fez. It took fifty years for those who had to stay to revolt against the overbearing influx of Castilians who were there as a result of the pressure by the monarchy and the church to make Granada, as they did Córdoba and Seville, into a Spanish Christian city.

How modern such brutal overkill sounds. I am reminded of two lines of William Butler Yeats:

> The best lack all conviction, while the worst
> are full of passionate intensity.

There is some hint that the queen may have regretted her decision. The cardinal was exiled from the court for a while as a reaction to his treatment of the people of Granada.

Queen Isabel cannot be judged for being of her time and under the influences she had been trained by since she was born. She had feared for her life; she had been the cause of a civil war; she had married judiciously against the wishes of the court of Castile. But the good influences which have given her the reputation as Spain's greatest queen do not outweigh the harm she did in the long run. Still, she would not be lauded as the great queen of Spain, as Elizabeth was in England, had she not earned it.

So it is an even greater tragedy for the country that her decisions in Granada after the triumph of which she was so proud and so praised should be so terrible a blot on her reign. Ferdinand seems not to have agreed with her. He saw it as a financial matter, not as a religious crusade. Besides, he had *converso* blood himself.

But Isabel, the little round fanatic Catholic queen was influenced by Cardinal Jiménez to set Spain on a course that would take centuries to get over, the expulsion of the most intellectual, of the best business community, and of the richest and most powerful groups in their kingdoms, who had been a part of both the Christian and the Moorish governments for centuries. She and Jiménez tore the intelligence out of the body of Spanish people and set fear in its place. If there seemed to be little reaction even at the time, the Inquisition was there to quell criticism as heresy.

In 1504, Ferdinand and Isabel ordered that a new chapel be built in Granada as their burial place and as a monument to the Christian triumph in Granada. Isabel left orders that her body should be buried quietly and that money from any extravagant funeral should be used for the poor. She died later that year. Her body was taken to the Monastery of St. Francis on the Alhambra hill until the memorial was finished.

Her wishes were far from being honored. The chapel seen today as an attachment to the cathedral in Granada, built on the place where the Friday Mosque had stood, is the most elaborate, finest example of early Gothic/Renaissance art found in Spain. The leading sculptors in Spain and in Italy were rounded up to decorate it when Charles V became king, and central European art married Isabelline gaudy to become a new architecture.

The two tombs, put there by Charles V, are of splendid Carrara marble, so intricately carved that they simply cannot be taken in quickly. American gold graced them; the finest Spanish grillework in Spain separated the two tombs from the chapel. Both the chapel and the sacristy are stuffed with saints, griffins, classic figures, apostles, and through a passage into what was a sacristy there are wonderful things: Queen Isabel's crown, King Ferdinand's sword, paintings by Hans Memling that are unforgettable treasures, a triptych by Bouts, both of these favorites of Isabel and left by her for the chapel. The paintings are Flemish; Charles and his advisors must have given them to her. Gold reliquaries, gold everywhere.

I am so sorry that I saw it first after seeing the Alhambra. I had to go again to realize how magnificent it is. There they lie, idealized on their marble beds, asleep, Ferdinand and

Isabel, and their hated son-in-law, Philip the Fair, and the ideally beautiful marble wife he and all the rest treated with year after year of brutal jailing and cold disdain.

But in the sacristy are three treasures more valuable to me than anything in the chapel. On either side of an altar kneel two life-sized figures. They are both small. Their clothes are painted, and their faces are obviously portraits from life or at least within the lifetime of many who could guide the sculptor. King Ferdinand is dressed in a red robe over a gold dress. His hands are clasped in prayer. His hair is cut like a sixties rock star. He looks like he has lived a fairly hard life; maybe the circles under his eyes are from riotous living, maybe they are from his wife, who kneels on the other side of the altar.

Isabel is dressed in gold. She has a healthy bosom. She is very young looking, solemn, her cheeks full, her mouth in a tiny smile. She stares at nothing. It was these two who did so much to change the world. There is a third figure, obviously by the same sculptor. It is Charles V, not the Holy Roman Emperor on a horse, not the old man at Yuste, but a boy of about eighteen before he could grow a beard, with the heavy Hapsburg chin that embarrassed him all his life.

It is said that even today there are families in Fez and Morocco who retain the keys to the houses they lost in Granada.

GRANADA

 Granada is the most beautiful city that I have ever seen. Years before I saw it I longed to be there—not to go, that is different. Sometimes when I am there I still long for its essence, its familiarity, the sight of it. No wonder the most familiar remark about the city is that of the Mexican poet Francisco de Asis de Icaza, "Give him alms, woman. For there is nothing in life so cruel as to be blind in Granada."

The beautiful green *vega* surrounds it for mile after mile, its protection in the womb of a valley among the mountains of the Sierra Nevada that keep it so contained, and so heart-breakingly lovely.

When I drove east from Alhama I took the narrow old road where so many armies, so many invaders, so many defenders, so many refugees had passed. I drove by a few old, small truck farms, called *huertas,* with vegetable gardens and livestock and the inevitable vines for grapes and flowers. *Huertas* once had surrounded Granada, fed it, and provided homes for families who liked to live quietly in the country near the city. So I approached the city as I wanted to see it first, unexaggerated, not as a modern city over a six-lane highway.

Granada has always been talked and written about as something alive, something human. A human size, a human history, good or sometimes terrible, both weighed as part of that sad white city in the distance in a green bowl under the snow-peaked mountains of the Sierra Nevada. In the background on what seems to be the first hill, nearer the mountains, the *Colina Roja,* the Red Hill, the towers of the *alcazaba,* the walls of the Alhambra.

It was ideal to arrive at sunset. The Alhambra is east of the city and the light pours down on it, the red and purple where low, dark clouds were brushed by the last of the sun. I drove around the city below, across the river, and up the mountain to the Alhambra, where millions of people have gone to see a jewel, or capture it, or destroy it. All of these things have happened.

My room in the hotel was an accident that was a miracle. It was only nine feet square, one wall a window to the floor, with a perfect view of the towers of the Alhambra, half buried in trees. A haven where I, too, could work. A nun's cell painted red. So by the next morning as I climbed the hill, I already had the picture of it all in my mind, a whole place in the distance unchanged in six hundred years. I did not know yet how wrong I was.

I joined a line of tourists from everyplace, in the kind of crocodile that sophisticated travelers in Europe avoid, often to their loss. The guide yelled directions, facts, and history censored by legend. The words drifted behind him, half-heard in the wind of the hill. When it was our turn to follow those who entered the Gate of Justice in French, in Spanish, in Japanese, in German, we trooped along in English.

We passed under the high semicircle of an arch, like a giant keyhole, the Gate of Justice. On the tower above it the faint outline of a large hand is carved. On the stone lintel of the great door the guide said there was a large key carved, but I could not find it, at any angle of light, even stretching my hand up to try to feel its shape. Maybe time, or the Castilians, or the French have removed it, and it exists only as part of the legend.

But the hand is still there; it has been explained and explained, so I will add my own thoughts. I think it is the Hand of Fatima, one of the most sacred icons in a religion that is supposed to have no human images. There is, of course, a legend, that when the hand reaches down and grasps the key and opens the Gate of Justice, the Moors will return to Granada.

We followed our guide to a large plaza, where we were another small huddle of strangers in a crowd. Hundreds of tourists waited, young and old. Some of them had been there for a long time, long enough to find comfort. They leaned on elegantly scrolled old cannons with Arabic designs in brass. They lounged on the pavement under the trees, some asleep with their backpacks as pillows, some eating their breakfasts. They didn't seem to be tourists at all, for they sat and lounged as people always do in parks and plazas in Spain, finding shade, choosing sun, in an ancient *plaza mayor* of a royal city called Alhambra that has disappeared.

Time has taken the name of the royal city of Alhambra and given it to the palace itself. Camp, fortress, village, it had been a place to live as "king on the mountain" and rule

the *vega* as long ago as the people who made the cave paintings of Altamira.

On one side of the plaza a vast unexpected alien building
interfered with the sky. It was made of blocks of gray granite,
built for power, dominance over delicacy, a thick, brute wall,
out of place in my expectations. On the other side, with a
view down toward the path we had climbed, beyond that the
trees, we could gaze into the distance at the city of Granada,
and beyond that to the west, where I had come from, the
Sierra Alhama. We leaned our elbows on an ancient wall, at
a height for humans to lean on and tell stories and lies, gossip, wait. Time didn't matter.

It was finally our turn. We followed the guide through
another gate, the Gate of Wine; the name itself gives the lie
to those who think that Muslims do not drink. There, in the
sun ahead of us, were the high rough towers of the *alcazaba,*
the timeless watchtowers over the *vega,* to the distant western mountains of Alhama. I thought it was the Alhambra and
sighed. This was no lovely fairytale palace. It was as strong a
fortress as any other hilltop castle all the way down the
Spain I had traveled, following the route of the *Reconquista.*

We did not go in. Instead we wandered slowly after our
guide along an esplanade to the right, past a row of trees.
Beyond the esplanade, we were shepherded along a small,
half-hidden path. There was a garden courtyard below us on
our left, a row of delicate columns that made a porch for a
small building. On our right a gray, harsh, obscuring high
wall diminished us, made everything seem small, the garden
opposite it, the building and the columns frail instead of delicate. It was the wall of the huge granite building that squat-
ted over all. Charles V, the grandson of Ferdinand and Isabel,

had proceeded to have part of the Alhambra palace and city torn down to build his own granite palace, which has remained unfinished ever since, its vast round courtyard empty, its rooms now a museum.

If that building were anywhere else it would be praised as one of the finest Renaissance buildings of his reign. I tried to imagine it with space around it, and I could see that it could be magnificent, massive, formal. But it is so out of place, thrust up against the Alhambra, too gray, too huge. Looming over the small Moorish palace, it looks like an elephant's footprint in a delicate garden. Only when I tried to forget, too, what lies behind it, and under it, the mosque to the palace of Alhambra, many of the private rooms, gardens, halls, and the Moorish white houses of the city that once housed ten thousand people, could I begin to appreciate its architectural value. Cold comfort. A vast indignity.

We entered the first room of the Moorish palace. If you cannot relearn wonder again at the Alhambra, you may as well stay at home and die. Even after centuries of destruction and change, there is still a miraculous oasis of beauty and calm, a silence that is felt even when there are crowds from all over the world, almost wall to wall in the rooms. The silence is there behind the murmur of thousands of visitors. They even stroll, almost body to body, quietly. I have never seen a place, including churches and tombs, that so demands silence. But not complete silence.

The Alhambra is never empty. It is inhabited by swooping, circling swallows, who fill the air with wings, high and at head height, though they seem never to touch the crowds below them.

I was beginning to see an architectural oasis. Literally.

The trees were the incredibly delicate columns' capitals with their pierced leafy foliage of marble. The water that is the center of the being of an oasis has come to the fountains and the pools for centuries from the Darro River, fed by springs in the Sierra Nevada. The most famous is the *Ainadamar* to the Muslims, the *Fuente Grande* to the Spanish, Fountain of Tears in English.

The Arabs named it for its effervescent sounds, its trickling water, and they built their summer mountain retreats around it, lacelike pavilions that are long gone. It is a large, stone-lined pond in the shape of a horseshoe, where, at one end, the water pours, as it has for all the centuries since it was confined by its wall, murmuring and muttering and sighing its course down the mountain to join the river and flow into the cisterns of the Albaicin, the Moorish section of the city, and the fountains of the Alhambra.

The water has been lifted to the top of the hill by a system that has been there since the thirteenth century, when the oldest part of the palace was built. Rivulets of it flow through the rooms in the runnels that lead to and from the floor-level fonts, and when the floors are wet, there is a reflection of the columns so that the rooms seem to float. The spray of the fountains feeds the gardens, the trees. Water from the mountain controls the sound, the scent, and has made a green haven of what had begun as a bare desert stone upthrust in a wild and fertile valley.

When I think of a palace I see grandeur, the one in Madrid of 1,800 rooms; the huge Escorial; in England, Windsor and Hampton Court; in France, Versailles. The palace of the Alhambra is small, intimate, truly a home, or once a home, human size, personal. That, I think, is what has haunted it ever since, the departure and the closing of the last door by the last Moorish king, Mohammed XII, Boabdil, the man they call in Granada King Chico.

But there are so many other reasons for the haunting reminders that are planted deep in the land and the people and the cities of Andalucia, in the language, the music, the dancing, the houses, the white villages, the decoration, and above all the names of the cities. The Moorish culture is still woven so into the Spanish soul that all the centuries of denial and of trying to remove it have failed. To have succeeded in removing it would have been like trying to remove a part of the heart from the human body. Thank God they have failed, for their sake and for ours. The Spanish people at last are seeing and honoring their true past, not that imposed by the legends of an authoritarian Gothic state.

We were led into the oldest of the rooms left, the public courtroom, where petitions and punishments were decided. The tiles are the most formal there, the columns heavy as ancient trees, with heavy crowns. With the crowded international flock there were only glimpses of the floor and the ceiling, part of the walls, at the end of the room a finely carved gallery that stretched from wall to wall.

The crowds were carefully herded so that there would not be too many people in any one of the frail rooms. But there are so many that every room seems full, and the languages were spoken softly, intimately to each little clutch of tourists gathered around their guide, as we shuffled past the Germans, the Japanese, many young Spaniards, Arabs whose ancestors had built it.

They, we, all of us stared at the walls, the ceilings; so much, so intricate, so delicate. The rooms seem all to be entered by evasive hallways, labyrinthine. It was our turn to follow slowly into a columned porch. In front of us, across a small courtyard, a gold façade reached to roof height. To see so grand a façade in so small a space is the kind of appearance that is the architecture of dreams.

We passed through one of two tile-framed doors in the façade. Beyond it we were led to the left into a wide corridor of an Aladdin's cave. The high ceiling was made up of a series of vaults hung with what look like crystalline stalactites. They are a form of hanging tile called in Arabic *muqarnas*. The series of ceiling vaults ended, not in a door, but a wall, that went no place in this crystal maze. There was a seat, and nothing else. But at the right sunlight showed another small door. We were herded through it, into the Court of the Ambassadors.

There was not a bare wall or ceiling in the interior of the entry and the room beyond. They were, literally, precious, glowing open sesames. The ceiling of the throne room was sixty feet high, the walls covered with graffiti—poems, mottoes, sayings, *sura* from the Koran—all in graceful gold Arabic.

In front of the Hall of the Ambassadors a long pool of still water stretched for fifty feet to the other end of the courtyard, where there was a line of columns. Down both sides of the pool green shrubs of myrtle were planted. We were in the Court of the Myrtles. This was where the visitors to the court could stroll and maybe pray for what they wanted, while away in the distance in the belvedere of the Hall of the Ambassadors the emir sat enthroned, cross-legged on a gold platform covered with brocade, and dispensed favors or death.

When we walked to the other end of the pool and stood looking back, the huge Comares tower that made up the top room of the Hall of the Ambassadors was reflected in the pool as in a mirror. From one of the high windows of a room below where we stood, Boabdil, when a young prince, had been let down seventy feet to the ground by his mother and her ladies on strips of scarves tied together to escape death at the hands of his father.

A very small round bird that could fit into my hand was strolling, completely at home among the feet of the crowd, paying no attention, disdaining being stepped on. It rose quietly and flew toward the Hall of the Ambassadors and disappeared into its nest, lodged in the white filigree of the façade of the throne room.

There were no impressive huge doors to go through in our labyrinthine walk. The camouflage of a maze was subtly there as we went from room to room. We were not there and then we were there, as wanderers within the Court of Lions, one of the most superbly beautiful man-made places that I have ever seen. If the palace has a heart, and it does, it is there, among the most delicate, most beautiful columns, as frail as air, surrounding a space that is the glowing center of the palace.

At each end pavilions define the shape of the open courtyard with copses of columns, their capitals marble lace. The whole court is as geometric as a poem, the pavilions at the end where there are floor fountains, the great fountain in the middle surrounded by twelve faintly gilded and painted, almost comic lions on guard. There are cross-channels carved into the floor from the fountain to the two most beautiful semiprivate rooms of the palace that are on show, for there is much of it still hidden.

On the right is the Hall of the Bencerrajes, the tribe that is mentioned in the lament of Boabdil. *"Mataste los abencerrajes."* "You slaughtered the Bencerrajes." It was they who had been invited to a banquet by the sultan, to make peace. As many as thirty were supposed to have been beheaded in this room. And it is said that it happened because they had backed Boabdil in the civil war against his father, Abu'l Hasan.

A huge crystalline eight-pointed star covers the ceiling, almost from wall to wall. Below it, a floor-level fountain reflects the star in the water. It was beside it that the guests of the sultan were beheaded. There are brown stains in the marble that are said to be their blood.

The Hall of the Two Sisters, opposite, has no such dramatic story, but it does contain the gold scrolling of calligraphy, and, looking toward the north to a courtyard below, is a jeweled belvedere that looks out over gardens, and other towers that may be as beautiful as this but are more mysterious, because they are not shown. But around the courtyard below the window is a balcony, and on the east side of it a series of rooms that look, even from the belvedere, somehow out of place.

They are the rooms built and decorated for the honeymoon of Charles V on his marriage to the beautiful and wise Isabel of Portugal, whom he fell in love with, even though it was a perfect regal marriage. This was the woman whose portrait hung with that of his mother Juana, whom he kept in prison for forty-four years, in the room were the old man died at Yuste.

But for me the rooms are much more then that. On my wandering from north to south, I had seen so much of Castilian grandness, royalty, and Isabelline gold ornament splashed over anything that would hold it that it was a joy for me to be in those simple rooms of the Charles V apartments, where a young American had lived for several months, looked out as I was looking, east to the Sierra Nevada. It was there that he sat at a table in the room and wrote down what he heard, what he saw, and what he researched in the Jesuit

Library with its forgotten records of the Alhambra in the reign of the Catholic monarchs.

The man was Washington Irving, then a young diplomat in the service of the new United States, and the year was 1829. He had ridden with two friends from Córdoba to Granada along roads that were "little better than mule paths, and said to be frequently beset by robbers." They were armed, and accompanied by a "guide, groom, and valet," one twenty-year-old man. "We were determined to travel in true *contra-bandista* style, taking things as we found them, rough or smooth, and mingling with all classes and conditions in a kind of vagabond companionship." Was I, not knowing, imitating Washington Irving as I, too, traveled, taking things as I found them? I hope so.

Washington Irving was to spend six months living in the Alhambra, which had been turned over to a housekeeper by the governor of Granada, who had moved the official residence down into the city below. She seems to have run it as a pleasant and down-at-the-heels boardinghouse. In Irving's time what had been decorations of royal apartments were, as is so much of the palace, covered with whitewash.

For those of us who see it as one of the most beautiful and magic palaces in the world, Washington Irving's choice of cheap lodging was the most fortunate choice ever to happen to the Alhambra. His book *The Alhambra* has been translated into more languages than any other American writer's. It has brought thousands of visitors to Granada through the years since, and its popularity shamed the nineteenth-century Spanish government into beginning a serious effort to revive the place. In effect, his book of memories, legends, and opinions, has been one of the leading influences in the effort to save this jewel for all of us.

His writing is, to me, as magical as the *Arabian Nights*, although much of it has been ignored by serious scholarship—it was written in a time when romantic language was taken for granted. But the language does not obscure the facts, it only tends to veil them. Think of the Court of the Lions, that haunted place at night at the dark of the moon. On the first night that he tried to sleep in his new rooms, Irving kept hearing sounds, and finally, to keep himself from panicking, he took a candle and went out to explore the Court of the Lions. From under the marble floor he heard moans and screams. He admitted to coming back to his room faster than he left it. He found out the next morning that it was "only" a family relative, locked up in one of the rooms below, who had gone crazy.

But my favorite of his exploits is when he went swimming alone in the pool of the Court of the Ambassadors to cool down on a hot summer night.

The Alhambra has been written about in pejorative terms by the English traveler Richard Ford, who was there in the 1830s. To him the Spanish were thieves, vagabonds, liars, ignorant and dirty. But, then, the English have forever been grumpy visitors to Europe. They have never gone with a "disposition to be pleased." The donkey is always too old, too frisky, or breaking down, the dragoman is lazy, the food is terrible, and the countryside is drab compared to England. Italy is one of the few countries to escape this, and even there they speak so little English!

But Richard Ford's picture of Spain in the early to mid-nineteenth century is the most complete to be found in English. What he said about the Alhambra is cold-eyed. He saw a slum. Minor government officials had torn the tiles from the walls of the palace and sold them; goats were penned in the courtyard, which was all that was left of the mosque; explosives were piled in the rooms. (Washington Irving reported this to the American chargé d'affaires in Madrid, and he brought pressure on the local Spanish officials to remove them.) For centuries the papers of Ferdinand and Isabel were piled to the ceiling of the Hall of the Ambassadors, locked up and protected against rabid historians, but not against rats and rot.

But most of all, Ford put down in detail the last awful destruction by the French, who had occupied the Alhambra for several years during the Peninsula Campaign of the Napoleonic Wars, from 1806 to 1814, in which France fought the Spanish *guerrilleros,* and later the British army under the Duke of Wellington.

A digression which is not a digression—I should not, at my age, by surprised by almost any connection I find, but the regiments sent to fight my great-grandfather, who was a Kentucky volunteer in the War of 1812, had fought for Wellington in that vicious mountain campaign in Spain, some of them so brutally that they faced courts-martial when they returned to England after the war.

Part of the palace and the little city that surrounded the palace—a public mosque, a market, and several mansions, some poorer houses—had been pulled down long since for the construction of Charles V's elephant's foot of a palace. Almost all the rest was destroyed by the French army to make a parade ground. So what you walk in now, a plaza between the palaces and the *alcazaba*, with its high towers at a western point of the Alhambra, was part of the French barracks.

But the most important fact that Irving points out and that Ford ignores is that the central rooms of the Alhambra were repaired and saved by the French commandant, who had decided to live in them. When the French retreated toward the end of the Peninsula Campaign, they destroyed everything they could, several towers, powder magazines, some more houses. But, fortunately for us, the retreat was so hasty that they didn't finish their planned destruction.

That was my first visit. The second was in another and more lonely time, as it should have been, for the Alhambra is a lonely place, a place of suppressed whispers and sighs, even when there are hundreds of people walking through it. But to be there in its essence is to be there alone, as I was alone in the last morning of my visit to Granada.

After most of the tourist crowds had left at the end of October, I went, on that last morning, to stand with the most intrepid and buy my ticket for a last few hours of living in the Alhambra. It was also the last day of daylight savings time, so that in the early morning it was still dark. Shadow people, only five or six of them, stood around, waiting for the ticket office to open. Later there were Japanese, Germans, several Spaniards, but I was the only American. I was first in a little cold line.

So when I had my ticket I walked alone up that deep morning twilight of the path that I had followed for days of seeking the woods, the ruins, the surprises of the red hill. Ahead of me the now familiar Gate of Justice was isolated in the half-dark.

I walked through the shadows between the Charles V palace and the little Alhambra, and at eight-thirty was there to be let in. Had there been voices in the Court of Justice, they would have echoed in emptiness, but there were no voices. It was silence that echoed there. Light had not yet found the gold façade of the Comares Palace. I went to the tile-framed door and opened it as if I lived there. I had a

sense that the Alhambra was, for a little while in a little miracle of time, my own.

I lingered as long as I wanted to in the rooms, the halls,
able to study them, more, begin to take them for granted as
familiar, the stalactites, the arches, the shadowed floors. But
this time there was little light to guide my way into the Court
of the Myrtles. The water was as quiet as a caught breath,
the reflected image of the Tower of the Comares absolutely
still. There were no birds. In the great Court of the Ambassadors there was only emptiness; it needed people. It was
almost nerve-wracking to be there alone.

Then I went into the paradise of the Court of the Lions.
This marble place of so much blood and so much past was,
in that morning and in that silence, as near to both mean-
ings of paradise as I have ever been. I was terrified. I needed
people, a friend, a human breathing. I could hear my own
heart. I stood in that space of time and the world while the
morning light began to touch the roofs, and then the
columns and then the lace of the columns' capitals, and then
the dew-wet floor, and the whole place was doubled, up and
down, reflected. There are some memories so strong that
they are always present, as places to go and come away from.
That room and that morning and that slowly opening light
are mine and in me as I sit here and remember. It only takes
getting up early enough on a morning in Granada.

I was there for three hours. Gradually I could see people
in the distance across the outside gardens, down the paths,
but there seemed to be no guards, and I went where I
pleased, along the narrow paths between the trees, to hints
of buildings once as marvelous as those I had seen, and for
that few hours of the morning, I saw them as full of life for a
while.

In one of the groves of trees, left wild, I found a marble room at ground level, its roof marble as well, stove in by the weight of time and neglect. A tomb? A prison?

The sun was high beyond the trees and it was late in the morning. A gardener called out, "Who are you? Do you work here?" I think I understood the Spanish by the surprised and nervous pitch of his voice. He must have been so used to working and dreaming alone. The only word I could think of to say was *"perdido."* I answered both questions by saying that I was lost, and did not lie.

DUENDE

 Duende. The dictionary translates it as goblin or charm. It is that and not that. What it is can be defined a thousand times, and a thousand times missed. It has to be experienced and, once experienced, never lost again. It can be an endless second, a black sound, a flame of passion in a song, a poem, a gesture, a place. One thing it is—it is totally and unmistakably Spanish. I had seen it, heard it, been caught by the *duende* all through my search in Spain.

I think it exists in the deep well of Spanish soil, in the rebels, the mystics, the poets, the singers, the music. When you try to define it *duende* is already gone. But the second, the pause, the stab, the chill down the spine when it is released is always remembered. It has been imitated by professionals who claim to evoke it and only succeed in being professional. It has in it the impishness of the sudden, the glorious precision of the perfect moment in a sport, a song, a dance, a poem. St. Teresa had it. El Cid had it when he stood up to his king.

And of all the cities in Spain, I found it in Granada among

its poets, its young, its memories, and the concise edges of its black shadows. Two poets in Spain beyond all others that I know have it. In poetry it is when sound and sense meet in one word. A critic once said, "It is given to few people to cry at the right word in the right place."

Both of these poets lived and worked in Granada, three centuries apart. Federico García Lorca and St. John of the Cross shared the gift of the *duende* of a profound simplicity of language and song. St. John in his prison cell in Toledo in the sixteenth century and Lorca with his visceral memory of what in Spain is called *cante jondo*, or deep song, were changed by the music. Lorca helped Manuel de Falla revive *cante jondo* in a festival of song in Granada in 1922. Out of that festival has come modern *flamenco*.

I have driven to Granada from the south and from the west. But when I drove down a small road from the northwest, I saw the *duende*, evasive among the olive trees. I passed through olive groves where the small dirt roads that make sandy ribbons among the trees disappear, this time not over a horizon as in the north, but over the round foothills of Andalucia's Sierra Nevada mountains, those mountains of snow that rise away in the distance. The mountains are a wild background to the groves below them: domestic and tame on their round hills of disciplined trees.

It was there in the calm of the olive groves, the vast design over the country of Andalucia, that I caught a shadow, a glimpse, as I sped by on the superb mountain road, of a small man, under five feet tall, in the tattered robe of a dis-calced Carmelite monk, on a slow burro, ambling peacefully through the olive fields.

This small man was St. John of the Cross, poet, the patron saint of poets, Doctor of the Church, the highest honor the

Catholic Church, heavy with honors and prayers and titles, can bestow.

In his lifetime, the Spanish precision of his black shadow bouncing along in the dirt, he traveled for years, thinking, praying, sometimes with a comrade monk, sometimes alone during the best part of his job, which was to inspect the new nunneries and monasteries that had grown up so quickly in the simple houses of the Order begun by St. Teresa. St. John then was poor, neglected, and, to the end, persecuted by his fellow Carmelite friars.

He had been captured and imprisoned in Toledo in 1577 by those of the Carmelite order who were violently opposed to the reforms of St. Teresa. El Greco's *View of Toledo* (*Toledo in a Storm*) shows the monastery where he was confined, in the forefront of the painting, by the Tagus River, which surrounds Toledo like a snake.

It was in the appalling circumstances of his imprisonment in the calced reactionary Carmelite monastery in Toledo, where he was beaten daily by the other monks as part of the ritual of punishment for having gone over to the reformed discipline, that he became a poet.

He had been in prison for months in a tiny cell, filthy, bitten by fleas, only one time given a gesture of human compassion by a new guard who let him have pen and paper. One night when he was praying he heard singing from a peasant passing in the distance, maybe across the river, maybe in an empty street beyond his window. A late-night lonely man was singing what we would call a folk song, and what in Spain is called *cante jondo*, deep song.

Deep song is usually a lament about death and love, risen out of the ancient depths of Spain, from tribal and Moorish and Roman gypsy immigrants from the east, who are said to have come to Spain fleeing from the hosts of Tamerlane. In Andalucia for nearly a thousand years, the new Spanish mingled song, rhythms, laments, and blood with the people they found there. Deep song. It is the perfect name for it; today some of its descendent songs are known as *flamenco*.

The song St. John heard from a stranger in the depths of night was a dialogue. The woman sings, *"Muerome de amores, Carrillo. ¿Qué haré?"* I am dying of love, my dear. What can I do? The cold answer is, *"Que te mueras, alahé."* Die, then. I am going.

Half-starved, his shoulders permanently crippled by beating, his body covered with sores, this nearly broken monk was possessed when he heard the voice, by an ecstatic revelation that led him into being the greatest poet Spain has ever produced.

In his poetry, he told through images of the senses, as in the Song of Solomon in the Bible, of love that transcended the senses. In his commentaries on the poetry, which he wrote while he was prior of *Los Martires* in Granada, he tried to explain the unexplainable and gave the world the finest work on spiritual good manners that has ever been written.

He was in Granada ninety years after its fall in 1492. The Muslims had been subjected to all of the brutality that the betrayal of their treaty with the Catholic monarchs had brought with it—slavery, contempt, theft of their property, the torture of the Inquisition. Finally, after years of forced conversion and broken promises, they revolted, and gave Philip II the excuse to exile them from Spain as his great-grandparents had the Jews.

Castilian emigrants, retired soldiers, mercenaries and their families had been sent to occupy the abandoned city. The green *vega* around Granada had become a brown waste left over from years of war and neglect. No one knew then or cared how to farm it. If there were any farmers among the emigrants they were animal herders, and they let their flocks eat down what was left of the *vega* to desert.

The water system used by the Moorish farmers fell into disrepair. The royal family neglected the place; Charles V's elephant's foot of a palace lay unfinished. According to Gerald Brennen, who has written an introduction about St. John's life, and translated much of his poetry, Granada had become a military outpost, full of soldiers and whores.

But around the lower slopes of the Red Hill that had been the royal city of Alhambra, Charles V had planted what is still today his greatest gift to Granada, a forest. It is still there, along the foothills of the Alhambra hill, the Alameda, a cool green oasis of trees where paths are tunneled by hundreds of years of walkers, animal and human, through shade and silence. The Hill of the Martyrs, at the east end of the Red Hill, where King Chico had surrendered the city to Ferdinand and Isabel, and where St. John lived, was on the edge of the forest.

These were the woods where he could wander, and tell his flock the knowledge that he shared with his friend, St. Teresa, that God was not only in her pots and pans, but in the trees, among the flowers, the birds, the air, the wind.

At the end, he was threatened with being defrocked not because of the usual accusations of heresy but because he had insisted on the right of the nuns to elect their own prioress instead of having one imposed from above. The seesaw between authority and democracy springs up all through history, as now, as ever. Instead of his being defrocked, it was decided that he should be sent as a missionary to the new world of Mexico.

Death interfered. He developed a tumor in his leg, and went to the Carmelite monastery in Ubeda for treatment. There, once again treated with contempt by the prior, he died. There is a Catholic fairytale ending of repentance, a "they lived happily ever after," for such happenings. It is said that the prior, at the end, was converted to sanctity, and forgiven for his cruelty. The body of St. John was declared sacred by the people long before the Church recognized it; there was a fight over the poor remains of the monk.

A leg was left at Ubeda; the rest of him was taken by night to Segovia across the southern *mesa* of La Mancha. There is a famous scene in *Don Quixote*, published in 1605, where Don Quixote and Sancho Panza see a funeral cortege at night, which is thought to be that of St. John.

In Ubeda today, there is a chapel and a tomb, but the recumbent statue on the tomb is a tall, slim *hidalgo* of a man, and the face is long, lean, and aristocratic. Still, because it is where he died, the *duende* of the man permeates the overdecorated chapel, more powerful to the memory than the splattered gold of the Indies that climbs up the *reredos* and around the walls. But outside, above the door of the chapel that covers the cot-sized bit of land where he died, there is a small man with a wide face, and it is more truly St. John of the Cross, whose lines live as Shakespeare's do in English, in the Spanish thoughts and in the sayings of Spanish poets. One of them was the man now recognized as the twentieth century's finest Spanish poet, Federico García Lorca.

When I drove down to modern Granada from the north, after the live groves and the snow mountains, after the fine road and the peace and the *duende* of that glimpse of St. John, I was shocked when I came to the northern outskirts of my beautiful Granada. In most of the cities I had seen in

Spain, especially those whose industrial sections were newly designed, the sections tended to be clean, well cared for. I never saw the eyesores you expect in other countries, including our own, until I came to the least used tourist entry into Granada. No matter how sophistic the presentation to the tourist industry is in the south and the west, the ugly hidden industrial sections in the northern approaches to the city of Granada are the worst, the ugliest I saw in Spain.

But once beyond them, none of that matters in those pauses when you find, in this city most central to Spain's history, its mistakes, its prejudices, and its love. The city of El Chico, of St. John, of Federico García Lorca is still there, still sad, still quiet.

The Granada of the mind and memory, the past and present, is more than a place; it is an intimacy, caught by Arabic and Spanish poets more than historians, and countrymen more than soldiers. Let Lorca speak, for it is his city, the city of his life and death. Lorca said, "I think of Granada as a sweetheart who has died."

He wrote,

... in the 17th Century, Soto de Rojas (who had returned, weary and disillusioned, to Granada from Madrid) writes these words on the title page of one of his books. "Paradise closed to many. Gardens open to Few." In my judgement this is the most exact definition of Granada: Paradise Closed to Many.

Wherever Lorca went he carried a countryman's heart.

The melancholic and contemplative man goes to Granada, to be all alone in the breeze of sweet basil, dark moss, and trilling of nightingales exhaled by the old hills near that bonfire of saffron, deep grey, and blotting paper pink—the walls of the Alhambra.

To be alone . . . to understand not the water's play as at Versailles, but the water's passion, the water's agony.

Neither the prodigious mound of the cathedral, nor the great imperial and Roman seal of Charles V have effaced the little shop of the Jew who prays before an image recast from the seven-branched candelabrum, nor have the sepulchers of the Catholic Monarchs kept the Crescent from showing at times on the breast of Granada's finest sons. The dark struggle continues without expression. Well. Not really without expression. On the *Colina Roja* [the Red Hill] are two dead palaces, the Alhambra and the Palace of Charles V, which continue to fight the fatal duel that throbs in the heart of every Granadan.

These were the texts chosen by his brother Francisco in his memoir, *In the Green Morning: Memories of Federico*. Lorca knew only too well what much of Granada had become. These are his words a few months before the army and the Falange, a Spanish version of the Nazis in Germany and the Fascists in Italy, rebelled against the elected government of Spain in 1936. In a radio broadcast that summer, speaking of the Moorish culture fragmented around him in the city of Granada, he said,

> An admirable civilization, and a poetry, architecture and sensitivity unique in the world—all were lost, to give way to an impoverished, cowed city, a "miser's paradise" where the worst middle class in Spain today is busy stirring things up.

It is one of the few negative statements in poetry or prose that he made about the city and the *vega* where he had been born and so loved.

Granada is still Lorca's city, but it is hidden from those of us who come to meet it. It can be found. To open that paradise takes wandering, and recognition, a departure from the oh-so-beaten tourist track.

I walked along the *Camina del Darro,* the narrow, ancient street between the Albaicin, the old Moorish quarter on the hill across the little river, the Darro, from the high hill of the Alhambra. The little street is so central to the *duende* of the city that I walk there again, even as I write today, so far away. On the side of the street opposite the wall and the river, there are several mansions built by the rich Castilians who came there after its fall in 1492. One of them has been turned into one of the finest small archeological museums in Spain, where I found a seated mother goddess so benign, so comforting, that I wanted to touch her arm, and draw her motherly attention like a child. She is from the seventh century B.C.

On the other side of the river, the highest tower of the *alcazaba*—the *Vela,* where Ferdinand and Isabel ordered the flag of Castile to be flown—seems to float against the sky. The river flows, deep below the street, the only place in Granada where it is not covered over by pavement.

That day, when a car came by, I, like the other walkers, clung to the stone wall to let it pass, and stared down at the stream, which has collected the water from the Sierra Nevada and brought it to Granada for centuries. It is lined with green flowered weeds, man-high, and small trees that are so green they are a reminder of the ancient *vega* that, like the river itself, is covered by the concrete of the city. It is that water, joined by the water from the Fountain of Tears, that moves and sighs in the fountains of the Alhambra and the Albaicin.

Old bridges, arched high like the Seljuk bridges in Turkey, lead from the *Camina del Darro* to the hill below the Alhambra that is part of the Albaicin. Over one of the bridges, up steep stone stairs, by the stone balustrades, the path of large paving stone winds from the river into what is left of the old Arab quarter under the Red Hill. There are small café bars, their one or two tables veiled by trees.

Out of the racket of the modern city, behind a church built as a symbol of the conquerors on the site of a mosque, I sat down at a small table under a flowering tree, and waited. Not for anything. Just there in that miraculous silence.

My only companion was a young, attractive girl, sitting on a high stool outside the door of the café, reading. From the size of the book I think she was a college student, maybe the daughter of the owner. She brought me tea, and went back to her book. What we shared was the silence, both of us there, the girl dignified and friendly in one of those small oases that are secret, all over Granada, hidden under the modern city with its tour buses and its traffic that seems at first to overlay the silence, the peace, the sadness of Lorca's Granada. But it does not conquer it, no matter how many buses and cars are shunting perpetual strangers to the Alhambra, the cathedral. No one has ever finally conquered Granada.

After I had rested and had tea, I walked along the narrow streets and alleys, testing my sense of direction to find my hotel without maps or guidance. Well, there was guidance. In the distance I heard, faintly, a song of Albéniz, played on the guitar. This is a section where students, musicians, the gathered, self-protecting young, live in Granada. I would have expected the latest rock, the new American music, and there was plenty of it in Spain and all over Europe. I remember almost running down a street in Ankara in Turkey trying to get out of step with Michael Jackson, blaring out on a loudspeaker.

The music seemed to change direction as it touched the high white walls of the narrow streets, sometimes in the distance, sometimes near. I tried to find it in turn after turn but I was being led by the *duende* as imp.

I finally came out on a street of shops. At the open entrance of a music shop a tape was playing Albéniz. The shop was obviously a meeting place for young guitarists; there were several of them, their guitars slung across their backs, beautiful classic instruments, polished, cared for. They were listening quietly to the music. One of Spain's most famous *flamenco* guitarists was playing Albéniz, the nineteenth-century composer who, even before Falla and the others, had found the font of Spanish sound, the true *flamenco*, which Lorca and Falla rescued from the bars and the brothels of Granada, giving back the recognition it had lost through gentility and imitation of accepted European classic laws of music.

There were for me so many of those moments, and for the rest I had a guide, the dedicated research and writing of Ian Gibson. His first book, *The Death of Lorca*, and his second, a biography of Lorca, set me over and over on Lorca's path there, his love for the city, his friends. Out of their memories, I found a young musician turned poet, an ebullient, friendly soul, whose joy hid a sadness that is reflected in his tragic poetry, in the depth of his plays. He, of all the poets in twentieth-century Spain, had the *duende* he once wrote about and gave as a lecture, failing, as we all do, to define it, as we all do, for it is a moment, and meeting, not a place or a time; a recognition, not a definition.

Maybe that is why I have thought since that it was in

Granada, led by Lorca and the work of Ian Gibson, neither of whom meant to guide me or anyone, that I found at last the unchanging well, sometimes heard, sometimes seen, a glimpse, a glance, of the depth of personal precision, in the culture, from Castile to Andalucia, in the art, the landscape, the essential Spain.

I think of Auden's poem on the death of Yeats when I meet Lorca in memory: "You were silly like us; your gift survived it all. . . ." Friend after friend described Lorca to Ian Gibson as childlike, and yet he had the courage to go into the depths of Spanish language and sorrow, and find a view of love and death that is, in Spain, an inevitable marriage.

Once, on a visit to the Alhambra, Lorca jumped up on the wall that looks down on Granada, where the valley, the city, the *vega* below, stretches all the way to the distant mountains. He recited the poem he had written in honor of Walt Whitman, one of his most profound, bitter, gentle, violent, a self-deriding cry, a plea. He shouted all the derisive words for homosexuals in Spanish that he had been called throughout his life, from his earliest school, when he was nicknamed Federica—*pájaros, jotos, sarasas, apios, cancos, floras, adelaidas.* His voice echoed over the city.

And with the ugly words came his loving, gentle tribute to Walt Whitman,

> And you, beautiful Walt Whitman, stay asleep on the banks of
>   the Hudson
> with your beard toward the pole, and your hands opened.
> Your tongue of soft clay or snow calls out for
> comrades to protect your ephemeral gazelle.

Lorca had seen the soul of that chaste man, Walt Whitman, as a gazelle.

It was a moment of *duende,* of honest immortality. There were so many such moments remembered by his friends, so much love and fear in the man's life. He had already, by thirty-six, become the best-known playwright in Spain, and he had given time and generosity and talent to a company of students. During the republic elected in 1931, they organized a traveling company, the Baraca. They traveled across Spain to small cities and villages, presenting Spain's classic theater. It was a revival of a theater that had become mundane, money-minded, dull. It is an irony that the boiler suits they wore on the Baraca tours were to become the unofficial uniforms of the Republican side in the war that followed.

Without the substructure of events that summer of 1936, it would be impossible to understand what happened to him. In that year the past and the present clashed in the worst and most decisive civil war in Spanish history, the great watershed that had been growing stronger for centuries. It was the first time that any country in Europe tried to stand up to the brutality of the false, outgrown myths of its past. To us who remember it so well, the first shots of the Second World War were fired there.

I will try, here, to give a framework of facts of what happened in Spain that summer in order to begin to explain what followed. That year was a year of extreme politics all over the European world. Those extremes have been recognized as warnings ever since, when the attempts at elected balance have been ignored. Hitler was in power in Germany. And it was in Germany that the old idea that had been a law in Spain five centuries before, *limpieza de sangre,* purity of blood, became an excuse for genocide.

But at the Olympics the high point of the games was the

victory of the American runner, Jesse Owens, who was black, as a David against the Goliaths of the Nazis in Germany. Stalin was dictator of the Soviet Republics of Russia. Mussolini was the dictator of Italy, and persuaded the Italians that they could revive the power of Rome. The fact that the trains ran on time (which became the joke of the regime abroad) covered the fact that Italy had invaded and decimated Ethiopia. Hitler's, Mussolini's, and Stalin's methods were the same: fear, discipline, nationalism, authoritarian power, and myth used as fact.

The terrible worldwide depression had made too many insecure people, frightened dupes to blind authority. People around the rest of the civilized world hated and feared all three of the dictators. But not enough. And not enough people.

In Spain, the young men's party to the right was the Falange, under the charismatic leadership of José Antonio de Rivera, the son of the Spanish dictator who had lost power in the first Republican victory in 1931. In 1936, the elected conservative government fell. It had replaced the liberals elected in 1931 in the first Spanish republic. When the conservative government fell in its turn, new elections were called.

The first attempt was almost a reign of terror to keep people from voting. The Falangists and the right-wing rowdies stormed the polls. There were riots from both the left and the right. The Spanish *Cortes* declared the election fraudulent.

In the second attempt at electing a Republican government the Falangists, much of the army, and the church hierarchy stayed away from the polls. The liberals won in a country where Spanish priests were instructed to teach children that to vote liberal was a mortal sin. Because the right had boycotted the second election, trouble had been expected ever since the liberal Republicans had won. With the exception of the strong Syndicalist Anarchist party centered in Barcelona, the rest of the left joined a Popular Front, the motto, the call to arms, the buzzword of the summer of 1936. The Spanish Popular Front included conservatives, liberals, socialists, and the small communist party.

In the first weeks of summer before Spain exploded into war, most of the intellectuals, the media, the university faculties knew that there could be trouble ahead from an embittered right. Neither side seemed to recognize the huge weight of historic hatred that had built up through the centuries of authority from the years of the *Reconquista,* and from so many centuries of privilege, church autocracy, anarchic uprisings, strikes, and the compromises between them that had tried and failed to bandage a gaping wound.

The newly elected republic asked for help from the democracies and got none. Claude Bowers, the ambassador from the United States, reported that the republic was weak but that the election had been fair. His words did not rouse much attention from official Washington.

For the right, Germany and Italy would send troops, equipment, planes; they used the Spanish war as a rehearsal for World War II. Nobody stopped them. Russia was the only country to give major help to the beleaguered republic, but at the price of an attempted Communist takeover of the government. But it had started, and it remained to the end, a Spanish war, a Spanish sorrow. But all of that was later, in the three years the war lasted, until the takeover by Franco.

That last summer, people began to take action for safety. Lorca, who had been a joyfully outspoken Republican all through the elections, and was listened to because of his fame, was persuaded to go to Mexico. He had even bought his ticket.

But something kept delaying him—his love for his country, not the noisy, violent nationalism of the right, and the naive delusions of the left, but a simple man's love for the place he was born, knew best, had kept within himself all through his life, wherever he went. The man, Lorca, knew he had to leave the country. But the child he had been, derided by his schoolmates and protected by his family, always a governing element in his living, yearned to return to where he had always felt safe and he was surrounded by familiar love.

There are, to me, two acts beyond coincidence—that both Lorca and St. John of the Cross might have survived in the new world, and did not go—that make the fate of both of them seem preordained.

On July 17, Lorca took the night train from Madrid to Granada to say goodbye to his family before leaving for Mexico, but, as deep as deep song within him, he had fled for home. He arrived in Granada on July 18, 1936. By the next morning he was trapped there. The revolt against the elected government had broken out at five o'clock in the morning with a call to arms from General Franco in Morocco.

His father was one of the very few rich men who was a known liberal. His sister had married Manuel Fernández-Montesinos, a young doctor, who had been elected in the second election by the Popular Front as mayor of Granada. On July 20, he was arrested in his office.

Granada was one of the first cities where the Falange took over the barracks, the district and city government. There were mass arrests of all known liberals, left-wingers, known Republican sympathizers, including a friend of Franco's, the commandant of the local barracks, professors, members of trade unions, personal enemies—the complete roster of right-wing hatred, fear, and prejudice. Bloodbaths, by both the right and the left, were beginning all over Spain.

What followed is curious and horrible, partly because many of the people involved had known each other since childhood, partly because it was so daily, so mundane and intimate. I have walked along the streets, looked at the houses where it unfolded, day by day, mornings and afternoons, after the first acts of rebellion. They do not look like places where death spread from family to family. I started at the *Huerta de San Vincente*, where the Lorca family had lived for years.

The *Huerta de San Vincente* was a comfortable, unassuming farmhouse bought when Lorca's father brought the children to Granada to be educated. It sat in an orchard and garden just beyond the edge of the city. Now it is in a park within a city that has long since engulfed the *huertas*. It is a shrine to Spain's most admired twentieth-century poet; it houses his piano, a few possessions that were not destroyed. To me, it is a poignant, sad, haunted place.

The house is surrounded now by a large park called the Federico García Lorca memorial park. It is formal, full of roses regimented into beds. Women push their children's prams through the clean walkways. It is beautiful, civic, a place of pride in fame, but it has no *duende,* and the signs tell nothing of Lorca's fate.

I wandered down behind the cathedral to the *Plaza de Bibrambla,* the once-great square where the Inquisition burned its victims, where the jousts were held in Moorish times, and where the little streets toward the university beyond it to the west were the scene of what happened. Little seems changed, except that everything is changed. Of all the places of trial in the deep past, then when Lorca was growing up, where he met his friends, and skipped classes at the university, this is the center of his world.

When Lorca's brother-in-law was arrested, his sister returned to the farmhouse, where the family huddled together. Squads sent by the Falange came to the house, tied the caretaker to a tree, and beat him almost senseless in front of the family. Finally Lorca, who had not been a physically brave man, could stand it no longer, and stepped in to try to stop the beating. He was thrown to the ground and kicked. When the squad left they informed Lorca that he was under house arrest.

The next day he took a basket of food to his brother-in-law in prison. At that moment few people had much idea of the horror that was unfolding. But when Lorca came back to the house, he was so shaken by what he had seen or what had happened to him he could not speak.

He obviously realized that he was a danger to his family. He decided to call Luis Rosales, an old friend and poet whom he had helped in the past. The Rosales family were leading Falangists. In a move a little like the purloined letter of Poe's story, Lorca and his family decided that the Rosales house would be the safest hiding place.

He had known the Rosales family for most of his life. They lived in one of those spacious houses in a narrow street near the Falange headquarters. I walked past it, now a hotel, still as secret from the street as it was when he was taken there by his horrified close friend, Juan Rosales, who came to get him, and drove him to what they both thought was a safe place in his own house on the street near the *Bibrambla*.

No sooner had he left the *huerta* than the squad of the Falange arrived again. It seems that in the first days of the

Falangist and army takeover, everything was so disorganized that people acted on their own, settled old scores all over Spain, acted on old prejudice on both sides, exploded with age-old hatreds. They took apart Lorca's piano looking for a radio they had heard was tuned to Russia; the whole thing would have been as appallingly tragicomic as the "communist menace" sold to the American people in the early fifties had it not been for what followed.

Some of the Falange found out where Lorca was hiding. They seem to have waited until the two brothers who were officers in the Falange, including Juan, were out of the way, both sent on inspection at one at the new "fronts" of a war that was waiting to happen.

On August 16, in the dawn of a Sunday morning, Dr. Manuel Fernándes-Montesinos, Lorca's brother-in-law, was shot. Lorca was arrested on the same Sunday afternoon. A small crowd had gathered, drawn there by the public display of the arrest.

Police, the army, and the Falange surrounded the street so that the dangerous poet could not escape. They even had snipers on the roofs around the house in *Calle de Ángelo*, where everybody knew everybody else, and which is so narrow that cars can only edge past each other, and so a picture of urban domesticity that there could not have been a place to escape without being seen by neighbors wandering in the streets. It was Keystone Kops. It was a B movie.

Lorca stepped out into the little street, surrounded like a dangerous fugitive by armed men, and was walked to the car to be driven for the few short blocks to the Falangist head-quarters. I see a man walking out of a door into the hot sun of a Sunday siesta, surrounded by armed strangers. Or did he know any of them? Had he been to school with them? Had someone been a friend? A bully? No one knows or remembers.

But much of what happened on that hot Sunday in August of 1936 in Granada is known. He was hustled into a car as if the whole Republican army were expected to attack and rescue him. He was driven to the city government building and shut in an empty room, alone. He disappeared for a while, left there while arguments broke out. The Rosales brothers threatened and begged for his release. The man who had taken over the government for the rebellion sat in his office. His hand could have signed the orders to let Lorca go into exile. The hand did not move.

Did Lorca know that his good friend and brother-in- law, the mayor of Grenada, had been stood up against the wall of the cemetery just beyond the Alhambra hill and shot that Sunday morning?

There were frantic attempts, by the Rosales family, by Lorca's other influential right-wing friends, to release him. When they went to rescue him the Rosales brothers were told the lie that he had been moved out of the prison room where they had put him. When, finally, Manuel de Falla, a well-known conservative and entirely safe because of his fame, went to the city jail to beg for Lorca's release, he was told it was too late.

Late into the night of August 18, the Black Squad came for him. The Black Squad was the name for the squad known after a month of civil war as the executioners. It was made up of volunteers, and of Assault Guards who were being punished for being slow to join the revolt against their government. A young friend of Lorca saw him handcuffed to a man with white hair, a one-legged cripple. The old man was a village schoolteacher, much loved by his students, a dedicated Republican, who had been reported as a dangerous red by an enemy. So much of that went on. To be reported was to be killed.

They were shoved into the fast car belonging to one of Granada's best known *machos,* a devil with the ladies, a fast driver, the 1936 idea of a real man, known as a "playboy." It was the new slang name for an international type, admired in 1936. I remember them well. In a dismal economy they were the good catches; their cars smelled of fine leather and cigarettes. They were family approved.

They drove away through the dark, narrow streets. It was three o'clock in the morning. They speeded by the church of Santa Ana, along the *Camino del Darro,* past the mansions built there when the town had been taken over by the Catholic monarchs, into the winding road that led up toward the unseen mountains of the Sierra Nevada. There is a village called Viznar in the foothills below the stark walls of the Sierra Alfacar, where an archbishop had built a palace after he had returned from Spanish America. There the Falange had set up headquarters.

Downhill to the west there was an old mill house that had been a pleasant refuge for the children of Granada when it got too hot in summer in the city. The rebels had made it into a prison. Someone told later that Lorca had tried to quiet his fellow prisoners, who consisted of himself, the old teacher, and two young would-be bullfighters whose apprenticeship was to half-kill the bull with darts by weakening its neck muscles so that it could not raise its head when the *torero* took over the show. They had been ardent anarchists, caught in the Albaicin.

A young man under the protection of the commanding officer was being hidden in the mill house His job was to tell the prisoners they were going to be shot. He said that Lorca had asked for a priest, but, expecting no more prisoners so late at night, he told him he had gone to bed. The boy helped Lorca remember the prayer of repentance his mother had taught him when he was a child.

In the deepest dark just before dawn, when the stars seem bigger than at any other time of the night, the four men were put into the back of a truck and bounced along the dirt road toward the next village, Alfacar, where the green of the *vega* downhill stopped at the steep, stony treeless Sierra Alfacar behind it. The village was beside the famous spring called the *Fuente Grande,* which since Moorish times had provided water for the Alhambra and the Albaicin. It had been a well-known place for Granadans to come to sit on the grass around the horseshoe-shaped pool and catch the mountain breeze.

The Moors had called it the Fountain of Tears, because in its center there was a plume of water that rose into the air, cooled the surrounding grassy hillsides, and seemed to sob faintly as the water fell. Did the men in the back of the truck hear it when the truck stopped? Did they smell the good smell of barnyard as the road passed an old farmhouse on the way there? Could they see the olive groves around them? There was no moon. There could only, when the truck was stopped, have been the whisper of the fountain and the predawn singing of birds.

The four men were shot on the hillside beyond the pool. Years later, one of the men who was in the Black Squad that night said that when the sound of the volley died down, he was frightened to hear the voice of Lorca, who had risen to his knees, "I'm still alive."

Did he whisper? Did he call out? Did the birds begin singing again after the first volley had died down?

The squad gave him the *coup de grâce.* Later that morning

the man who had driven his fast car with the prisoners swaggered into a bar and announced for everyone to hear, "We shot Lorca this morning. I put two shots in his ass because he was a queer, a *mariposa*."

All of this was word of mouth over the years. Nothing was written. It would have been too dangerous under the dictatorship of Franco. For years it was an open secret. At first the Franco government pretended to know nothing. Finally they issued a death certificate. It said that Federico García Lorca had died of wounds during the war. But it was not until Franco's death in 1975 that the full story was made public.

Sunday mornings are quiet in Spanish cities. There are few cars, only a walker now and then. I drove through the empty streets where, during the week, I would have been shunted aside for the tour buses, the taxis, taking money and money up to the great hill, the Alhambra, which has now become one of the most popular places to see in Europe.

Through the small square of the Santa Ana Church, which is at the end of the Plaza Nueva, I drove into the narrow *Camino del Darro,* that ancient lifeline by the river of Granada. The street name turned at the end of the river street into the *Calle de Triste,* the Street of Sadness. I wondered then who among all the people who drove and dodged cars to go to the archeological museum realized the import of the name. For this, in 1936, would have probably been the main way, and still is the easiest way, to drive to Viznar, and to Alfacar.

The road switched back and forth around the small foothills of the Sierra Nevada. It began to climb. For a few miles, I was driving on one of those wonderful Spanish roads, so beautifully engineered, until I came to a sign that said Viznar. It was simple, only a little under five miles up from Granada into the mountain passes, and to the perched village. The guidebooks are right. It is a beautiful village. It must be a summer colony still for Granadans. The houses are bright white, the walls flower-covered. There is even, once again, a summer place for children to go away from the Granadan heat for a few days of relief, or at least I took one of the signs to be that. Nineteen-thirty-six was in my mind so fused to the morning, I questioned little. I had to ask the way to Alfacar.

West, down a steep decline, and onto a well-paved road that had been the rock-strewn dirt road the truck had taken, I drove past the *barranca*, a shallow gully between the mountain heights, without seeing it. There were so many trees. Where olive groves had been, I saw none. It seemed only to be a pine-rich mountain pass down toward the small village of Alfacar.

The road went through a farmyard, one of those roads you see so often where farmers share the rare flat ground with travelers. The clean farm smell of hay, manure, and grass seemed a comfort.

I was surprised to see on the left-hand side of the road a large apartment house perched above the steep mountainside with what must have been a superb view of the whole valley, the *vega* of Granada far below. Well-kept cars, some large, were parked in front of it.

Just beyond, on the right, I saw the sign, PARQUE FEDERICO GARCÍA LORCA (1981). The entrance to the memorial was up steep steps and through a gateway, the grille of the gate fixed into a large, imposing entry of brick. On either side and on the hill behind the memorial there were the funereal formal yews. I saw no olive trees at all. It was a public municipal monument. Around a large circle of black and white stones, paved in the same kinds of patterns that have been laid for so many centuries along the pavements of Spain, were pine trees.

In the center of the circle was a fountain that at first I took to be the *Fuente Grande*, but it was not. It was shut off, and the place was empty, given over to the singing of the birds. On a semicircular wall behind the paved circle were a series of plaques, all of them with quotes from Lorca's poems. I could not read them. My eyes were too flooded, and they were, of course, in Spanish. For some reason I don't want to find out what the municipality of Granada had chosen of Lorca's poetry.

There are still disagreements about where the four men were shot. I expected to find an olive tree with a marble marker under it that Ian Gibson had said was there. I did not find it. But I think I know where the men are. It would have been a small grave. The young man who was forced to bury them laid the bodies one on top of the other. Today, the only way to identify these men would be that one of the skeletons would have only one leg. At the right of the paved circle, facing the plaques, there are two pine trees among so many, but these are carefully planted a grave's-length apart, and they are set in gravel, unlike the rest.

I sat in my car for a long time, partly to recover from what I had seen. I know that not all the municipal planning, not the heavy design, not the wrong trees and the wrong weight of things could disguise the fact that I had stood in a place so—not haunted, not mystic, but completely and terribly alive.

I decided to drive back the road I had followed, for I had forgotten the *barranca* where over two thousand people had been shot and thrown into shallow graves, and I was suddenly ashamed of that. Lorca had been finally one of two thousand, the only one named.

I parked the car at the beginning of a little dirt road that disappeared into a beautiful thick stand of green pine trees that stretch farther than I had the courage to go along the huge graveyard. That is what the *barranca* is.

On the left side, up a shallow incline, the young trees look like one of those forest mosques that were the early way of building, oases of stone, like the mosque at Córdoba. On the right, downhill and up the other side of the graveyard, the rich trees seem endless.

The irony of this beautiful memorial of trees to the people whose bodies have fed them and become them is overwhelming. At first, after the war, members of the families who had lost fathers, mothers, brothers, sisters slipped up, eluding the civil guards and, unable to find any place where they could be sure that the ones they had loved were buried, put stones at the heads of all the unmarked sunken grave-shaped shallows. The government came and took the stones away, but someone had the bright idea of obscuring the ground so that none of the graves would be remembered. They planted the trees.

Now it is one of the most beautiful monuments to the dead who have fed it that I have ever seen.

Alfacar is a fairly large town. There are post–civil war *cármenes* that are the hallmark of Granada, houses within walled gardens on hillsides so steep that I could not imagine climbing up to build them. There are several restaurants. Before I left I went down to the *Fuente Grande*. The grass-covered hillside is gone and in its place is a concrete surround, no place to lounge and have a bottle of wine and a picnic, no easy pleasure. In the distance, across the road, on the left side of the Lorca monument, there are more pines, and a few cottages. Changed and the same, what the Franco government tried to hide stands there, not the same land-scape, but the same place, one of those places where man's inhumanity to man was acted out, over and over, in a coun-try that in so many miraculous ways no longer exists, not through fighting but through diminishment. Now the best of it is the stuff only of nostalgia.

The road that runs between the *Fuente Grande* and Lorca's place of death has been named. It is called the *Calle de Martires.*

Except for dead monuments, these mountains, this *vega,* these pines, Granada's hidden places are in his poetry still, and in the new life of Spain. The *duende* that guided his life and work, the quiet places, the narrow old streets, the *ram-blas,* the boys and girls at ease with each other, walking together, the quietness of the early morning at the Alhambra, the *paseo* in the evening has become, or the best of it, his city again.

HOLIDAY

 It was time to stop and stay a while—someplace easier, unknown, unimportant, and that did not remind me of death and civil war. I had known the facts and much of the propaganda of the war since I was young; but knowing it was clean and mental, and something far away. Intelligence is bloodless.

I hadn't known about Lorca, only facts. Now I had made myself walk in his streets, from his boyhood home to a lush forest of pine trees, and it was familiar in a different way, as if a dear friend had died. I saw him as he had seen Granada.

I found out, driving alone west across Andalucia, what "Mine eyes dazzle" meant. For when I thought of Granada from time to time along that featureless highway I was engulfed in what I had seen, and then my eyes would dazzle, tears but not crying, like rain left on a window. I would have to slow the car until the moment passed. I prayed that my favorite city would become beautiful again in my mind, as it had been before I had gone up on that terrible mountain. It has now. As always, I want to go back.

I was tired of sorrow. I wanted to do nothing for a little

while. Having followed war, kings, queens, caliphs, saints, and then one I had been close to by reading since I was eighteen, I wanted to go where no place was. A rest. A week; it sounded like the luxury of the world, no driving, no past, just sea and sun. Lovely. There was only one problem. I hate the Costa del Sol.

It is the most un-Spanish of places. It has been invaded for too long by the northern Europeans escaping fog, rain, and puritanism. Oh, the buildings are there, and buried deep below the sand, a fascinating past obscured by beautiful Swedish girls in their topless bikinis, and pale English girls imitating beautiful Swedish girls. Hard rock, soft rock—no, not sandstone, limestone, marble—but music, and commercial *flamenco*, the noise of tourism at its worst over the beaches. It is the only part of Spain I know where Spaniards have, through fatigue and exposure, learned to be rude. Crowds are so thick in summer and early fall that they seem not so much to move as to be stirred. I have just described a perfect holiday for an eighteen-year-old modern Visigoth.

I was already in the south, so there was no going to the English Channel for a little restful mist, or to the Bay of Biscay for saints, shrines, and treacherous sea. I consulted the map and the guidebooks I carried. I found it. I thought I found it, a small resort referred to condescendingly as a place where Spanish families went in the season.

It was a long way from Granada, all the way across the south of Spain. I didn't care. Between Córdoba and Seville, I found the drive was too long, and stopped, I thought, just for the night, at Carmona. I stayed three days. I found the minor road that passed through where the two-hundred-year frontier had been in the thirteenth century. That was the reason why the towns I passed through were called Arcos de la Frontera,

Jerez de la Frontera, and, later, Palos de la Frontera. I remember best the mile after mile of sunflowers; all their heads watched in one direction, regimented by the sun.

Sanlúcar was not on the Mediterranean coast but on that Atlantic shore between the frontier of Portugal and the Pillars of Hercules, now called the Straits of Magellan. It sounded wonderfully uninteresting. Little to do. Not really recommended. Perfect. A place where there might be the sun and the silence I craved.

In a great half-circle of shore in southern Atlantic Spain, fed by three rivers, is the Costa de la Luz, a lovely name, the Coast of Light. There is, they say, so little there to see. Sanlúcar de Barrameda sounded, and was meant to sound, like a boring little resort. Imagine it! Dull, quiet, and pastless, not fascinating. I couldn't wait. I drove west from Arcos de la Frontera, still driving away from Granada, not toward anything, but gradually, after Carmona, I began to be in the present again, avoiding fascinating cities.

There was no sign for Sanlúcar de Barrameda; I was prepared for that by my trusty dragoman, a Michelin atlas of every road in Spain there had ever been, and I saw that if I got off at the sign for a place called Lebrija, and headed southwest on a little pencil line on my map, I would finally arrive at Sanlúcar.

I couldn't find it. For mile after mile it simply wasn't there. I passed sand dune after sand dune. I was lost in a space of sand and sky and a hint of the sea. Sanlúcar was nowhere, signs but no city. I finally got to a traffic circle in the road. Those circles in Spain have to be learned and, once familiar, are a godsend. Driving around the circle I almost missed another small sign, Sanlúcar, and had to go around again. This time I made the turn at the sign that said I had arrived in Sanlúcar.

There was still nothing there. Oh, there were some filling stations, a few roadside eating places, a few houses. Nothing else. No sea, no resort. I knew it had to exist, or had arrived at hope, which is the stop before knowledge. After all, I had a reservation at a hotel, and any traveler knows that means a place exists. Behind hope I found fatigue, and behind that, a little touch of despair. I pulled into a filling station. One of those blessed, well-dressed English-speaking college girls came out to the car. She smiled. "You are looking for Sanlúcar, are you not?" she said before I could speak. I simply nodded.

She gave me perfect directions into the town, the turning toward the hotel, the hotel itself, with a warning that it was in the center of a cat's cradle of Moorish walking streets, off to the side of a large church, across from a nunnery, behind the *plaza mayor*. Of course. I followed her directions exactly and was lost for three hours in a little Moorish Christian medieval ancient town. At first I was fool enough to try to drive around to find my hotel. Then I parked at a little square and walked. I realized later that for at least one of those hours I had been within a hundred feet of the hotel. Once, I passed it. How could I get so lost in a little, old mild resort where nothing happened?

I was to find out later that it wasn't little, it wasn't medieval, and it had one of the most fascinating pasts in all of Spain. So many roads I had followed led there, from the *Reconquista*, the Indies, the *conquistadores*.

Then, quite suddenly, I recognized the hotel, a blank white wall across from a high, blank brick wall, behind the blank white stucco of an ancient church with one small baroque circular window in a monastery plaza. It was the time of *siesta*. There was not a soul around in the street. In the hot part of the day Sanlúcar was, sensibly, asleep.

I tried the only large double door I could find, and there it was, a small sign, *Los Helechos,* The Ferns. I walked into the door that led to two Moorish houses combined into a hotel, with two white courtyards filled with plants, an old well, a quiet within it that I could not believe. It was as pure an *Arabian Nights* scene as I could have found, a simple hotel, with a lobby full of plants, a desk where another young college student spoke enough English to guide me. I followed him through a corridor to an opening into a lovely white courtyard with a fountain and green, tree-sized plants. This was what my room looked out on from a barred window with a green plant of my own on the sill. I had found an ideal place just to be for a while after the hurly-burly of wars and mountains and all that I had hoped for in Spain except a place to sit and think. I was to find out that I had arrived at the best hotel, the most attractive, and the cheapest of all the places where I had been living.

Every evening after their classes were over a group of young college students, men and women, made the unassuming hotel bar their *tertulia.* They drank very little. They played chess and Chinese checkers and discussed quietly whatever they were discussing. I began later to see the *tertulias* all over the town, always at the same table: businessmen in one of the outdoor restaurants, the farmers at the medieval market, the retired fishermen who have had their own meeting place since the fourteenth century. I saw them in the mornings, always at the same time.

In the early evening on my first day there, when the sun was low, I walked back out of the magic door to see where I was. I wandered into the *plaza mayor,* where the people of Sanlúcar sat all evening, some with baby carriages beside them, with contented, sleeping babies. For the first time in

Spain after dark I was not a stranger. Everybody around me knew everybody else around me and included me in the smiles, the greetings.

There were discussions and soft laughter. The half-light of lamps from the little local bars and restaurants was just beginning to color the twilight. Down a narrow street I walked toward a second plaza and, dividing the two plazas from one another, a small palace which had been turned into a hotel, not grand, just another genteel old house the color of age and neglect beside a street too small for cars, so narrow that I could touch both walls that bound it. A man with his dog seemed to live in a doorway. I thought of Unamuno's story of two sisters, a family seething with silent passion, marooned in parlors with heavy curtains, the pathetic notion of local snobbery, the same theme as Lorca's *The House of Bernarda Alba*.

I escaped into the second plaza, where there was a breeze that promised the sea. In front of me was a quarter-of-a-mile walk on an elegant, almost formal esplanade as wide as the city blocks that had been laid out between the medieval town and the sea. It was lined with trees, with fine modern houses. It was another city, new and white, this one with beautiful gardens, this far south; semitropical blooming plants that leaned over white walls.

Sanlúcar was not one town. It was two. They lay beside each other. Nothing seemed to have been destroyed to build new buildings. The medieval town where I had wandered, lost, was still there, behind me, where I lived.

Ahead of me the water was turned white by evening. I could hear it, and I walked toward it, aware of the Atlantic Ocean. But it was not the ocean in this deceptive, ancient, magic town. It was the estuary of the largest river in Spain, the Guadalquivir, its name from the Arabic name for great river. Away in the distance was the vague shore of the largest natural habitat in Europe, the Doñana National Park, a place of birds, wild animals, islands, swamps, old paths, and, I found out later, where Goya spent the summer with the Duchess of Alba in what was then the most famous aristocratic watering place in Spain.

I also learned, in that first evening, that the food there was perfect, that Sanlúcar was the center for the finest, lightest sherry blushed with gold in that ring of towns, including Jerez de la Frontera, that make most of the sherry that comes from Spain. It is called manzanilla; to me it is to most sherries as single malt is to ordinary Scotch whiskey. I knew none of this. I only knew that I was where I most wanted to be, and that the air was clean, the little town the right size for a kind of gentle wanderlust, and that there was little to discover.

There is the most honest pamphlet about the Costa de la Luz. It simply says, under gastronomy, that the best dish there is fried fish. (No complicated sauces, no fabulous traditional local messes.) So every evening after sharing the *siesta*, I ate the finest fried fish in all the Mediterranean, red mullet, *barbounia* in Turkey, *triglia di fango* (slime mullet!) in Italy, *salmonete* in Spain. This superb fish was so fashionable in ancient Rome that people lost fortunes buying it to impress their guests at banquets. There was, at one time, a law that only the emperor could eat it.

So there I sat in the evenings at an outdoor restaurant on the esplanade in the gathering darkness as the night came down, alone but never lonely, eating red mullet, the emperor's fish, drinking manzanilla, the lightest sherry known. To paraphrase Thoreau, it was not sherry I drank nor

I who drank sherry; it was the wine of the Hesperides and I was served it by the wind from the west.

As I began to learn to be in Sanlúcar, the place where nothing happened, I was finding out that it seemed to contain all that I had begun to learn in my traveling—unsought, secret roads of the past and the historic changes of Spain, as if all those roads led to it. I was more and more aware that I was in one of the places in Spain that I would go back to again and again.

I had, on that first evening, seen two cities. Now, in the daylight I found the third. Overlooking the medieval and the modern cities, the *barrio alto* had once been the aristocratic summer resort of Imperial Spain. The long, high palisade followed the eastern shore of the river, a steep sentinel over the lower cities. There was the castle, there the once-great houses, on watch over the markets, the fishing boats, all the way to the sea, where the ships from the new world crossed the bar of the Guadalquivir.

Sanlúcar lay at the main entry from the Atlantic Ocean to the rich, newly discovered Indies, America. It had been there that the ships laden with gold and silver crossed the bar at last after the dangerous Atlantic crossing, the entry to what Fernand Braudel called the most ancient and treacherous of all the shores of the Atlantic, the nursery of Atlantic exploration.

Instead of a quiet town, I had discovered once again that, like Columbus, I had found what I had not looked for— the beginning of the upriver voyage to the city of Seville where every ship from the Spanish Main had to report at the *Casa de Contratación*, the government register and customs house. What a relief it must have been to cross the bar at Sanlúcar after the perilous Atlantic voyage, to moor at last beyond the danger of the pirates from England and North

Africa, gathered offshore like flies around honey. No wonder Sanlúcar had the reputation of being a wild port, the place in Spain where the vagabonds gathered in bands. In the days of the American voyages, poets, runaway students, thieves, the poor, the starving, and those called by a new word in the sixteenth century, *pícaros,* all sought passage on the outgoing ships, and gathered in the riotous taverns.

Crossing the bar. It is one of those phrases we use without considering what it means. It has been a metaphor for death and turned into a joke . . . Tennyson's "and may there be no moaning of the bar when I put out to sea." No. Not a pub or a café or a down-and-dirty bar. It was a sandbar, and it was at the ocean entry to a river where the current flowing into the tidal estuary moved the underwater sand into, literally, a high sandbar the ships had to cross to get into port. The bar at Sanlúcar controlled the size of the ships that plied to and from Seville for well over a hundred years from 1500, just after the discovery of America, to the late seventeenth century when the great galleons came into service and the *Casa de Contratación* was moved to Cádiz. No ship over two hundred tons could cross the Sanlúcar bar; the great galleons that we are so familiar with from movies and popular stories were built for a thousand or more tons.

A ton is a huge barrel, as high as my head, for freight and, in Sanlúcar, for aging the manzanilla sherry. I saw a huge display of sherry barrels one evening when marquees were put up along the esplanade. The *bodegas,* the sherry factories, showed their wares in barrels black with age, with the *bodega*'s names of their sherries on them. The one I remember is Goya.

The reputation of Sanlúcar as a major port for ships to Seville and for fishing still has hints of its more fashionable past, not only the memory of a famous love affair of Goya.

The past is still represented in the names of the owners on the racing forms for one of the oldest and most famous horse races in Spain. The race is on one day in August. Spanish people come from all over the country to see it and bet on it. Sanlúcar is never more crowded. It is claimed to be the oldest horse race in Spain. There, as they would have when the races began in the mid-nineteenth century, the fishermen, the street poor, the punsters, the vagabonds, the poets, the *hidalgos,* the *caballeros* gather. Groups share ownership of many of the entries—*"Los Insolventes,"* the broke, have entered a gelding called Sir Castrates; "The Fishermen," a horse called Philippi. The Count, a horse called Olmeda. The horse belonging to the group called *Picota,* the pillory, is named "The Winds of the South."

The races are run near sunset at the evening low tide for over a mile along the flat sand shore of the Guadalquivir. Thousands of spectators stand in the shallow water on one side and the sand beach on the other. It must be one of the most beautiful sports events in the world. And it was started by a group that may no longer exist, the Aristocrats, at least not as the powerful, arrogant Goths they were for so long. It was in Sanlúcar that I had the greatest clue to what had happened to so many of them as they began to die out.

There is yet another of those narrow streets that goes toward the high bluff. I went there first without an idea of going up the hill. I was trying to find the market. The outside wall of it was forbidding, dark, a low, medieval doorway, a carved escutcheon over it. I thought it might have been a monastic building or at least a charity hospital. A woman entered the door, and I followed her.

Inside, busy women fingered vegetables and fruit under bright lights. Someone haggled over a chicken. The place had all the noise and color of an Andalucian market, the smell of raw meat, fresh vegetables, of figs and apricots and oranges. I wondered how long it had been there. Once again, everybody seemed to know everybody else, sharing the morning. The walls, the ceiling, the large counters seemed very old, but the flowers, the vegetables, the fruit were so fresh they must have been picked that morning, and not far away. Even better was the friendliness, good coffee, and the fifty-cent lunch. I tried it because I reasoned that the people who brought vegetables and meat to the market would not be satisfied with bad food. I was right.

The street beyond the market was so steep that it had wide steps, and to go onto it was to sink back into a deep and unexplained past of ancient gargoyle carvings on columns against a wall or a building at the beginning of the long flight of steps; maybe it was an abutment that must have been fourteenth century, rising against a perpendicular bluff. I had to guess. There was no way of knowing.

At first at the top, I went to the right of the road, where a grand Mudejar folly had been built, probably in the late eighteenth century. It was more "Moorish" than any Moorish building ever was. Neat and gaudy, wonderful colors, and a sneaking look at a plant-gorged courtyard, it tells much about the secret, ironic attitude of Sanlúcar toward its own past, that it is this building that has been chosen as the *ayuntamiento,* the town hall. It was a pleasant, lively place; the people lounged around it, walked in the fantasy of a garden of old trees.

Not so beyond it. On the crest of the hill, there was a sense of frailty, of death, decay, neglect in the once-fine houses. Some of the carved doors sagged, some of the windows were broken, some of the houses had obviously been broken into. There was one house with a sign so old that it, too, sagged with rain and wind and age; I think it was called the *Caballeros* club. A faded sign put there some years before said, "closed for repairs."

The people who had made the hill the power center of the town of Sanlúcar had gone away, or died or grown old or gone broke, or some of them may have moved down into the shore city and built fine houses there. Whatever had happened to them, it was for me a memorial to a way of living that shut out the common world, and drew its fatal strength from a privilege that every year in Spain before the civil war had meant less and less.

But the center around which they had clustered was still there, still cared for, still lively. It was the seat of one of the greatest land owners ever in Spain, the Duke of Medina Sedonia. It was the ninth Duke (and first of a new line), who had been dragged kicking and screaming by Philip II into being the Admiral of the Glorious Armada, and still, in that house, there are archives of probably the greatest value to Spain's history outside of officialdom.

The ducal palace, which looked attractive but unassuming on the street side, the rear of the estate, must have been bordered by the strange creatures like gargoyles on the decorated wall I had passed when I climbed the stairs of the street. Above it must have been wonderful gardens and a spacious ducal lawn. But that could only be imagined. All I could know of the present Dukes of Medina Sedonia, if indeed they lived there, was that they had clung to a place they loved while all around them was desertion and loss, and because they had done it, they had presented Sanlúcar with a grand presence that was, to outsiders like me, a well-kept secret. I honored that, for it was this house where the archives have been opened to leading European historians, perhaps for centuries, notably in the twentieth century to Fernand Braudel.

Behind the evasive, unassuming side of the ducal palace was a church that told the story of the last years of the *Reconquista,* that two-hundred-year secession of any but border raids in the thirteenth and fourteenth century. It had been built by Moorish artisans, and its door was of Mudejar carving.

But even more for me, in what I had thought was a dead place, was the Discalced Carmelite Convent. It keeps the most authentic copy, made by nuns during the lifetime of St. John of the Cross, of his writing. He had read it and copy-edited it, so his imprimatur shows how valid a text it is.

On the last day I was there I decided that I really ought to have seen Cádiz, not see but have seen, or "done" as some tourists say, marking off lovely old after lovely old, museum after museum, capital after capital. So I drove for an hour to Cádiz, east of Sanlúcar, the port of the high galleons of the Spanish Main. Before new archeological evidence was found, it was reputed to be the oldest city in Europe.

In the museum I saw what I expected, the slightly fat-faced Phoenicians with their tightly curled hair, carved on the lids of their coffins. These were the first known traders to open up the Costa de la Luz to the Middle East. Before they ventured beyond the Straits of Magellan into the Atlantic, it was believed that if you went beyond the Pillars of Hercules, you were in danger of falling off the edge of the world. Here and there were mysterious figures that were not Phoenician, and when I examined them I saw, again, the word Tartessan. The carving was more delicate, the wit more evident, but their identity was still a mystery to me— Tartessan. It brought back the first time I had seen the name, at a stop on my way someplace else. It was to lead me into yet another Spain,

I wandered into the park that was the main square in front of the museum and found the huge monument, with almost photographic life-sized images, of the men who had met in Cádiz during the Napoleonic Wars when the rest of Spain was torn apart, and had written the first constitution for a republic. Can a huge marble monument be touching? Yes, it can. This tribute is to a republic that was destroyed by the heavy foot of reaction after Napoleon's exile.

On the way home, for I thought of my hotel room as home by then, I remembered a story that I had heard of a soldier from World War II who had been caught by the retreat from Dunkirk in 1940. He had hiked with his company twenty miles to Dunkirk in new boots, and his feet hurt "something awful." When asked years later what he had done when he got to the English Channel, while the defeated British Army was being strafed and dive-bombed by Stukas as they waited for boats, he said, "Ooh, I took off me boots and I had meself a lovely paddle."

It gave me an idea. So when I got back to Sanlúcar in the early evening, I went down to the wide, beautiful, nearly empty sand beach where there had been through the day so many swimmers, took off my shoes, rolled up my pants, and had myself a lovely mile-long paddle where the horse races were run, and the ships of Magellan had set out to the Spice Islands in 1529 and ended up circling the world.

I had found the place that, having opened the rest of the south to strangers, the Spanish wanted to keep to themselves. So don't go to Sanlúcar when you are "doing" Europe. There is nothing there to do.

TARTESSOS

When I had stopped for the night in Carmona on the way to Sanlúcar I stayed there for several days. This can happen when you are alone, not over-organized, willing to waste time, and face exhaustion. I stayed at a *parador*, built in the ruins of a fourth-century fortress, and its descendant, a palace fortress built by Peter the Cruel in the fourteenth century to house his mistress.

Carmona was on an isolated, sharp hill, rising out of the valley. It looked like a man-made pyramid in the distance. When I began to climb it beyond the spread of the modern town, I got myself stuck in a street so steep that there were steps down it. One of my side mirrors scraped a flowerpot on a windowsill. A little cat scratch sound. I was already in the habit of asking the nearest man to get me out of trouble. Men are men, thank God, and along with the native polite-ness of Spaniards, I was banking on *macho*, after all, a famil-iar, untranslated indigenous Spanish word. The Turks call it *erkek adam*, manly, virile, courageous man!

I liked Carmona, so I wandered, and one day I came to a small museum. I had already found that the local museums of

Spain are treasure houses, partly because there is a movement to keep artifacts in the locality where they are found instead of sending them all to the huge central archeological museum in Madrid.

The result of this new policy is that the artifacts found make up a map of their own by where they are dug up. It is possible to guess the size of an ancient country by where its artifacts are found. Here I was, west of Córdoba and east of Seville, a fact that would become important in the game of "seek the legendary country" I was pleasuring myself by playing.

The museum at Carmona was in an old palace with a fourteenth-century doorway, and a pleasant series of small rooms, the usual Roman torsos, and Muslim carvings found in that part of the country. In the third room I found it: a vase nearly two feet high that I first thought, from its graceful flights of decoration, was Minoan, which would have put it near one thousand B.C. It was not. It was labeled Tartessan. The label on the vase was, for me, the first proof I found that the kingdom of Tartessos had at last been lifted out of legend into recognition as reality by archeologists and scholars, the imprimaturs that Schulten sought. Later, when I saw the second group of artifacts, in Cádiz, I swore that I would somehow find more. But the first I saw, ever, to know what it was, the vase at Carmona, began a search that has not yet ended.

Here on my wall, I have hung enlargements of my photographs, so I can study them, three sides of the vase, so light in design after the squat Roman matrons, the Phoenician pots, and the tribal kitchenware. And it has that essential Spanish quality of movement. I could not believe that it could have been in the eye of Spanish artists for that long, that passion for movement, that mixture of precision and wit.

Large griffinlike creatures moved around the vase, one pausing to gaze, one almost dancing, one walking. There were three of them, with high, waving animal tails on bodies that might have been oxen, or deer. Their legs were long and slim and as graceful as flamingos. Their heads were birdlike but like no bird, their wings abstractions, proud and graceful. They were not in step, their movements were casual; one had its head down, one looked straight ahead, one reared up toward a sky. There was a geometric square that may have been a feeding trough, for one of the creature's heads was lowered to it. If an aspect of *duende* is the inability to forget the shock of a beautiful thing at the moment of first seeing, it is for me in the recall of that vase. It was umber and subtle orange and black, and it may sometime have been brighter, but it still held life in its colors, its movement, the shapes of its imagined animals or birds, or dancers, or simply figures of dreams incarnate.

I was to find many more objects with this quality. That is what is different about much of the art of Tartessos. It shows individual vision beyond the usual formal images. There was caprice instead of the orthodox ritual forms, which have appeared in so much of the world from dim time past to the present day, the demanded orthodoxy of vision, often so blindly mundane.

That large vase was the object that started me on a search that would end, if it ever does, on the west side of the Guadalquivir, where it goes into the ocean, across the wide river mouth from Sanlúcar. I was no longer looking for "proof" of the kingdom of Tartessos. That is for scholars. I was looking, by the best means I could, to see who they were from what they had created, and what of it had survived. I was finding that if there was any similarity to what I had seen in the past, and in other places, it was what had been found in Ur of the Chaldees, in Nimrod, in Crete, and, strangely, in Urartu, that short-lived kingdom in the east of Turkey in the shadow of the mountain that bears a form of its name, Mount Ararat. All of these recovered places pre-date 700 B.C.

For so long Tartessos had been a legend, to cynics a place that could not have existed. So many lost cities. So many legends. As Troy had been turned from legend to reality by Schliemann, Tartessos had a dedicated German archeologist, Adolph Schulten. He was convinced by his own desire that he find what he thought might be Atlantis, somewhere in the southwest of Spain. A mystery.

He solved the mystery, and Tartessos has still not been found. But Schulten was sure he had stood on the land where it was hidden, and so am I. I had caught the virus of hope as you catch the lottery virus; just one ticket, just once, that I could find a shard, a map, a fragment. I had a few days left to go to a place that had hidden itself for millennia. So with the same surety I would have for winning the lottery, I went west as far in Spain as I could go.

I studied my topographical map, my top sheet. There it was, a kingdom, or could have been, in the southwest of Spain, between the Portuguese border and the narrow passage into the Mediterranean from the Atlantic. It was a semicircle with its shore along the Atlantic. Behind it, in a second semicircle, were the western reaches of the Sierra Nevada. Its main river, the Guadalquivir, flowed into it from deep in the northeast to Sanlúcar, the no place I had chosen.

The shape on the map told me more than any historic hints, or a legend that has caused academic argument since the sixteenth century at least, about where and why a kingdom, a settlement, or a city might have begun with its few huts, its first walls. There it was, a valley fed by fresh water from three rivers, with protecting mountains behind it like citadels. All around the Mediterranean and the Aegean can be found the same natural harbors and fields, where ancient cities have flourished and then disappeared under meters of earth or water. In the Aegean off Turkey I had dived over them, those man-sculpted building stones, piled or flung across the sea floor by some long-forgotten catastrophe, the home of sea urchins and little, bright shallow-water fish.

I have seen strange shapes that could be the ghosts of ancient boats, shapes of sand, traces of lost trade long past, and death without date. There are places that are, as Troy was for so many centuries, sunken legends, cities that have come down as tales of vast riches, that we still know little about, in Spain, in Africa, in the Americas. Where, still, is El Dorado? Xanadu? The capital city of Tartessos?

Although volumes have been written within the last forty years about Tartessos, I found that its most valid history, added to what we now know from archeological digs and works of art, is in the Bible, where the kingdom is taken for granted as part of the ancient seascape. The Old Testament also acts as a calendar.

For centuries proud ships sailed with cargoes of gold and silver and bronze from the country of Tartessos, which the Bible had called Tarshish. The first mention is in I Kings, chapter 10. "Once every three years came the navy of Tarshish, bringing gold and silver, ivory and apes and peacocks."

To read the whole of the chapter as a series of clues, and fabulously rich ones, is to put the mention of Tartessos, or Tarshish, into a context. It appears in the story of the visit of the Queen of Sheba to see the wonders of Solomon's court.

Treasure after treasure is mentioned as well as fine food, a happy court, the king's wisdom. Visitors brought gifts of gold and spices and precious stones from all over the known Mediterranean world. There were sandalwood trees to use as columns in his palace among the cedars of Lebanon. There were two hundred shields of "beaten gold," a throne made of ivory, covered with gold, with statues of lions (or live lions?) on either side of it. In other words, along with sandlewood, and gold from Ophir, a ship brought ivory, and apes and peacocks from "Tarshish." The voyage took three years. I Kings is said to have been written around 990 B.C. So the city-state was established then, already famously wealthy, in touch with the east, and also with Africa, since apes, ivory, and peacocks came from there.

By the eighth century B.C. Tarshish was used as a metaphor by Isaiah for God's wrath and condemnation of pride and riches ("Howl, ye ships of Tarshish") and for those trying to hide from God's wrath ("Pass ye over to Tarshish; howl, ye inhabitants of the isle"). When Jonah tried to escape God's orders to warn Nineveh that it would be destroyed if it didn't mend its ways, it is to Tarshish he took ship, to get as far away from the orders of his God as possible.

These were the main hints that Adolph Schulten used to begin his search. He is said not to have found Tartessos. But I think he did. I think that he found it across the river mouth from Sanlúcar where he said it was, and where I gazed while I had my paddle upriver along the shallows. The next clue I found that this might be true was another map, this time an archeological map. Long after Schulten's work in the 1920s, modern archeologists had made a path around the Doñana National Park by pointing out the places they had chosen to dig for that ancient city or country.

The shape was what the ancient geographers and the Roman engineers said about the land they called Turdentania, their new name for the Tartessan homeland. The shoreline and the main interior of the land closest to what Schulten said was the capital has changed so radically that it was impossible to see how any such fabulous city-state could have been there.

A huge lagoon covered most of what is now the Doñana National Park, the greatest bird and wild animal habitat in Europe, a vast wetland with pastures that once were islands. The lagoon reached from Lebrija, over four miles from the shore at Sanlúcar, west to what is now the city of Huelva. Two rivers brought vast mountain riches into the great lagoon—the Río Tinto and the Guadalquivir. The mountains they flowed from also made Tartessos and destroyed it by invasions from envious exploiters, the Carthaginians and the Greeks, and later the Romans.

The Hercules myth tells me something else about the shore of Atlantic Andalucia. From before the Greeks, the natural land- and skyscape was seen as a god, with the shape of a human. There were thousands of gods of streams and mountains, lands and emotions. The Greek culture saw abstractions and natural phenomena as human images. Hercules was given the credit for being the founder of the south of Spain, Seville especially, upriver on the Gaudalquivir from the Atlantic.

Hercules is said to have fought and killed Geryon, the triple-bodied monster who ruled over the west of Iberia, modern Spain. Hercules had stolen his famous cattle. Fine cattle were a staple of the kingdom, as today the land is grazing home to the most famous breeds of fighting bulls. The Guadalquivir, up through the time of the Romans, emptied into the great lagoon, which had three rivers as outlets to the Atlantic.

Tartessos was a culture with a language and an alphabet, an ancient literature, mostly poetry, and laws in the form of rhymed poems, on the face of it very sensible since it would have been easier to memorize them. These things are what historians of this ancient world have found in ancient texts, facts that are as fragmented as the physical evidence of their shining culture. It is said that they were peaceful, regal, and rich, three qualities that would draw aggression.

Perhaps Tartessos did last over a thousand years. No one can be sure. All the evidence that lies where the national park starts is the memory line of rivers, and the catastrophe of mud and slag that threatens to pour down from the Sierra Nevada, which had been the protecting barrier for the kingdom. Such a catastrophe, caused by earthquake, is said to have sunk Tartessos—and Atlantis—and in the twentieth century played havoc with the park and the fields and marshes within it. Like the Bible stories of Sodom and Gomorrah, and very like the legend of Atlantis, which it imitates more closely, Tartessos is said to have been destroyed in a single night.

There are, of course, modern believers who are convinced that Tartessos was Atlantis. But their evidence has to be seen as hyperbole. Such exaggeration can falsify what might be true. They publish the accounts of scuba divers and underwater submersibles of vast walls, roads, even massive sculptures, under the Atlantic near where it enters the Mediterranean.

It all sounds valid until one remembers that the same discoveries have been made, and reported in the same words, at the island of Cancún in the Caribbean, and even in the depths of the rainforests of South America. The latest report I could

find states firmly that Robert Ballard, in his underwater exploration of the Black Sea coast, found a "vast" city ruin from
before the biblical flood. He did not. He did find evidence of
human habitation, but it was not the dramatic find that the
new "Atlantans" claim.

But yet? The mind flies into myth again. After all, the
Aztecs expected white people to come from the Atlantic to
their cost. What if the Atlantic, long before it was known in the
east, was the central sea for an older culture, that the southern windblown route from east to west, where Columbus
sailed so blindly, had been known and used for centuries.
Thor Heyerdahl, who became famous when he built the *Kon-
Tiki* of native reeds and sailed it across the Pacific, tried to
prove the east/west crossing when he successfully sailed a
papyrus boat based on Egyptian models from the west coast
of Africa to Brazil.

What if it is all true—what if Atlantis is in the sea off
Cancún, hidden in Brazil, or under what has been estimated
as thirty meters of sand, mud, and river silt in the place
where Schulten said it was, and which he couldn't reach
because the pumps he used could not pump out the flowing
ground water?

In Plato's Dialogue *Timaeus*, and in *Critias*, the story of
Atlantis is told as a tall tale, a legend, with an expert to
prove its validity, a ploy that has been used ever since—witness the "experts," medical and political, in modern advertising, who are quoted without names, " unnamed sources,"
rumor sworn as truth. The expert for Plato was an ancient
Egyptian priest who told the story to Solon, who told the
story to Plato's great-grandfather, of a kingdom immeasur-
ably wealthy, the size of Asia, swallowed by the sea, nine
thousand years before his birth.

"There was an island in front of the Straits which are called the Pillars of Hercules," Plato begins his half-remembered half folktale.

> There came violent earthquakes and floods, and in a single day of misfortune all the warlike men in a group sank into the earth, and the island of Atlantis . . . disappeared into the depths of the sea. For that reason the sea in those parts is impassible, impenetrable since there is a shoal of mud in the way, and this was caused by the sinking of the island.

So this wild tract of swamp and grazing land, of forests and old hunting preserves that has gone back to the birds and the animals from whence it came, could have been, for a while, the mythic kingdom. It is now the Doñana National Park. What if it did sink eons ago and was given, in Plato's words, back to the "fowls of the air and the beasts of the field"?

The islands that would have been the natural protection for the Tartessan cities did sink. And the Atlantic Ocean's wild currents have pounded the floor of the shallow water near the coast to create a miles-long submerged sandbank, curved in an ironic imitation of the shoreline. The surf off the coast of the Costa de la Luz is well known as some of the most exciting and dangerous for scuba diving and for surfing in Europe.

There is no greater sculptor than the ocean's waters. What is the world's largest port today may be one day a nameless swamp. Or, as Shakespeare wrote, "Full fathom five my father lies. There are pearls that were his eyes. . . ."

So I set out like a fool to find what could not be there, not so much the land, that too, but the people, those who had produced the art, and the splendid elegant objects that they used which may be all that is ever found.

I went around the natural park, the salt marshes, in the same direction that an ancient Tartessan merchant might have gone by wagon and mule around the great lagoon, from Sanlúcar north to Lebrija, where the north shore of the lagoon had once been, along the double highway, the *autopista*, to the outskirts of Seville, around its southern ring road and onto the *autopista* west toward Portugal.

The road was lined for miles this time, not with sunflower fields but with shrubs in bloom, some with pink flowers and some with white. I had studied a tourist map to guide me. It had all of the local museums marked where I might find what I was looking for. But if I had not learned already that what I was seeking was not what I would find, it happened again.

I glanced down in the middle of a joyful morning speed across a bridge along the highway to see a shallow river filled and its shores stained with blood. It was what I was looking for, the Río Tinto, the Red River. The red I saw, which might have been blood, for all the fighting that went on over it, was one of the most valuable metals in the world, copper sulfate.

I had marked the streams in the Sierra Nevada that ran into the Río Tinto; they were like hundreds of small veins that told where the gullies were, between the pile on pile of mountains. This was the place where the riches of Tartessos had made and destroyed a kingdom. The mountains were sharp, stony, filled with gold and silver and copper and iron, high natural pyramids, harsh shapes of truly untold wealth.

The road had to be narrow, and it cut through sometimes in short tunnels. There were exposed cuts as well, where, on the surface of the rock, fragments of silver caught the sun. I got on the wrong road, found a place to stop and study where I was not, found a turning place where a tavern was poised on the edge of a cliff. I have seldom been so frightened of simply turning a car as I was at that moment in that sharp landscape of glittering stone.

I found a road that promised to take me past the Río Tinto mine on the way to the first of the towns marked with a local museum, high in the mountains. On the way I wanted to see an abandoned copper mine run by a British company in the late nineteenth and most of the twentieth century.

The Spanish had been amused by the fact that they had built a little English town for their workers, with a cricket pitch, a Church of England church, and rowhouses like the outskirts of English industrial towns in the north. There was also a museum promised there, but it was a mining museum, and I knew too much about mining. I knew what an abandoned mine looked like. I had grown up seeing them abandoned, forgotten, the slag heaps left, the slowly falling board-and-batten houses built and then abandoned by companies whose presidents hardly knew where the mines were. So an ugly abandoned little English town was to be expected, even in the heights of the Sierra Nevada.

I got to the mine before I was ready, if I would ever have been. The whole top of the mountain had been sheared off. There was a round chasm where it had been. It was the size of a huge lake, of a volcanic calderon, and it looked as deep as a pit of hell. All I remember as I drove along beside that terrible space is that huge pit that seemed to have no bottom, where human slaves had mined for gold and silver and copper and iron and tin, for these mountains have or had them all, for five thousand years. It is the oldest mine in the world that has been worked continuously into the twentieth century.

I forgot the little town and its museum in an effort to get away from the place, and when I pulled into Aracena, famous for its cave, I was still shaking. I tried to go into the cave with a quiet group of Spanish people having a Sunday treat, but I had, for the first time in my life, to turn back, and sit in the shade of the main square for a while, and stop remembering.

In the distance in front of me there was a life-sized horse's head of cast bronze. Its changeable colors caught the sun. It was reared up against the sky, spirited and graceful. I was sure I had found a Tartessan sculpture. It was modern, not a copy, but a new vision so old that it was without time and simply there and simply made by a Spanish eye and hand.

One day I drove from Sanlúcar to Huelva, a fairly modern port on the Atlantic where much archeological research is centered. It's a pleasant little city, once bigger, once rumored to have been one of the places where there could have been a capital of Tartessos. Unlike so many old Spanish cities where the streets wind round and round a hilltop, Huelva is laid out in the familiar checkerboard pattern of a modern city. Its eighteenth-century cathedral and some of its buildings look like they could be in South America—Spanish colonial architecture, the grillework, the massive planting.

In one night in the late eighteenth century, Huelva, like the more famous destruction of Lisbon, was flattened by the same earthquake that destroyed Lisbon. Being a port, much of Huelva was buried in mud and sand and the raging rivers that are usually so quiet, flowing down from the Sierra Nevada. Atlantis and Tartessos were supposed to have been destroyed, in the same way, on the same fault in the earth that makes an earthquake zone.

The archeological museum in Huelva has almost all of the products of archeological digs that are still going on there in the constant search for Tartessos. It is, along with Madrid, the most telling and exciting of all the museums that hold those hints of Tartessan life for which I searched, and will again some day. Here was some of the stuff of legend, a small chariot, its sides, its platform where a driver must have stood—to race? to fight?—covered with shining silver. Even the spokes of its wheels were bound with silver.

In a wall exhibition there is a modern column with the head of a man who wears a formal beard. On his head is a diadem, or a cap. It is a simple series of welded gold circles and upright columns, very light, no hint of the heavier, more brutal-looking crowns that would come later to this part of Andalucia. The figure wears a gold necklace with acorn amulets hanging from a pendant chain. It is like a necklace found near Seville, another as far north as Cáceres (and, later and heavier, the large acorn amulets around the neck of the most famous unknown woman in Spain). On the wall are two bracelets shaped like five-inch cuffs of gold, and around an abstract waist, the links of a wide belt of gold. Beside him, the black, life-sized silhouette of a bull is decked with a pectoral of gold shaped like a bull's hide between his horns, and around his body a wide belt of gold.

That bull's-hide shape is found wherever there are artifacts from Tartessos. In the castle museum at Bodrum in Turkey is one of the earliest ships ever found. Some of its cargo was bronze, shaped like bull's hides. Was the bronze from Tartessos? And when did the influence of Tartessos or Tarsus disappear? It could have been when the country was cut off from its Mediterranean trade by the Carthaginians, who made a barrier of ships along the Pillars of Hercules, destroyed the Tartessian trade routes, and then took over the mines that sustained them.

In the archeological museum in Seville I found a hoard of

gold that had been dug up near the city: two three-foot-high slim candlesticks, simple, elegant, and looking modern enough to place on any banquet table today. Beside the candlesticks were bowls and cups of gold, a large belt buckle so finely made it looked almost frail, and beside it, a jewel, a bracelet with the same acorn-shaped amulets, a fine necklace with a pendant of what could be flower petals or leaves, bracelets of gold, belt links of gold, and two large gold pectorals shaped like bull's hides.

I think it is fatally easy to throw these objects all into categories marked "ritual." It seems to me as faulty to say they show this or that influence from the Orient. There were strong connections with the eastern Mediterranean, but they were commercial, and I have not seen Middle Eastern art that shows Tartessan influence. But I have seen the same qualities in earlier and later Spanish works.

I think I love most the shapes and movement of people and their animals, some in bronze, some in limestone, many on fragments of vases. Of all the statues of animals found in Spain, from the heavy primitive bulls of Guisando to the massive animal on the bridge at Salamanca and the elephant in the courtyard at Córdoba, the Tartessian animals alone have a sense of wit and movement. A lion's mane flows in an imagined wind, or he is running, his mouth a snarl. A man is riding a lively bronze horse, not sitting on but leaning toward its withers, urging it on, its head and tail high, its front leg elevated in the high graceful pace that you can see today in the Spanish Riding School in Jerez de la Frontera. The bronze, man and horse, is about two inches high.

In the archaeological museum in Madrid, the upright of a table base, a slim bronze column trimmed with a swirling gold design, is balanced on the slim body of a horse, with its long, arched neck. The same litheness, the same stance, can be seen in the modern fields of this horse- and bull-raising Andalusian countryside.

In the archaeological museum in Córdoba, the marble figure of a deer lies down, feet tucked in as lithely as a dancer's. A bull's head with graceful horns, the face of a Nubian in terra-cotta that was a portrait of a living human being, a slave girl, an obcious portrait of a living person, with her braids hanging down on either side, is in the archaeological museum in Madrid. They all show that the artist had chosen his or her subject, not bent to any formal ritual demand. There was, as a part of these discoveries, the mother goddess in the archaeological museum in Granada, a necklace with the acorn amulets made of bronze and amber in Huelva, dancing and fighting birds, and lotus blossoms as "modern" as some of the designs in the Popular Art Museum in Salamanca.

In the *Museo Arcqueológico* behind the lovely tree-lined *Paseo de Prado* in Madrid, there is the bust of a woman, *La Dama de Elché*. She is a stone funerary vessel. Or maybe she is not. There have been more arguments about her century, her provenance, who she was, goddess or queen, than about any other work of art in Spain. Is she influenced by Greek art, Roman art, or is she a face from long before such influences were thought of there? One scholar even accuses her of being a late-nineteenth-century fake, salted in an archeological dig. But there is no doubt of the genius of the creator of this face, one of the greatest works of art in Spain. She is stunningly beautiful, with one of the most unforgettable faces I have ever seen in a work of art. But from the other end of the gallery where I first saw her from a distance, she projected what I thought at first was a cruelty and contempt beyond any I had ever seen. I was so bemused by her that I took photographs of her and, when I got home, had one enlarged. There she hangs on my wall to be studied. I no longer see her as contemptuous or cruel, or sad, or even sleepy. These at least require emotion, which, for good or bad, is recognition. Like the spectators at a glimpsed bullfight on the television, I see her as finally, completely, utterly, terrifyingly without mercy.

But one thing is certain. Even under foreign domination, Carthaginian, Greek, Roman, or Visigoth, there was always that Spanish eye and hand. Sometimes, often, it had to be hidden from deadening authority, like the frog on the front of the great university façade at Salamanca, or the copulating nuns hidden in the choir at Zamora. Sometimes it was exiled as Goya was, or Unamuno. That anarchic wit, that passion, that precision, from deep song to classic *flamenco*, from the Tartessan horses to Picasso's *Guernica*, has *duende*.

PALOS DE LA FRONTERA

 I have ended where this book began, only I didn't know it was going to begin there. I went with my cousin for a holiday. We arrived during the week of *Semana Santa,* Holy Week, Spain's most famous week of penitence, prayer, and *fiesta,* for Spain celebrates death as passionately as it celebrates life, often at the same time.

A dear friend who had lived in Spain advised us not to miss a little port called Palos. So on the way to see Córdoba and Granada, we stopped in Palos de la Frontera. It was very small. The only thing of great importance, to us at least, was that Columbus had sailed from Palos on his first voyage to go west to reach the east. My knowledge of Columbus was about the same as most Americans. I knew that Queen Isabel of Spain had given him the money to go, that he had discovered America when he was looking for India, and that America wasn't named for him but for an Italian called Amerigo Vespucci, which seemed odd.

We had followed the advice in Michener's book *Iberia,* to the letter. His fervent praise of the celebration of *Semana*

Santa in Seville convinced me to stay as far away as possible and still be in Spain.

The spiritual intent of his description came from his own experience—the horses, the bullfights, the Sevillian snobbery, which was highly advertised. You were allowed to look at the Sevillian aristocracy in their boothlike pavilions, but not to speak and not to touch. It sounded to me like the Indy 500 or the Kentucky Derby, with a religious "theme." To Michener and to most who have seen it, it can be, as it was for him, the most profound experience in Spain. So pay no attention to me. We went to Palos.

Palos was also an escape, a pause, just a way to get over jet lag with as little trouble as possible. The hotel was called the *Pinta,* which did not surprise us. It was small, on a street near the local university, but then everything was near the local university. Spain had a university in every major town that I saw. They must be the best-educated people in Europe.

I wondered how little the size of the town had changed, and the population, since the days of Columbus. There was an atmosphere of forgetting, waiting, being poised for something that wouldn't happen. They had not yet renamed the new Franco plaza with its colonnade. There were no other tourists. I suppose they were all standing on each other's toes in Seville "doing" Holy Week.

No matter. I remember a joy in being there that had begun as we drove onto the side road from one of the Spanish *autopistas* which, with jet lag and a strange car, was scary that first day, but never a day after, for I love to drive. The Spanish were keeping to the speed limit, about eighty miles an hour.

So we turned with pure relief off the main road onto a little road to what had to be a little town. The road was narrow and empty between fields, where we saw fighting bulls, magnificent animals, and the horses of Andalucia they say have Arab blood. Certainly they must since this was Muslim country for seven hundred years, but they also have the grace and style that I would see later in the pre-Roman statues. The horses and colts we saw free in the fields were slim, high-stepping Spanish horses.

As soon as we had stumbled our way into the small hotel, we ventured out beyond our attempts to be understood in the usual survival Spanish. I had listened to tapes in my car before we left, sitting at stoplights saying *gracias*. Most of it hadn't stuck. In other words we were as everybody who goes to a new country, wandering around, a little lost. I see now, as I think of it at the end of this search for Spain, how much I saw there that first few days, and how little I understood.

As naïve as pups, we walked down the narrow street in the strange little town. There were two taverns. One we could see at once was the "nice people" tavern; a shining Spanish small car was parked in front of it. What make we didn't know. But we discussed the fact that being small it must be light and cheap, and wasn't it a nice sign of new Spain that there seemed to be one of these kiddie cars in front of almost every house. It was only one of the many things we were wrong about. Many of the small cars seen in Spain are powerful and expensive. They have to be small to get around the tiny streets and the sharp corners of the old sections of towns, which was, of course, only one of the many things we were misunderstanding. I found this out later to my embarrassment at the signs of struggle in Cáceres left on the car paint.

There were also, in front of the tavern, several shining smaller motorcycles, with wheels half the size of a regular motorcycle, the most familiar vehicle in Spanish towns. They zip by you, buzzing like bees. What seemed to be college students were coming and going, in and out of the open front. We could see them crowded at a long bar. The other tavern had bicycles and a few small motorbikes in front of it. There were mostly men sitting inside, except in the evening, when wives or girlfriends joined them. It was domestic, easygoing, cozy. They both smelled of *tapas* and wine, the most familiar smell in a Spanish street.

After a day or so we realized that the same people tended to meet at the same time, pull tables together beyond the open doors and talk, quiet talk and a lot of it, but it was Spanish talk, and only from the faces could we see that they were at serious business of some sort. We were seeing our first *tertulias*, the intimate, habitual, almost formal meetings of people who have much in common. The first thing I noticed that first day was that there were men and women together, something that would seldom have been seen in the days of Franco. It was one of the subtle measures of a new Spain that I would see over and over. The atmosphere of Palos, the ease, the cleanliness, was new to me, too. Franco had been dictator at my own first time in Spain. This time, years later, and within days, I knew that I was in a new country.

We walked under a series of those thin arches that look as if they are embroidered with wire. They were stretched across the street by our hotel, looking so sad in the daytime with their little dead lightbulbs and their wires showing. How was I to know that this first street would tell me more than I could take in about the towns and the people I would see later in my search? But, looking back, it did. I was to find out that the Spanish love a party, whether it celebrates a tomato, strawberry, or asparagus harvest or the death of

Jesus, a sacred bull, or the bullfighter killed by it. The one in Tordesillas for the Bull of the *Vega* was one of the most delightful I would join, but that was later, when I had learned to ramble around with the crowd and taste things and say good evening and thank you in Spanish.

We were the only guests in the hotel, and we were hungry, of course, much earlier than the Spanish families who came in later in the evening. We ordered *sangría,* of course, and *paella,* of course, which we drank and ate because we were in Spain.

Then, on our second evening, we were asked by a priest in English if we would mind moving our car. We took it where he told us to. This was done with pointing and smiling, for by that time, only two days, everybody greeted us as friends. I found such easy hospitality later in every unspoiled and not overvisited Spanish city. It is odd, and somehow right, that I should have to travel all over Spain in my search in order to begin to understand what we saw and were welcomed to in the first three days of our stay there.

That evening the street in front of the hotel was closed to traffic. There was much walking and consulting in the roadway as we went into the hotel. We suspected that there would be something to watch, so we got our drinks from the bar and went back up to the little balconies outside our rooms. The balconies were side by side directly over the street door. They were draped with flags that blew in our faces. Note: The first words we learned to say beyond good morning, good evening, please, and thank you were *"vodka y naranja natural con hielo,"* vodka and fresh orange juice with ice.

We sat watching and waiting as people began to gather on the sidewalk below. The regulars had come out of their taverns. Children ran back and forth across the road. A young man sitting on a beautiful horse with all the high-handed assurance of a *hidalgo* pranced it up and down the street through the gathering crowd. Its head was high, its pleated, knobbed tail high, its neck arched like the sculptures I would see of the Tartessan horses.

As it got dark the lights on the frail arches came on and, of course, as they always do, changed the little world. They glittered, festive; the crowd calmed and was more silent than I have ever heard a waiting crowd. Away in the distance, beyond where we could see from the balconies, came solemn music, near and nearer, pierced with the wail of fifes and the crash of drums.

It was completely dark by the time the procession reached the street below. Ahead there were the anonymous *penitentes* in their black robes with the pointed hoods that rose high over their heads, and were hung with black cloth that draped over their faces so they saw only through slits cut into the masks. It is said that the Ku Klux Klan copied their robes and hoods, but in white so they would seem like ghosts at night.

Candlelight from what seemed to be hundreds of candles, at the front of the floats that followed, danced across the gold staffs and the faces of the silent crowd. I am sure that every able-bodied person in the town who was not part of the procession was watching. And, unlike in Seville, there were no hired professional porters to carry the sacred images on platforms that must have weighed as much as two tons.

This was the night of Palos's procession as part of the mourning for the death of Christ in the days of grief and *fiesta* that would be celebrated in every town and village in Spain during the Holy Week before the Easter Resurrection. The Spanish may no longer be fervently Catholic, and they have much historic reason not to be, for the Church has too often been a tyrant, but on the night of their procession they celebrate something that goes back way beyond Christianity, *Reconquista,* the Holy Virgin mother, to the benign aspects of the Mother Goddess herself, the earliest of all the images that have been worshiped in the most ancient of myths and metaphors, from the Middle East to the shores of the Atlantic.

The tradition of the procession we were seeing was begun in the thirteenth century when Ferdinand III captured Seville from the Muslims. The *hermandades,* those brotherhoods formed during the *Reconquista* to succor the wounded and bury the dead in that centuries-long series of battles, were then and are now the organizers and the caretakers of the procession. They march in the robes of *penitentes,* carrying banners, candles, religious relics.

Down below we could see the first of the platforms, with lanterns of glittering gold at its four corners, a figure standing on it, life-sized. Around the platform was a red or purple brocade skirt that fell to the street. It was hard to see some of the colors in the candlelight.

There was a curious and almost frightening sensation that the body itself was walking, for it swayed as a body would, taking step after step under a heavy load. Was it because the men underneath the platform walk in unison? As the form came nearer we saw that it was a life-sized polychrome statue of Christ carrying the cross. He looked nearly dead with exhaustion and grief. His face was streaked with blood from the Crown of Thorns. His body was bent under the weight of the heavy cross. But he was dressed in imperial velvet, trimmed with gold, which was such a contrast to the suffering face that it made it worse than if the statue had been naked. Candlelight flickered and licked across that suffering face, and I turned my eyes away.

I heard a tap of something like a mallet carried by one of the leaders. The platform was stopped, and lowered to the street. It was impossible not to see that face. There is one like it in almost every town or city in Spain; some are seventeenth century, some carved by local woodcarvers, some by famous sculptors. They have *duende,* for the apex of suffering to anyone who was born and brought up a Christian is a historic communal memory of that moment.

The platform rested on its table-height wood posts. The men who were carrying it were squatting under it, behind the platform skirt, resting. We looked down. The proprietor of the hotel was carrying out a large tray of glasses of beer. He flipped up the skirt and passed the tray inside to the men. After a little while they passed the empty glasses back, lifted their burden, and the procession began again. All the way to the church, when they stopped to rest at the sound of the mallet on the front of the platform, there were bottles, food, gifts pushed under the platforms.

Behind the Christ came the platform of the Mother of God. It was larger than the Christ, for this is mother goddess country. She stood high above her platform, her face washed in tears made of jewels or glass, her body in magnificent robes, blue, like a great pyramidal tent with that small weeping face above it. She was crowned with a huge glittering crown.

It takes years in those smaller towns to create and care for these processions. They are paid for by the *hermandades,* who of course are the leading citizens of the town. I had a wicked thought that some of the *penitentes* were bank managers who repented being so mean to their customers.

But it was people as local as these—two mariner brothers, a hundred and fifty men born to the sea, some the ancestors of those who carried the Christ and the Holy Mother—who had the guts to go to sea with Christopher Columbus as long ago as 1492.

We went to see the replicas of the little ships of Columbus. That is what you do in Palos. It is also what crews of polite Spanish children do. There were few if any other Americans. I found myself being a little ashamed.

There they were: the *Niña*, the *Pinta*, the *Santa María*, riding at anchor in a small marina. The shore had been made to look a bit like a tropical port. The ships were so small. They shone in the sun with new paint. The ropes, coiled perfectly, were pure white. The bow and stern of the biggest, the *Santa María*, were high in the Spanish way, and the masts were tall. Her displacement, fully loaded, was two hundred and eighty-five tons. The average seagoing ship of the day was two hundred tons.

We joined a queue to walk up a steep gangplank. There was something touching about her smallness. She was at sea for two months in a strange endless ocean, a ship that today would be about the size of a river ferry, or a coastal pleasure boat. Life-sized replicas of sailors coiling rope, hoisting sail, loading, were poised in mid-movement. They were, I am sure, a lot cleaner and more finely dressed than the original "motley crew" that Columbus must have picked up to go out into the most frightening ocean, the wrong way. Eons of genetic memory must have warned them all against it. The maps of the far-reaching edges of the Atlantic Ocean still warned, "Here be dragons."

A man sat at a simple table made of thick board, supposedly noting the charting, or manifests, or whatever records needed to be kept. Latitude? Longitude? The instrument for longitude would not exist for another two centuries. They could know by the sun at noon how many days they had gone, but not how far. The length of the voyage could not be reckoned until they got there—in Columbus's case, wherever "there" was.

They steered by the stars and the sun's arc across the sky as men have steered since the boats had ventured out eons before through the Pillars of Hercules. I thought I would be cynical about little authentic replicas with little authentic men, most of whom were about five feet tall, but I was not. I was as moved as the children before and after me.

The *Pinta*, for which our hotel was named, was the middle-sized boat, about the size of the largest pleasure boats you see in marinas, for shoreline sailors and their friends and their bottles of wine and their stops to swim in quiet coves. She was one hundred and forty tons.

As for the smallest, the *Niña* (little girl), she lay low in the water and I could see her swimming along after the others like a faithful dog. She drew only one hundred tons' displacement.

They carried food, armaments, sailing equipment, men, crosses to convert the natives of the Indies, which was where they hoped they were going. They also carried a year's supply of goat cheese.

It has been said that the main reason they sailed from little Palos de la Frontera instead of one of the great ports of Cádiz or Seville was that Columbus had lived and planned his voyage at the monastery of Rábida, only a few miles away. The little line of towns along the lower Río Tinto were fishing towns, and a ship's complement was easy to pick up. Columbus knew the fishermen, the coastal sailors; who was unstable, who he could trust. The monastery of Rábida is still there, little changed from the days when Columbus and his son lived there, and where he took his last communion and made his last confession the night before he sailed.

I like to see him in his fine new clothes, letting his fine sleek mule walk slowly along the little road we had taken by the Río Tinto, through these little towns where he had been so broke and owed so much, hiring his crew among the fishermen.

But there may have been another reason why Columbus did not sail from one of the major Atlantic ports, Seville or Cádiz. Both of them were already overcrowded with ships of all sizes, including a full complement of ships from the Ottoman Turkish navy.

Seven months before he sailed, Ferdinand and Isabel, pushed by Cardinal Cisneros, had exiled the Jews from Spain. The ports were full of families trying to get out. The Inquisition, with its death dealing and its confiscating of fortunes from the earlier *conversos,* was behind them. In front of them, out to sea, the pirates had gathered like sharks to steal the goods they depended on to resettle, and put them up for ransoms that nobody could pay. Many of them who had gone before were captured and sold into slavery.

When Bayazid II, Sultan of the Ottoman Empire, the father of Suleiman the Magnificent, heard what had happened, he ordered that the Jews be rescued. He was a quiet, pious man. He followed the Koran, which honored the Jews and the Christians as "the people of the Book," the Old Testament, honored in the Koran, for Islam is a religion of tolerance written into the Koran, as compassion is written into the New Testament, no matter what violent turns they have both taken through the centuries.

Bayazid considered Ferdinand a fool. He is said to have

announced that he had thought Ferdinand a more sensible man than to exile or murder his most able, skillful, and clever citizens.

He ordered four hundred ships of the Ottoman navy, under the command of Admiral Kemal Reis, to sail to Spain and take the Spanish Jews to cities and towns all around the Ottoman Empire, where they were needed as citizens. They were to be resettled. So over a hundred and fifty thousand Jews, families, scribes, the educated, the artisans, were added to the Ottoman Muslim population. They brought education, brains—in effect, a viable urban middle class, so needed by the Ottoman conquerors, who had taken Constantinople in 1453 when Mehmet II rode into the city with a rose, they say, in his teeth, and declared the church of Sancta Sophia, the oldest church in Christendom, a mosque, as the Christians had made the mosque at Córdoba into a Christian church.

There was little left of the great Christian capital of the Byzantine empire, which had lasted over a thousand years. It had been sacked and looted long before by the Venetian Crusaders. The famous "Venetian" horses over the entry to San Marco in Venice were found in Constantinople in the hippodrome. The icon of the Virgin in the church had been carried before the Byzantine armies. So there must have still been room for all, and a building boom even forty years after its surrender in the city that was renamed Istanbul. The Ottoman capital had been moved there from Bursa.

Descendants of these Spanish exiles still live in Istanbul, still are honored as citizens, according to the Koran. The Jewish community in Cairo, and many or most of the Jews who returned to Palestine so long ago and became an integral part of the communities there, were Spanish Jews, welcomed by a Muslim community who were following the Koran as their sultan did.

But that was 1492, when a reactionary and power-driven clergy manipulated the rulers of the country of Spain. This is now, and maybe little has changed, except the names of the religion: once Christianity in the hands of manipulative zealots, now a loud minority of Muslims.

At the beginning of this book I told about what I had carried with me to Spain. I did not, and do not, speak the language. Are there more ways to meet and know a country? I think so. There is another way, without words and without the too easy familiarity with a place that takes things for granted and misses so much.

To be a stranger in a strange land, as travelers have been for centuries, is to keep astonishment alive, see as a child sees, retain one's awe, astonishment, and wonder.

I will go back to Spain. There is always, in this elegant country with its brutal sunlight and its concise shadows, so much to discover. I will, if I can, recognize its people, its music, its art, its dancing, and, above all, its dignity and good manners wherever I am in the world, which can take me back to a street, a building, a half-caught glimpse of that essence which is Spain.

ENDNOTE

BEAR WITH ME. When I am working on a book, with its attendant isolation, this phrase covers all the time, requests, generosity, and early reading that sustain me.

So to those generous souls who consented to bear with me through the planning and the writing, I dedicate this book with all my heart.

To my editor and publisher, Starling Lawrence, not only for backing a ridiculous idea long before it was anything but an idea, but for seeing to it that at every point I had what I needed, including a second voyage of discovery back to Spain that made the last chapters of this book possible. His careful editing and his faith in the results were a strength and an ever-present help in times of trouble.

To my dear old friend and agent, Michael Carlisle, for being there, for watching out for me at the stumbling blocks, and, above all, for helping me to see. As Joseph Conrad wrote, "That—and no more—and it is everything."

To the Tourist Office of Spain for their never-failing politeness, help, and hospitality far beyond any request I would have made.

To David Gies, editor of the forthcoming *Cambridge History of Spanish Literature*, Cambridge University Press, whose enthusiastic reading of an early draft gave me joy and direction.

To my late dear friend, Staige Blackford, who shared his Spanish experience, and whose reading of an early draft gave me the approval I needed for staying with a complicated subject.

To Kathrine and Stanworth Brinkley, who lived in Spain for three years, for their never-failing daily gifts of encouragement, care, and strength.

To Morgen Van Vorst, assistant to Starling Lawrence, who accepted with grace and carried out one request after another, however dumb or difficult or goofy, without a hint of surprise.

RECOMMENDED BOOKS

Burckhardt, Titus. *Moorish Culture in Spain*. Translated by Alisa Jaffa and William Stoddart. Louisville, Ky.: Fons Vitae, 1999.

Cervantes Saavedra, Miguel de. *The Adventures of Don Quixote*. Translated by J. M. Cohen. New York: Barnes and Noble Books, 1999.

Fuentes, Carlos, *The Buried Mirror: Reflections on Spain and the New World*. New York: Houghton Mifflin, 1977.

García Lorca, Federico. *Three Plays*. Translated by Michael Dewell and Carmen Zapata. New York: Farrar, Straus & Giroux, 1993.

St. John of the Cross, *Poems of Saint John of the Cross*. Translated by John Frederick Nims. Chicago: University of Chicago Press, 1979.

O'Callaghan, Joseph F. *A History of Medieval Spain*. Ithaca, N.Y.: Cornell University Press, 1975.

Orwell, George, *Homage to Catalonia*. New York: Harcourt, Brace Jovanovich, 1952.

Payne, Stanley G. *A History of Spain and Portugal*. In two volumes. Madison: University of Wisconsin Press, 1973.

Note: The following books contain such excellent pictures of certain parts of Spain that I found other places to discover:

Hughes, Robert. *Barcelona*. New York: Alfred A. Knopf, 1993.

Nooteboom, Cees. *Roads to Santiago: A Modern-Day Pilgrimage through Spain*. New York: Harvest/Harcourt, 2000.